PRECIPICE OR CROSSROADS?

Precipice or Crossroads?

Where America's Great Public Universities Stand and
Where They Are Going Midway through Their Second Century

Edited by
Daniel Mark Fogel
&
Elizabeth Malson-Huddle

Photograph of Morrill Hall at Cornell University, Ithaca, New York
taken by Deborah Schmidle.

Published by State University of New York Press, Albany

© 2012 State University of New York

All rights reserved

Printed in the United States of America

For information, contact State University of New York Press, Albany, NY
www.sunypress.edu

Production by Ryan Morris
Marketing by Anne M. Valentine

Library of Congress Cataloging-in-Publication Data
Precipice or crossroads? : where America's great public universities stand and
where they are going midway through their second century / Edited by Daniel
Mark Fogel and Elizabeth Malson-Huddle.
    p. cm.
 Includes bibliographical references and index.
 ISBN 978-1-4384-4492-5 (pbk. : alk. paper)
 ISBN 978-1-4384-4493-2 (hardcover : alk. paper) 1. State universities and
colleges—United States—History. 2. Education, Higher—United States—His-
tory. I. Fogel, Daniel Mark, 1948– II. Malson-Huddle, Elizabeth.
 LB2329.5.P74 2012
 378'.053—dc23
                                                        2012003677

10 9 8 7 6 5 4 3 2 1

To colleagues—faculty, staff, and administration—
at Louisiana State University
and the University of Vermont
still fighting the good fight

number of students. Higher education is a public good—an investment in society's future—not just a private good.

There can be no argument for the status quo for public universities. Most need to find less expensive delivery models for some of their educational programs. For example, universities probably need to make more use of self-paced computer courses that students undertake individually or of hybrid classes, combining Web-based, solitary work with live interaction with teachers and fellow students. Universities must simultaneously drive quality improvement and cost containment, as has been successfully done by other sectors in the economy.

Land-grant and public universities have often been able to provide an elite education for the nonelite as well as others, and we must find a way for them to continue to do so for an even larger number of increasingly diverse students. Member institutions of the Association of Public and Land-grant Universities (APLU) include all the land-grants and nearly all the other public research universities in the country, and together they have 3.5 million students. The country needs those institutions to continue to provide quality education for increasing numbers of students because there is nowhere else that this can be done. In fact, student numbers at APLU institutions have been growing. Community colleges and for-profits have their roles, but they are not going to substitute for what the public universities are, and for what they must do. Public universities and society must find a way, or we will fail our history and the future.

Land-grant and public universities must continue their contributions to research, innovation, development, and problem solving. It is estimated that at least half of the advances in the gross domestic product of the United States since 1945 have come from technical discovery from all U.S. universities. Public universities have a critical role for future increases in income and standard of living for the American people, not to mention for maintaining our competitive position in the world. Our contributions must be in a panorama of areas, including health, national security (not only traditional areas of national defense but also food systems and safety and bio-security), and environment (including climate change and water supply).

The role of U.S. public universities in problem solving is critical not just for the United States but also for the whole world. For example, without the help of our public universities, particularly the land-grants that helped to spur the global "Green Revolution," it is very unlikely that the world will be able to find a way to double food production by 2050.

Almost everyone agrees that doing so is absolutely necessary. Without progress on this goal, food prices at home and abroad will spike well before 2050, and the world will be even less safe for us than today.

In state after state, governors and legislatures are finding that public universities are key institutions to drive economic growth and solve local problems. It is true that the states have often decided not to pay fully for that work, but the need for sustained contributions by public universities to state and regional well-being and their capacity to make those contributions are widely understood.

Reduction of state funding is a major problem for many universities, and in some places truly harmful cuts are being forced on universities. This is true, for example, at the University of California. It is also true that these cuts are forcing public universities to consider some constructive options that would otherwise be impossible to contemplate. As we consider options, it is important that we remain deeply committed to advancing our core missions.

In brief, I think that the next several years are going to be both trying and pivotal for land-grant and public universities. But I do believe that, after a foreseeable period of considerable trials, the institutions can and will make their way beyond these challenging crossroads and will move forward, somewhat different, stronger, and forever adapting, while continuing to serve core public purposes. It is this generation's responsibility to see to it that it happens.

The essays in this volume—specially commissioned by the editors in connection with a full program of activities organized by the Association of Public and Land-grant Universities to honor the 150th anniversary of the Morrill Land-grant Act—make abundantly clear why we must do so. They demonstrate the massive contribution of public universities to the well-being and strength of the nation. And they point the way to what must be done to keep these indispensable institutions of American democracy sustainable and globally competitive.

PETER McPHERSON
President, Association of Public and Land-grant Universities

Acknowledgments

This book had its inception in my service as a member of the board of directors of the Association of Public and Land-grant Universities (APLU), in connection with which I was asked to chair a group planning the association's commemoration of the 150th anniversary of the Morrill Land-grant Act. When I retired from the presidency of the University of Vermont (UVM), the planning baton was passed to University of Florida president Bernard Machen, allowing me to concentrate my effort on the completion of *Precipice or Crossroads?* Throughout the process of putting the volume together, I have benefited from the support, encouragement, and advice of colleagues at APLU, and, in particular, its president Peter McPherson. For those good offices I am grateful to Peter, and also for his helpful counsel and support as I sought to obtain assistance for the project from the National Endowment for the Humanities. A timely NEH grant has been of great value in the preparation of the volume, and my particular thanks go to NEH chairman Jim Leach for his personal interest in the project.

Intensive work on *Precipice or Crossroads?* got under way toward the end of my tenure as president of the University of Vermont. My colleagues in the Office of the President and in the UVM Office of Federal, State and Community Relations were of great assistance, notably my professional executive assistant Michelle Atherton; Vice President for Federal, State, and Community Relations Karen Meyer; and Director of Federal Relations Wendy Koenig. Wendy worked with me closely on Morrill Act Sesquicentennial planning with APLU and was of great assistance in preparing the materials for the NEH grant application, as were Associate Vice President Ruth Farrell and her colleagues in the UVM Office of Sponsored Programs. I am also grateful to colleagues in the UVM

English Department, including department chair Antony Magistrale and staff members Katherine Layton, Tilza Buschner, and Justin Griffing.

The NEH grant allowed me to engage someone to help out with the editing of the volume, and I was fortunate to find that Elizabeth Malson-Huddle was able to accommodate working with me into her teaching schedule at UVM. Her editorial skills and impressive substantive contributions to the development of the volume led me to invite her to join me as co-editor of *Precipice or Crossroads?* I am very grateful to her for having agreed to do so.

Drawing together on tight deadlines a book co-authored largely by heavily scheduled and often hard-pressed university presidents and chancellors seemed at first blush to be a steep hill to climb, but thanks to the energy, conscientiousness, and expertise of our chapter authors, we were able to get it done. We are especially indebted to all of the contributors to the volume. They worked with us closely in honing their essays to ensure that we were able to pursue our goal—with what success readers must judge—of creating a book that, while authored by many hands, still constituted a sustained, cooperative approach to a well-defined and pressing topic.

We are grateful, too, for good counsel, guidance, and highly professional execution from SUNY Press acquisitions editor Beth Bouloukos, from accelerated publishing editor Ryan Morris and from copy editor Alan V. Hewat. We also wish to thank Nancy Gerth for the insight and expertise she brought to the indexing of the volume. When the book was already under contract with SUNY, APLU offered the SUNY Press a subvention in order to accelerate production by several months so that copies would be on hand in time for a planned National Convocation on the Land-grant Act Sesquicentennial in June 2012. We are grateful to APLU for that support, and to SUNY Press for stretching to accelerate delivery of the finished book.

Both of us are grateful for encouragement and forbearance on the home front from our spouses, Nicholas Malson-Huddle and Rachel Kahn-Fogel. Without their love and support, our task would have been much harder. Rachel helpfully critiqued my contributions to the volume, as did my mother, Charlotte Fogel, my sisters Rebecca Anderson and Jessica Fogel, and my children, Nicholas Alden Kahn-Fogel and Rosemary Kahn-Fogel Luttrell. We ascribe whatever merit *Precipice or Crossroads?* may be found to have to all who have assisted us. For its demerits, we accept sole responsibility. Finally, we are both products of land-grant universities, Elizabeth of the University of Vermont and the University of Wisconsin-Madison, and I of Cornell University and of the two institutions where I have pursued my academic career, Louisiana State University and the University of Vermont. Like millions of others, we each owe a profound debt of gratitude to that great son of Vermont, Justin Smith Morrill, whose name will be forever tied to the enormous benefits conferred on America and the world by public higher education in the United States.

DANIEL MARK FOGEL
University Of Vermont

Introduction

DANIEL MARK FOGEL

This volume poses a question of pressing importance to the American people. Today, 150 years after the Morrill Land-grant Act generated the reigning paradigm of public higher education in the United States—a model combining accessible and inexpensive undergraduate, graduate, and professional education; research, discovery, and innovation; a commitment to the practical application of knowledge to address economic and social challenges; and a mission of service for the public good—our great public universities are under threat, and some would say they are facing their hour of maximum peril.

They are among the finest centers of education and knowledge creation anywhere. Seven of the top twenty research institutions in the world according to a recent ranking are American land-grant universities (see, in this volume, Yudof and Callaghan, n. 3), and as such they strongly support, with their private peers, Fareed Zakaria's observation that "Higher education is America's best industry" (190). America's public universities greatly exceed their private peers in scale and in the importance of their contribution to national prosperity, competitiveness, and security. They perform more than 60 percent of the academic research and development in the nation. They educate some 85 percent of the students who receive bachelor's degrees at all American research universities, and 70 percent of all graduate students. They award more than 50 percent of the doctorates granted in the United States in eleven of thirteen national needs categories—including between 60 to 80 percent of the doctorates in computer and information sciences, engineering, foreign languages and linguistics, mathematics and statistics, physical sciences, and security. Without the expansive capacity they provided after World War II to receive returning veterans and, later, the children and grandchildren of the veterans' generation, America's postwar prosperity and power would have been unthinkable and unattainable.

But today the nation's public research universities are looking down a dark vista of decline, with few discernible paths forward that would effectively sustain, let alone enhance, the public mission forged when Abraham Lincoln signed the Morrill Land-grant Act on July 2, 1862. It is a vista defined by steeply declining state appropriations, by wavering, at-risk federal investment in research, and by aging physical plants that are less and less adequate to meet the educational needs of a growing population and national needs for research-based problem solving. Reduced public funding, moreover, drives relentless upward pressure on tuition, undermining the historical commitment to a low-cost college education for all and putting public higher education on a collision course with a growing body of feeling and commentary that college may simply not be worth it. And thus the question posed in the title *Precipice or Crossroads?* comes into focus: Our public research universities are the nation's most productive centers of education and talent development, not just of physicists, engineers, biologists, and computer scientists, but also of the practitioners of virtually all of the professions and callings that together weave the fabric of our society, from nurses, social workers, accountants, and physical therapists to designers, artists, dancers, and writers; they are our most prolific sources of research, discovery, and innovation, not just in science and technology but also in philosophy and ethics, in public policy, in education itself, indeed in almost everything; can the nation, then, remain prosperous, strong, and healthy if these critical institutions have been sent careening toward a cliff edge, and can that hair-raising course be changed?

Of course, we have not yet reached the verge of the precipice, and in many respects our great public universities have never been stronger and more effective. But here is the paradox: we know that these powerful institutions, their missions of accessible education, knowledge creation, and service, and their world-leading quality are at risk when we look at the unsustainable trend lines in public funding and tuition pricing. As I was writing this introduction, I paused to read a just-published news story on public higher education reporting that nationwide "[s]tate appropriations per full-time equivalent student dropped by 4 percent in constant dollars in 2010–11, after dropping 6 percent in 2009–10 and 9 percent in 2008–9" while in-state tuitions rose an average of 8.3 percent (paced by a 21 percent increase in California), and, moreover, that "in 2010, average American income in every quintile of the income distribution was lower in inflation-adjusted dollars than it had been a decade before" (Supiano). We only have to juxtapose these data points with the observation of Michael Crow and William Dabars in their chapter of this book that "there is a direct correlation between fiscal robustness and the capacity of an institution to pursue excellence in teaching, research, and public service, as well as its potential to contribute to the standard of living and quality of life of communities and regions" to see the vicious downward spiral threatening our public universities and American well-being as economic and political forces increase institutional reliance on tuition, pushing student costs toward levels beyond the reach of many families. Either students will be squeezed out, or institutions will lack the fiscal robustness to sustain excellence, and, in time, both of those undesirable consequences will come to pass. So the first part of the question this book poses is frankly rhetorical, the answer implicit in the question itself: the nation's public university sector, the most important source of renewal of the nation's human resources and of its capacity for innovation, problem solving, and economic competitiveness, is at risk; ergo, so is the nation.

The second part of the question—Can we keep from going over the precipice? Can difficulty and challenge become opportunities for the change in course symbolized by the crossroads in the title of this book?— is an open one, no doubt as open as a variety of questions that might be posed about the fate of the nation itself. Despite the forces at work at the moment that militate against government funding of any number of public goods, from high-speed rail and broadband access to health care and education, it is my belief that our great public universities—and, in turn, the nation—will decline if the political currents are not reversed, and specifically if the tide does not turn on state and federal support for public research universities. It is my hope that this volume will help to inform and fortify the efforts and voices of those who campaign for such a turn. For while it is incumbent on the leaders, the faculty, and the staff of public universities to manage the resources entrusted to them as effectively as possible, and while private giving will always play an important role in supporting the pursuit of academic excellence, only sustained, robust, and predictable funding from the states and the federal government can ensure that the nation will continue to derive at globally competitive levels the numerous benefits that public higher education provides.

A few years ago, the *New York Times* reported on China's effort "to transform its top universities into the world's best within a decade . . . spending billions of dollars to woo big-name scholars . . . and to build first-class research laboratories," an essential element of China's project to "raise its profile as a great power." The *Times* quoted Wu Bangguo, Chairman and Party Secretary of the National People's Congress in the People's Republic of China and the nation's second-highest-ranking leader, as saying, "First-class universities increasingly reflect a nation's overall power," to which I would add that they not only reflect but to a significant degree build that power (and if power *per se* is not your thing, substitute prosperity, health, quality of life). It would be tragic if the American people were to forget this lesson in nation building, inscribed in the Morrill Land-grant Act at a crucial turning point in American history, just as other nations on the rise are taking it to heart (French, A1). "The only way to gain more leverage on China," writes Thomas Friedman in a recent *Times* column, "is to increase our savings and graduation rates—and export more and consume less" ("Barack Kissinger Obama"), and let us say amen to the graduation rates, a concern indicative of Friedman's agreement with Wu Bangguo's view of the relationship of higher education to the strength of nations.

The essays in *Precipice and Crossroads* are by several hands, but it has been our aim for them to function together as an integrated, systemic treatment, on a collaborative basis, of a well-defined and pressing subject. The volume was conceived as part of a broad-ranging effort to recognize the Sesquicentennial of the Morrill Act. Every one of its chapters thus has significant reference to the history and legacy of the Act. But our notion from the start was that the book would look forward more than backward. In addition, we aimed to expand its scope beyond the particular institutions that carry designations as land-grant institutions to all of the public research universities that in important ways have been shaped, in their character and their missions, by that powerfully generative legislation.

We open with "Democracy, the West, and Land-Grant Colleges" by historian Coy F. Cross. Cross provides the historical context for the Morrill Act. He shows how westward expansion, tied to the belief of nineteenth-century Americans in opportunity and democracy, infused the commitment Morrill inscribed in the original legislation to the democratizing of access to higher education. Cross also shows how science-based European challenges to American agriculture, a mainstay of the American economy in the years leading up to the Civil War, played into the thinking of Jonathan Baldwin Turner, Horace Greeley, and Justin Smith Morrill himself about the need for bringing agricultural sciences into the postsecondary curriculum. The most influential editor of his time, Greeley campaigned hard for agricultural colleges in what was effectively the nation's paper of record, the *New York Tribune,* arguing that Americans needed to "make the most of what we have, by diffusing, studying, discussing, criticizing, Liebig's *Agricultural Chemistry,* Dana's *Muck Manual,* Waring's *Elements,* and the books that each treat more especially of some department of the farmer's art, making ourselves familiar, first, with the principles, then the methods, of scientific, efficient, successful husbandry." Greeley established his own farm at Chappaqua as an "experimental station."

In 1857, when Justin Smith Morrill first introduced a land-grant bill to create agricultural colleges, the Vermont congressman argued for the constitutionality of his proposal against massed Southern opposition, making the case well enough that the legislation passed both houses of Congress, only to be vetoed by President James Buchanan. Not until Abraham Lincoln had taken office and Southerners had deserted the U.S. Congress for the Confederacy was Morrill able to pass "AN ACT Donating Public Lands to the several States and Territories which may provide Colleges for the Benefit of Agriculture and Mechanic Arts" (the official title of the Morrill Land-grant Act). The 1862 legislation was broadened from its 1857 version by adding to agriculture the study of the mechanic arts and military tactics, by a commitment to "the liberal and practical education of the industrial classes," and by the stipulation that the colleges thus funded would not exclude "other scientific and classical studies." Early in his essay, Cross invokes the famous 1893 address Frederick Jackson Turner delivered to the American Historical Association on "The Significance of the Frontier in American History," and, toward the end, he cites Turner's 1910 Commencement Address at Indiana University, "Pioneer Ideals and the State University." In what must be one of the least platitudinous and longest specimens in the history of commencement addresses, Turner presents (in fifteen densely argued pages in the reprinting of his address in the *Indiana Magazine of History*) an argument that the nation's state universities are expressions of its democratic spirit and essential agents for the maintenance and success of American democracy (Ridge 210–19).

That democratizing and uplifting force is clearly evident throughout Carolyn R. Mahoney's "The 1890 Institutions in African American and American Life," an informative essay about the eighteen historically black colleges and universities (HBCUs) that received land-grant designations as a result of the second Morrill Act of 1890. The 1890s, as they are known for short, have been exemplars of the land-grant ideal of democratic access, making it possible for hundreds of thousands of African Americans (and nonblack students as well) to earn bachelor's, master's, doctoral, and professional degrees (including law and veterinary medicine) regardless of race and socioeconomic status. Their contribution to developing the human resources of the African American community and of the nation has only increased over time. Without the impressive roster of their highly accomplished graduates—from Ralph Ellison and Wilma Rudolph to Ronald McNair, Oprah Winfrey, Jesse Jackson (Sr. and Jr.), and James Clyburn—the nation would be far poorer, and its prospects dimmer. Through research, graduate, and professional education, and through their extension services, they address a wide range of fields and of community and national needs, ranging from sustainable agriculture and waste management through the biomedical sciences to food and nutrition sciences and international development. Mahoney's is simply the best survey I know of the breadth and scale of these institutions and of their historic and continuing contribution to American life.[1]

In the following two chapters leaders of two of the nation's largest universities address the purposes of public higher education in terms that are distinctive yet highly resonant with each other. In "The Modern Public University: Its Land-Grant Heritage, Its Land-Grant Horizon," E. Gordon Gee, president of The Ohio State University (with some 56,000 students on the main campus in Columbus), emphasizes continuity and change. He sees America's public research universities as continuing the original Morrill Act vision of democracy and access through their stewardship of the nation's "founding promise to create a meritocracy based not on wealth or family connections but on ability, determination, and effort." At the same time, Gee challenges universities to be open to fundamental change, insisting that they must be highly flexible and adaptable in order to build to the highest levels their capacity to develop solutions to the "wicked problems" before the nation and the world—problems that are complex, long-term, and resistant to traditional linear analysis and that therefore require solutions forged through the multidisciplinary resources of complex universities: "To connect and extend the original ideals of the land-grant institutions to the modern era, we whose business it is to mind the mighty engine of a public university must reimagine, reinvent, even reconceptualize the university, not merely re-thinking what we do, but, more fundamentally, re-thinking what we think, re-thinking what the American university is and what it is capable of achieving." The public and university leaders have in Gee's view a "sacrosanct social compact" that today requires a "full-scale recommitment."

The higher education budget passed in California for the current year (2011–12) cut the University of California System by $650 million, the California State System by the same amount, and the California Community Colleges by more than $500 million. For the University of California and its ten campuses, the cut came to a little more than 23 percent of the appropriation in 2010–11. Little wonder, then, that tuition in California rose 21 percent for the current academic year, and no wonder, too, that the chapter by University of California president Mark G. Yudof (co-authored with his colleague Caitlin Callaghan) unfolds against a backdrop of crisis. In "Commitments: Enhancing the Public Purposes and Outcomes of Public Higher Education," Yudof and Callaghan endorse as strongly as Gordon Gee the Morrill Act's spirit of democratic access and opportunity, but that spirit, they declare, is "under threat" due to cuts in public funding of such magnitude that the institutions are struggling to maintain quality and are being pushed willy-nilly toward privatization. Privatization is not only out of synch with the democratic and egalitarian spirit public research universities have embodied for the last 150 years, but it also curtails access and shifts enormous burdens to students and their families: "Even with scholarships," observe Yudof and Callaghan, "full pricing limits access for many families. And when students from less affluent families do find ways to attend, their educations can suffer from the demands of part-time or full-time work, the pressure to graduate on time, and the strain of growing student loan debt."

Yudof and Callaghan describe public higher education as a hybrid public-private good, but they see the balance in public policy and perception shifting heavily toward the private side, fueled by the increasingly prevalent feeling that "only students should be responsible for their educations." America's great public research universities "all arose from the extraordinary nature of the state government-public university compact," and the ongoing crisis has developed because "more and more Americans no longer believe the compact is important." Tellingly, Yudof and Callaghan note that it is less the economy than the political process that is broken, at least in California, where the $26 billion budget gap is just 1.3 percent of the state's $2 trillion economy. Yudof and Callaghan close, accordingly, with a call for a "new national higher education compact" in which universities are committed to subjecting their operations to a "private sensibility" in order to "establish realistic priorities, eliminate weak programs, adopt money-saving information technology services, and aggressively reduce waste"; in which states "rededicate themselves to supporting . . . universities' core functions"; and in which the federal government finds some way to contribute to the support of core institutional costs without creating a pretext for further state disinvestment. Such a new compact would demonstrate "a public commitment to, and understanding of . . . [the] societal value" of public higher education. Meanwhile, I would add, the middle class is increasingly squeezed out in a travesty of the land-grant ideal of access for all: "Over the past 10 years," reports the Orange County Register (Schaefer), "the proportion of middle-income students attending the University of California has declined at nearly twice the rate of California middle-income households, while the share of lower- and upper-income UC students has risen."

David E. Shulenburger's chapter on "Challenges to Viability and Sustainability: Public Funding, Tuition, College Costs, and Affordability" is a data-rich exploration of the funding, operating costs, and pricing of public research universities. In addition, Shulenburger enlarges on a theme touched on in other chapters in *Precipice or Crossroads?*, the growing resource disparity between public and private research universities. Shulenburger's data and analysis support conclusions that contradict many oft-repeated pseudo-facts and truisms in the national dialogue about higher education. He adduces a variety of studies, for instance, showing that the return on investment (ROI) that students and families make in educations at public research universities is significantly higher than the ROI at elite private universities, and that employers have a clear and decisive preference for graduates of the former.

Return-on-investment calculations, of course, focus on higher education as a private good, but Shulenburger provides a context by opening his chapter (after a helpful "Overview" section) with a summary he terms the "baseline" of the "incomparable contribution" public research universities make to society as well as to individual students. When he enlarges on that theme in a later section of his chapter, the private and public goods are writ very large, including, on the public good side, references to studies showing the "neighborhood effects" of higher education: for instance, "research findings that increases in the proportion of college degree holders in a given population lead to significant wage increases for those who do not hold college degrees," illustrating "why public subsidy that serves to increase the proportion of the population with college degrees is good for all of us." Other public goods—beyond the significant role of public research universities in research, innovation, and technology transfer supporting regional and national competitiveness and economic vitality—include "reduced poverty; reduced public assistance expenditure; improved health (including a reduced propensity to smoke); greater cognitive skill development of children living with educated parents; increased willingness to volunteer, to give blood, to vote, and even to understand the opinions of others."

Shulenburger's data on the cost of operations at public research universities over time and on the cost and affordability of attending those institutions for students and families are eye-opening. For example, he shows that public higher education revenues per student have been almost flat in real dollars from 1985 to 2010 (the increase over the twenty-five years covered in that span comes to a little more than $1,000, or roughly $40 per year [Shulenburger's Figure III]). He shows that public universities have controlled costs much more effectively than private universities (the rate of increase in the cost of education and related expenses per student at publics was roughly one-half the compounded annual rate of cost increases at privates from 1998 to 2008 [Shulenburger's Figure XIV]). And he shows (see his Figure XV) that the cost of attendance as a percentage of median family income at public research universities remains quite low—and dramatically lower than at private universities: at the most research intensive private universities, sticker price in 2010–11 came to 74.3 percent of median family income, and the discounted price (after financial aid) came to 49.8 percent of median family income, compared to 15.7 percent (sticker price) at the most research intensive publics and to 12.9 percent (discounted price at research intensive publics after aid). These data provide a general context for the observation by Yudof and Callaghan that "four of our campuses, Berkeley, UCLA, Davis, and San Diego, *each* enroll more Pell grant recipients than the entire Ivy League combined."

Shulenburger is not the only contributor to this volume who notes the growing resource gap between public and private research universities. Yudof and Callaghan point out that federal, state, and local appropriations to private not-for-profit and for-profit colleges and universities have grown steadily even as funding from those same public sources has declined as a percentage of all revenues at public institutions, drastically so at the University of California. Duderstadt observes that public research universities "now find themselves caught with declining state support and the predatory wealthy private universities competing for the best students, faculty, and support" and that "a serious competitive imbalance has arisen in the marketplace for the best faculty, students, and resources, with private research universities now spending almost three times as much to educate each student." Like Yudof and Callaghan, he suggests that this imbalance is in part due "to the degree to which current federal and state policies in areas such as tax benefits, student financial aid, research funding, and regulation tend to preferentially benefit and subsidize the high-cost nature of private institutions." Shulenburger's data put sharp teeth in such concerns. In 1980 there was rough parity between faculty salaries in public and private doctoral universities, but as Shulenburger shows (Figure VIII) by 2008–09 the gap was moving toward a 20 percent advantage for privates, and indeed data from the American Association of University Professors published in *The Chronicle of Higher Education* show that by 2010–11 that gap had widened farther, to about 25 percent (for example, the average full professor at a public doctoral university earned $118,054, or 75 percent of the average of $157,282 at private doctoral universities) ("Faculty Salaries Vary by Institution Type, Discipline"). It is hard to avoid the conclusion that as this trend continues the public institutions educating the vast majority of the nation's undergraduate and graduate students—and conducting the great majority of the nation's academic research and development—will increasingly find they can attract and retain only lower-quality faculty. Shulenburger shows other enormous resource disparities, including endowments per student at private research universities that average more than four times those of their public peers (Table 3) and expenditures per student at private universities that beggar those at the publics: for instruction at the most research intensive privates, $49,286 per student in 2008–09 versus $11,552 per student at publics; for academic support (for instance, libraries), $10,804 per student at the privates versus $3,290 at the publics; and for student services, $5,833 at the privates versus $1,291 at the publics (Figure VII). As Shulenburger is at pains to show, our great public universities still compete extremely well, arguably with better outcomes than the privates on some key metrics despite the resource disparity. But if these trends continue we may well ask whether the door to a democracy of opportunity through higher education opened by Justin Morrill in 1862 will become a passage to the cut-rate and second-rate, and, if it does so, whether the decline of public institutions in relation to the much less inclusive and much less capacious elite private universities will glare out as yet another sign of destructive inequality in the United States.

Certainly, as we move to the next chapter, Michael Crow (who presides over the largest campus enrollment in the nation at Arizona State University) and his colleague William Dabars have no question that America's research universities have been indispensable in lifting the nation up. Their discussion of "University-Based R&D and Economic Development: The Morrill Act and the Emergence of the American Research University" derives from a broad body of research supportive of their view that "[t]he science-based technological innovation and industrial application that are the products of academic research are widely held to have been requisite to the trajectory of economic development that led the United States in the second half of the twentieth century to become what has been characterized as the 'world's superpower.'" And while their central thesis is there in a nutshell—without academic research there would be no innovation and industrial application, no economic development, no prosperity, no national preeminence—they also emphasize the importance of institutions that in America have led the world in combining basic and applied research with the education of students: "The economic contribution of research universities is closely tied to the basic and applied research conducted on their campuses, but of inestimable significance is their function in the production of human capital, which represents a critical national asset because of its impact on the creation of innovation capacity and thus the competitiveness of the American economy."

Crow and Dabars focus explicitly and almost exclusively on the little more than 2 percent of American colleges and universities classified by the Carnegie Foundation for the Advancement of Teaching as Very High Research Activity institutions, just 108 universities, of which 73 are public and 35 are private not-for-profit (including two private land-grant institutions, Cornell University and MIT).[2] Of great interest is their discussion of the importance of the Morrill Land-grant Act in the evolution of the modern research university, in part due to the "contemporaneity of the emergence of the modern American research university and the land-grant system"—six of the fifteen American institutions that emerged after the Civil War as the first modern American research universities were designated land-grants—and in part due to the paradigms and salient features of the land-grant institutions that in many respects shaped the ethos, emphases, and themes that weave throughout the history of the

American research university. One of the most important of these formative elements identified by Crow and Dabars is the decentralized nature
of American higher education, which can be traced back to the rejection
by the Constitutional Convention in 1787 of James Madison's proposal
for the establishment of a national university. The Morrill Act reaffirmed
and, as it were, extended and institutionalized decentralization, for the
"land-grant system" is really not a system in any true sense: each land-
grant institution operates independently of the others, and, with respect
to governance, along the full spectrum from high degrees of institutional
autonomy to significant elements of state-based (but not federally or nationally based) oversight and control.

The heterogeneous nature of American higher education fueled what
Crow and Dabars (drawing heavily on the insights of Hugh Davis Graham and Nancy Diamond) term a "trajectory toward a decentralized and
competitive 'academic marketplace,'" driven "particularly in the late nineteenth and early twentieth centuries . . . by regional competitive rivalries"
and greatly accelerated and intensified after World War II by the competition for federal research dollars. Here, too, the land-grant ethos was
a shaping force. The emphasis of the Morrill Act on such "useful arts"
as agriculture and mechanics was foundational for the ascendancy of science and engineering in research universities and for the entrepreneurial
bent of these state-based institutions that sought to be responsive to their
economic environments, in service to the "shifting landscape of agriculture, business, and industry." While the utilitarian and scientific emphasis
fostered by the Morrill Act could find expression in private universities as
well (Harvard, Yale, and Dartmouth all established scientific schools in
the mid-nineteenth century), Crow and Dabars remark that "in the estimation of some of the foremost experts in university-industry relations,
public universities and 'especially those established under the Morrill Act
affected the direction of the academic research enterprise during this period to a greater extent than the private Ivy League institutions.'" Cornell
University, with its founder's motto that "I would found an institution
where any person can find instruction in any study" and "its novel integration of the traditional humanities curriculum with science and 'practical'
fields, especially engineering and agriculture . . . represented a new vision for a 'modern' university." When rising American research universities such as Cornell and MIT married the utilitarian bent for hands-on
problem solving inscribed in the Morrill Act to the institutionalization of
academic research pioneered in America on the Germanic model by The

Johns Hopkins University, the die was cast. By the early decades of the twentieth century, "[t]he rise of academic science . . . fostered the growth of science-based industry, which in turn increasingly correlated with economic development."

While the federal land-grant under the Morrill Act was an important precedent for federal investment in academic research and development, massive federal investment that aimed not only to "maintain American military preeminence but also drive economic growth and improve the quality of life through the production of science-based technologies" was forged in the crucible of World War II and institutionalized through the creation of numerous federal agencies under the guiding spirit of Vannevar Bush, who had directed the wartime Office of Scientific Research and Development. In addition to the rise of federal agencies such as the National Science Foundation and the National Aeronautics and Space Administration (both founded in the postwar years), of the National Institutes of Health (which predated the war but which was massively expanded and reconfigured, as suggested by the pluralizing of Institute in 1948), and of great national laboratories staffed by university-trained scientists and technologists, Crow and Dabars emphasize the importance of the Bayh-Dole Act of 1980, which allowed "universities for the first time to patent the results of federally funded research," thus transforming "relations between academic institutions and business and industry." The Bayh-Dole Act was one of the critical elements that ensured that "the trajectory of economic competitiveness that marked the postwar era" would continue to be "primarily the product of the teaching and research that take place in our universities."

Crow and Dabars follow the historical discussion in the first half of their chapter with a detailed, informative treatment of approaches to assessing and quantifying the contribution of university-based research and education to local, regional, national, and global economic development and competitiveness. They treat not only the contributions of research universities to economic development through discovery and innovation but also the important role of research universities in human capital production through their programs of undergraduate, graduate, and professional education and training. Throughout, they emphasize the key role of advances in science-based technology for economic productivity. They cite authorities who have calculated that some 85 percent of the gains in productivity and standard of living in the twentieth century arose from technological advances. Throughout, they stress the preeminence of research universities in the "'Triple Helix' of university-industry-government innovation" and in the broader ecology of entrepreneurship and national systems of innovation. They also warn that "[e]ntrenchment in discipline-based departments" promotes "individualism over teamwork and the discovery of specialized knowledge over problem-based collaboration" and advise that "[t]the amalgamation of transdisciplinary and trans-institutional frameworks has the potential to advance broader social and economic outcomes."

Crow and Dabars close with an alarm and an exhortation. The alarm is clear and present: with "[t]he American economy . . . at a crossroads," with "the prosperity we have known during the past seventy years . . . increasingly imperiled," and with "nations worldwide . . . investing strategically to educate broader segments of their populations," "America has allowed its research universities . . . to lose their adaptive capacities": "For the first time in our national history, we risk broad decline as a consequence of the insufficient adaptation of our institutions and the disinvestment that characterizes our policies toward higher education." The exhortation brings them full circle to the service mission integral to Justin Morrill's land-grant vision. Research universities, say Crow and Dabars, must "explicitly embrace a broader societal role" in highly innovative ways: "If research universities are to create knowledge that is as socially useful as it is scientifically meritorious, they must integrate their quest to advance discovery, creativity, and innovation with an explicit mandate to assume responsibility for the societies they serve," which might entail "ambitious and multifaceted public outreach and engagement programs dedicated to societal advancement and regional economic development" and which must include "a commitment to the production in sufficient numbers of scientists and engineers and artists and philosophers and economists and doctors and lawyers—in short, the human capital from which we draw our future leaders in every sector."

For John Hudzik and his colleague at Michigan State University, President Lou Anna K. Simon, it is imperative that the Crow and Dabars call on research universities to assume responsibility for the societies they serve be extended beyond locality, region, and nation to the world. They urge, as the title of their chapter proclaims, that research universities move "From a Land-Grant to a World-Grant Ideal: Extending Public Higher Education Core Values to a Global Frame." Hudzik and Simon frame the core land-grant values as "quality, inclusiveness, and connectivity": "the pursuit of quality in teaching and research relevant to societal needs, inclusiveness to diversify student access and widen the content of subject matter for higher learning, and connection of higher education missions to community needs and aspirations." Today, they urge, the "backyard" of the community a given institution serves must include the world, for "[i]n a world as interrelated and complex as ours, it is increasingly difficult to imagine any significant challenge in the context of a single location." They illustrate this point with numerous examples, including, among many others, transnational food systems affecting food safety; the house-of-cards interconnectedness of global financial and banking systems; and the borderless dimensions of such matters as infectious disease control, energy consumption and management, and environmental sustainability. Clearly, they suggest, applied problem solving of such global challenges requires universities to embrace global engagement and responsibilities.

As in other chapters in this Sesquicentennial volume, Hudzik and Simon provide some historical context, both affirming a continuity of values extending from the original land-grant ethos to their world-grant ideal and allowing that for much of the nation's existence "a powerful inwardness drove U.S. social, political, and cultural frames of reference" and that "[i]t was not a global environment to which the Morrill Act originally responded." They observe that World War II and its aftermath—including the imperatives of the cold war, concerns about American scientific and military preeminence (crystallized in the nation's consciousness by the launch of Sputnik in 1957), and increasing disquiet about America's place in the world (captured in 1958 in Eugene Burdick's best-selling *The Ugly American*)—made for "a massive reorientation of the American frames of reference" and a decisive departure from the nation's historic isolationist bent. Thus began what Hudzik and Simon describe as Stage 2 of the institutional engagement of land-grant universities (Stage 1 was, of course, domestic, both local and national). Stage 2 was characterized by expanding engagement abroad both in postwar reconstruction and in international development work in other parts of the world. By and large, such work was "more assistance than partnership per se," conditioned by an assumption of American superiority and a belief that we had much to teach but little if anything to learn from those with whom we worked abroad. Even so, Stage 2 was marked by the expansion of international engagement opportunities for faculty, students, and staff and by internationalization of curricula, some of it in language and area studies supported through the cold war–driven National Defense Education Act.

Hudzik and Simon describe Stage 3, now under way and still developing, as distinctive in several ways. Globalization—our recognition of "factors and forces that transcend borders and sovereign states"—calls

on universities to pursue a much more "comprehensive internationalization," a commitment, confirmed through action, to infuse international
and comparative perspective throughout the teaching, research, and service missions of higher education. It shapes institutional ethos and values
and touches the entire higher education enterprise. It is essential that it be
embraced by institutional leadership, governance, faculty, students, and all
academic, service, and support units. It is an institutional imperative, not
just a desirable possibility.

Comprehensive internationalization requires American institutions
to embrace true partnerships abroad, with reciprocal teaching and learning and mutual benefits, or, in Hudzik and Simon's terms, co-creation
of co-prosperity. Engaging in this way, American research universities
face a variety of challenges outlined by Hudzik and Simon, including,
among others, the acceleration of research productivity in other nations
(they report that "[t]he increased output of scholarly publications in the
sciences and engineering between 1988 and 2008 was about 17 percent
in the United States, about 60 percent in Europe, and in triple digits in
Asia") and the "rising inability globally—and clearly in the United States
as well—for traditional public funding mechanisms to meet and sustain
growing capacity needs."

Hudzik and Simon lay out very clear rationales—a "Business Model
Rationale," a "Client/Customer Rationale," and a "Social Needs Rationale"—for why American research universities should rise to meet these
challenges through "world-grant" comprehensive internationalization.
They detail what comprehensive internationalization would mean, when
fully realized, for the education of students and the work of faculty and
staff, for academic curricula and programs, for research and scholarship,
and for the local communities universities serve. Universities should routinely provide "opportunities to connect local constituencies to global opportunities and learning." They describe a variety of assets and attitudes
that universities must develop in order to meet these challenges. And they
review in detail two sets of "tensions" universities must address to move
successfully from a land-grant to a world-grant orientation. "Constructive
tensions," including such pairings as "global/local, liberal/professional, ru-
ral/urban," may inspire innovation that "bends and penetrates political,
geographical, disciplinary, and cultural borders." "Disruptive and counterproductive tensions" include our comfort with old ways that have yielded
success in the past; disciplinary arrogance; the assumption that internationalization is the business of other people's disciplines but not of one's

own; elitist ranking schemes that affront values such as democratic access and that privilege theoretical and abstract work over practical and applied work in many fields, including some of the professional disciplines; and a misguided tendency to pit efforts in the domestic and international domains against each other, framed as a "zero-sum" game. In the last third of their chapter, finally, Hudzik and Simon survey ways to reduce and overcome internal barriers to realization of the world-grant ideal, including the promotion of cultural change; the thorough documentation of desired outcomes in many domains (learning; research, scholarship, and engagement; and inclusiveness and connectivity); the promotion of faculty engagement; the design of portals for global collaboration (partnerships, hubs, and networks); and the thoroughgoing promotion and implementation of an "assist model" of collaborations without borders. Throughout their argument, the land-grant ideal flows into and feeds the world-grant vision precisely because, in their view, it is the "combination of research and engagement that holds the greatest potential to address local and world challenges."

Networks of collaboration—in this case within large, statewide systems of public higher education—are also the theme of the chapter by Nancy L. Zimpher, Chancellor of the State University of New York, the nation's largest system, and her colleague Jessica Fisher Neidl. In "Statewide University Systems: Taking the Land-Grant Concept to Scale in the Twenty-First Century," Zimpher and Neidl lucidly and compellingly make the case that statewide systems such as SUNY are better positioned than other institutions—than single land-grant campuses themselves— to fulfill the mission and aspirations Justin Morrill envisioned for higher education in 1862. Frankly addressing the tensions that at times erupt between systems and campuses, particularly the flagship research universities—a theme touched on by James Duderstadt in our next chapter, where we read that "many public research universities today find themselves constrained by university systems, characterized both by bureaucracy and system-wide policies for setting tuition levels and faculty compensation that fail to recognize the intensely competitive environment faced by research universities"—Zimpher and Neidl present a case for striking a balance between high degrees of campus autonomy and appreciation of the special identity of each unit within the system, on the one hand, and, on the other hand, system-wide, coordinated policies and services that allow for the efficient and effective attainment of the public policy ends of appropriations for postsecondary education. Theirs is a compelling argument, particularly if one has any qualms at all about the elite public land-grant research universities having become selective in admissions (in several notable cases, highly selective to the point of being exclusionary) against the grain of the democratic and egalitarian aspirations of the Morrill Act. A system such as SUNY can address this concern even while harboring and supporting several increasingly selective institutions heavily invested in research and graduate education because, as an integrated system with a wide array of four-year and two-year institutions, including community colleges with open admissions and vocational as well as liberal arts and general education programs, it can address the needs of the citizens, the communities, and the state it serves accessibly and affordably along the full range of aptitudes and career paths that Morrill intended the land-grant colleges to cultivate.

The State University of New York is massive. Today it includes "sixty-four schools, a mix of twenty-nine state-operated campuses, and five statutory colleges—including research universities, liberal arts colleges, specialized and technical colleges, health science centers, land-grant colleges—and thirty community colleges," and it enrolls more than 465,000 students served by some 88,000 faculty and staff. Zimpher and Neidl have many points of reference in their chapter, including the recommendations made roughly a decade ago by the Kellogg Commission on the Future of State and Land-grant Universities, Clark Kerr's exemplary California Master Plan for Higher Education (1960), and policies and initiatives under way in university systems from Florida and Texas to Wisconsin and California. But one special value of the Zimpher-Neidl chapter is that its central example, the living laboratory in which they have tested their concept of "systemness," is the SUNY system itself, which Zimpher is actively engaged in transforming along a number of vectors, all of which illustrate the contention that statewide systems, through their "systemness," can fulfill the historic land-grant mission of public universities more completely and successfully than individual institutions. One of these is a cohesive and coordinated commitment to statewide economic and community development responsive to changing workforce and societal needs, with the network of SUNY campuses serving as "anchor institutions" in their communities. Those campuses effectively cover the state: "93 percent of New Yorkers live within fifteen miles of a SUNY campus, and nearly 100 percent live within thirty miles. In many communities, SUNY is the region's largest employer." Cohesion and coordination of the system's community engagement requires regular assessment of community needs and of the responsiveness throughout the system of curricula and programs to those needs. Also required is attention to the development of programs for which there is rising demand and regular review of programs for which there is less or no demand and which may be outmoded—and a willingness to terminate them. The system is able to address state and national goals of improved retention and degree completion through intensive attention to articulation protocols that allow students to transfer general education credits and many credits earned within majors according to rules that are consistently and equitably applied at all system campuses. Such procedures greatly facilitate student progress and student advising. And while granting increasing autonomy to campuses in academic matters and internal resource allocation, the system is able to offer shared services in areas such as information technology, procurement, and risk management that produce material dollar savings, resources that can then be reallocated to the core mission of teaching, research, and service.

James J. Duderstadt, who has led another of the nation's truly world-class public research universities, the University of Michigan, focuses in "Creating the Future: The Promise of Public Research Universities for America" precisely on those institutions most likely to feel constrained by the centralized "systemness" Zimpher and Neidl espouse—on the major research institutions that were also the focus of Crow and Dabars. Duderstadt is currently serving on a Research Universities ad hoc committee of the National Academies, the charge of which is to answer the following question: "What are the top ten actions that Congress, the federal government, state governments, research universities, and others could take to assure the ability of the American research university to maintain the excellence in research and doctoral education needed to help the United States compete, prosper, and achieve national goals for health, energy, the environment, and security in the global community of the 21st century?" (National Academies). While the report of that committee will not come out for some months (like this book, during the Sesquicentennial year of the Morrill Act), and while Duderstadt in his chapter is speaking only for himself, and with a focus on public research universities (whereas the National Academies committee is considering all research universities, public and private), the argument he presents is informed and shaped by deep and long immersion in efforts to address the tightly framed and extremely critical question with which the ad hoc committee has been grappling. That question, furthermore, is set forth in language that recalls the visionary power of the Morrill Land-grant Act, which engaged

Congress, the federal government, state governments, and universities in a very American, decentralized way in actions designed to help the United States "compete, prosper, and achieve national goals."

Duderstadt swiftly and lucidly recapitulates the history that made public research universities what they are today, the "backbone of advanced education and research in the United States," noting the irony that these state-based institutions "were not created by the states themselves but instead by visionary federal initiatives," the Morrill Land-grant Act of 1862 and the post–World War II expansion of federal investment in "campus-based research and graduate education" championed by Vannevar Bush. Duderstadt summarizes the challenge before us—"[T]today, despite their importance to their states, the nation, and the world, America's public research universities are at great risk." The risk arises from multiple causes: in the states, not only increasingly inadequate funding but also "intrusive regulation and governance" and, in the broad universe of higher education, rising, indeed "predatory competition" from wealthy private universities at home and from "rapidly evolving international universities" that threaten the capacity of public institutions "to attract and retain talented students and faculty." Yes, the states' budget challenges are "painfully apparent," and, yes, "the highly competitive nature of American higher education is one of its strongest features," but "public research universities are critical national assets" and "[i]t would be a national disaster if the crippling erosion in state support and predatory competition among institutions were to permanently damage the world-class quality of the nation's public research universities."

Duderstadt's analysis of current challenges is telling. First, changing public priorities and demands have put public research universities between the rock and hard place of being asked to do more with less: "[P]ublic support of higher education and research is no longer viewed as an investment in the future but rather as an expenditure competing with the other priorities of aging populations" and, on the heels of cuts in appropriations in many states ranging from 20 percent to 50 percent, "state governments are urging their research universities to wean themselves from state appropriations by developing and implementing strategies to survive what could be a generation-long period of state support inadequate to maintain their capacity, quality, and reputation." Second, the relationship between universities and government is changing along very damaging lines, with governments intensifying their regulatory and accountability regimes in part, apparently, in an effort "to retain control over the sector through regulation even as their financial control has waned." Governments and governing boards are more invested in oversight than in "stewardship to protect and enhance their institutions" for the benefit of "present and future generations." For Duderstadt the heavy, constraining hand of bureaucratic higher education systems is another symptom of the changing relationship with government. And Duderstadt sees something else at work, perhaps more fundamental and insidious: "While it was once the role of governments to provide for the purposes of universities, today it is now the role of universities to provide for the purposes of government." In demanding that universities "provide the educated workforce and innovation necessary for economic competitiveness," "[g]overnments increasingly regard universities as delivery agencies for public policy goals in areas . . . that may be tangential to their primary responsibilities of education and scholarship." Finally, there is the problem of an increasingly destructive disequilibrium in the competitive environment, so that "serious imbalances . . . in available funding, policy restrictions, and political constraints" threaten "the national interest": we are in danger of creating "an intensely Darwinian winner-take-all ecosystem in which the strongest and wealthiest institutions become predators, raiding the best faculty and students of the less generously supported and more constrained public universities and manipulating federal research and financial policies to sustain a system in which the rich get richer and the poor get devoured."

Duderstadt's prescriptions for what to do are multifaceted and highly nuanced, ranging from institutional strategies for the near term (streamlining, cost-containment, and productivity enhancement) to a compelling pitch that the federal government should become the primary patron of research and graduate education, a conjoined enterprise increasingly focused on national and global needs and issues rather than, as in much of the first century after the Morrill Act, on the needs of local agriculture and industry. In return for federal support, universities should commit to reforming graduate education, addressing its well-known shortcomings (e.g., low completion rates and lengthening time to degree). With limited resources, state governments should focus on their priority for workforce development by renewing their commitment to undergraduate education at the associate and bachelor's degree levels with more adequate subsidies. The nation, by one calculation, cannot support more than about sixty major public research universities; states therefore should guard fiercely against "mission creep," the inveterate pressures from public campuses that aspire to expand beyond their historic missions in undergraduate education in order to attain research university status. Duderstadt calls, too, for relief for research universities from "the constraints of politically determined governing boards, the tyranny of university systems, and the intrusive regulation of state government," for the research institutions must be "provided with the autonomy and agility to restructure their operations to enable them to survive with their quality intact what is likely to be a generation-long period of inadequate state support." Duderstadt suggests that there is such great power still in the land-grant paradigm that it should be extended into the twenty-first century in transformative ways, including, for example, the development of "new university-based paradigms to conduct translational research" linking "fundamental scientific discoveries with the technological innovation necessary for the development of new products, processes, and services." Such translational research is particularly important because of "the disappearance of many of the nation's leading industrial research laboratories." Recent federal initiatives such as the creation of innovation hubs as the locus of focused collaborations among research universities, national laboratories, and industry, Duderstadt suggests, are "simply the repurposing of the land-grant agricultural and industrial experiment stations established by the Hatch Act of 1887."

Above all, Duderstadt emphasizes the importance of a "national strategy," for the United States stands apart from the rest of the world in having no "comprehensive policy for enhancing and sustaining its research universities in the face of growing international competition." Such a comprehensive policy would encompass the division of funding responsibilities already discussed (federal responsibility for research and graduate education, state responsibility for undergraduate education); fixes to the multiple flaws of the current system, including, for example, "the failure to cover the full costs of federally funded research projects (indirect cost recovery, cost sharing requirements), a research appropriations process that favors political influence rather than national priorities, and regulatory constraints that discourage the recruiting of international students and faculty"; provision of sustainable, predictable support for research, putting an end to damaging fluctuations; adjustment of federal and state policies that "tend to preferentially benefit and subsidize the high-cost nature of private institutions"; and, for long-term faculty development, "a federal program of matching grants to establish endowments for the support of faculty positions, modeled after highly successful programs at the University of California Berkeley and in Canada." Importantly, Duderstadt rejects the notion that our great public universities should privatize. Rather, as their missions in research, graduate education, and service extend beyond state borders, their public missions expand "into 'regional,' 'national,' or even 'global' universities with a public purpose to serve far broader constituencies than simply the citizens of a particular state." The research universities need to work to shift public perception so that they are seen by the public as what they are, producers rather than consumers of state resources—offering their states very high returns on increasingly modest investments—and the states, in turn, "would be better off if they encouraged their flagship public research universities to evolve into institutions with far broader missions (and support), capable of accessing global economic and human capital markets to attract the talent and wealth of the world to their regions."

As president of the University of Michigan, James Duderstadt was—and remains as president emeritus—a strong supporter of the arts and humanities, and in his pitch for federal support of research and graduate education he remarks that "both the unusually broad intellectual needs of the nation and the increasing interdependence of the academic disciplines provide compelling reasons why such federal support should encompass all areas of scholarship, including the natural sciences, the social sciences, the humanities, the arts, and professional disciplines such as engineering, education, law, and medicine." Sadly, however, many who advocate for support of public research universities make the pitch (whether in all sincerity or because they feel compelled to do so) solely on the basis of the contributions to economic development of university research and training in science and technology, sometimes without any mention of other disciplinary domains. As a poet and literary scholar who has been engaged for decades with the Association of Public and Land-grant Universities and who recently finished a term as chair of its board of directors, I felt that, wise observations such as Duderstadt's notwithstanding, *Precipice or Crossroads?* required, to avoid a grievous imbalance, at least one chapter centered in the value of the arts and humanities in public research universities, and I took it upon myself to write that chapter to close the volume.

In "Challenges to Equilibrium: The Place of the Arts and Humanities in Public Research Universities," I have tried to exhibit a number of facets of a very real problem. I want to make clear why university presidents and other higher education advocates, even if they are poets and literary scholars, are very unlikely in the current political climate to foreground—perhaps more often than not these days are unlikely even to mention—the arts and humanities (and, for that matter, the classical social sciences) when seeking funding for their institutions at legislative committee hearings. I drafted the chapter well before the governor of Florida, Rick Scott, vividly illustrated my point by suggesting that Florida does not need to put taxpayer funds into the social sciences at the state's public universities, saying, of anthropology, "It's a great degree if people want to get it. But we don't need them here" ("Scott: Florida doesn't need more anthropology majors"). I also wish to show that liberal education, including the study of literature and the classics, was an integral part of Justin Morrill's vision, both when he brought the Land-grant Act forward in Congress and when he looked back on its passage years later. My chapter surveys the development of the modern research university with special attention to those aspects of its character, history, management, and partnerships (for example, after World War II, increasingly with the military-industrial complex) that privilege some disciplines, especially science, technology, engineering, and mathematics (the STEM disciplines), marginalizing other disciplines and thus demoralizing faculty and students in those disciplines. I discuss the ways in which the culture wars of the 1980s and 1990s turned the humanities in particular into favorite targets of ideological critics of the academy, a battering that coincided with a deepening crisis in the employability of new PhDs in virtually all of the humanities disciplines. And I seek to make a case for the indispensable role of the arts and humanities without recourse to utilitarian rationales such as the oft-heard claim that the study of English, for example, is important because good communication skills can help one succeed in business. Much is rightly made of the "value added" that research universities provide to our society, and in the end my argument is that it is only through the humanities that we are able to determine what value is in those often most important domains of human experience in which, as M. H. Abrams has put it, "valid knowledge and understanding are essential, but certainty is impossible" and that it is only through the arts that human beings fully express and know their own humanity. In the absence of such knowledge and understanding, how are our scientists and technologists to know the ends to which their innovations should be directed? Or, to pose the question in another key, I have always believed in the great, original land-grant mission of ensuring the efficient provision to humanity of food and fiber, but once we are fed and clothed how much more than brutish would we be if we were condemned to huddle at the bottom of the Maslow hierarchy of needs, content with food, shelter, sleep, and warmth, and unable to understand and enjoy art, music, literature, dance, philosophy, and yes, Governor Scott, anthropology and political science?

Burlington, Vermont
November 3, 2011

NOTES

1. Another set of land-grant institutions, the thirty-three American Indian schools belonging to the American Indian Higher Education Consortium (known as 1994 land-grants for the year in which they received the designation, which carried with it long overdue equity funding through the U.S. Department of Agriculture), lies outside the scope of this volume since none of its member institutions are in any sense research universities (typical AIHEC members are small community colleges enrolling a few hundred students in associate and certificate degree programs).
2. Carnegie classifies an additional ninety-nine institutions as Research Universities High Research Activity, of which seventy-four are public and twenty-five private not-for-profit. In the main, the High and Very High Research Activity institutions are distinguished from each other not by quality and importance of the research and scholarship they generate but by scale and breadth of field coverage ("It is important to note that the groups differ solely with respect to level of research activity, not quality or importance," http://classifications.carnegiefoundation.org/methodology/basic.php, accessed November 1, 2011).

Democracy, the West, and Land-Grant Colleges

COY F. CROSS II

> The note of American life was hopeful, exuberant expansion, and, as
> for two centuries past, the exuberance was founded upon a sense of the
> freshness, wealth, and future greatness of the West.
> —Allan Nevins, *The Origins*
> And we say today, as we have ever said to the young man or woman
> light of purse but willing of hand, to the farmer or mechanic of increas-
> ing family, slender means and dubious prospects, Your true home is in
> the West!
> —Horace Greeley
> The most important idea in the genesis of the land-grant colleges and
> state universities was that of democracy, because it had behind it the
> most passionate feeling.
> —Allan Nevins, *The Origins*

Viewing the Land-grant College Act from the perspective of the 150th
anniversary, one can see it as the greatest legislation affecting higher education in American history. But truly to appreciate its full dimensions, we
must consider it in the context of its time and the ongoing movement to
strengthen American democracy. In 1862, with the outcome of the Civil
War very much in doubt, Abraham Lincoln signed three bills that greatly
enhanced western settlement and development: the Homestead Act on
May 2, the Transcontinental Railroad Act on July 1, and the Land-grant
College Act on July 2. Although nearly three more years would pass and
additional hundreds of thousands of soldiers would die before the war's
end, Lincoln and Congress believed American democracy would survive

1

and its people would continue moving west. The Transcontinental Railroad and Homestead Acts had an immediate impact, but neither contributed more to today's America than Justin Smith Morrill's "Bill Granting Lands for Agricultural Colleges."

At the 1893 American Historical Association conference, historian Frederick Jackson Turner read his paper entitled "The Significance of the Frontier in American History." Turner quoted the recent census concluding there was no longer a clearly defined "frontier line" of settlement in the United States. The end of the frontier closed "a great historic movement." Turner concluded, "Up to our own day American history has been in a large degree the history of the colonization of the Great West. The existence of an area of free land, its continuous recession, and the advance of American settlement westward, explain American development." Turner, reflecting the attitude of most nineteenth-century Americans, discounted the presence of Native Americans on the "free land" (Turner 1). There were exceptions, including Helen Hunt Jackson, whose *A Century of Dishonor* (1881) was an impassioned appeal for American Indian rights. But these were rare and politically inconsequential.

Turner cited Lincoln's three great acts in the spring and summer of 1862 to support his thesis. Although subsequent scholarship has contested, corrected, and amended parts of Turner's "Frontier Thesis," from our country's beginnings Americans accepted the connection between western settlement and democracy. Thomas Jefferson among others believed the availability of western land made possible the creation of a democracy free from the degrading conditions affecting Europe. Accepting the teachings of Voltaire, Montesquieu, and others in this Age of Enlightenment, Jefferson suggested that given the right conditions people could improve themselves. A democratic government provided the greatest opportunity for its citizens, but the rights of citizenship did not apply equally. Jefferson and nearly all the founding fathers considered only educated, property-owning white men as qualified to vote in this democracy.[1] Women, blacks, and Native Americans occupied descending rungs on the social ladder. Having seen the impact urban, industrial life had on British factory workers, Jefferson thought America could avoid those appalling conditions by becoming a land of yeoman farmers, an image many Americans held throughout the nineteenth century, long after it proved unfeasible.

In his *Notes on the State of Virginia*, Jefferson called "those who labor in the earth" "the chosen people of God." America had sufficient western land to make individual farm ownership achievable, while also overcoming the problems of tenancy in the South and subdivided farms in New England. Independent farmers could grow food and raw materials for European markets. The Ohio, Mississippi, and Missouri Rivers could carry their produce to New Orleans, where waiting ships would haul it to Europe to exchange for manufactured goods.

When drafting the Land Ordinance of 1784 to prepare western territory for eventual statehood, Jefferson hoped to provide cheap land for individual farmers. His 1785 Ordinance priced the land at $1.00 per acre, but other interests ensured the land could be purchased only in lots of 640 acres or more. Federalists, who envisioned a self-sustaining America manufacturing its own goods, raised the price to $2.00 per acre in 1796. After Jefferson became president in 1800, the Republican-controlled Congress reduced the minimum purchase first to 320 acres and then to 160 acres, decreased the price per acre to $1.25, and allowed payment over four years.

The 1790s seemed to confirm Jefferson's economic vision. The French Revolution in 1789 and the ensuing war pitting France against a British-led coalition disrupted European farming. America remained neutral and profited. Wheat prices nearly doubled and American farmers significantly increased their grain exports. Newly mechanized British textile mills needed more cotton, and Eli Whitney's cotton gin helped Southern growers meet the demand. The American shipping industry prospered, too, as the nation's merchant fleet became the largest in the world.

In 1803, Jefferson reaffirmed his vision when he approved the Louisiana Purchase for $15 million, even though his actions strengthened the central government, a position he opposed. More than 800,000 square miles, the Louisiana Territory nearly doubled the size of the United States and greatly enlarged the western area available for yeoman farmers. The added territory included the vital port of New Orleans, the key to western river transportation. Everything seemed to be in place for Jefferson's ideal nation to become a reality.

The very Napoleonic Wars that stimulated American agricultural expansion, however, soon revealed the weakness in Jefferson's yeoman-farmer national ideal. For Jefferson's plan to work, European nations had to cooperate. As the Napoleonic Wars expanded in 1802, both England and France refused to respect America's neutrality. France detained American ships that had stopped in British ports. The British Royal Navy seized American ships carrying molasses or sugar from the French West Indies. The Royal Navy's practice of searching American ships for deserters and

impressing them into British service further exacerbated U.S.-British relations. Between 1802 and 1811, Britain apprehended nearly eight thousand American sailors, many of whom were not deserters, but United
States citizens. This insult helped provoke the American-British War of
1812 and undermined the notion that the United States could prosper as
a nation of small farmers reliant upon trade with Europe. Still, a roman-
ticized version of Jefferson's dream lived on throughout the nineteenth
century.

The ensuing half-century preceding Morrill's introduction of his Bill
Granting Lands for Agricultural Colleges brought profound change in
the lives of most Americans. The period could be seen as "The Age of
Internal Revolutions." Historians have described "The Industrial Revolution," "The Economic Revolution," "The Market Revolution," "The
Social Revolution," "The Agricultural Revolution," and "The Education
Revolution." Our young nation experienced these "revolutions" simultaneously, with each contributing to and relying on the others. In a masterful
essay commemorating the Land-grant College Act's 100th anniversary,
historian Allan Nevins described how these "revolutions" naturally led to
this revolution in higher education (Nevins, *The Origins* 24).

During the same period, a wave of bankruptcies beginning near the
end of 1836 plunged the United States into the worst depression of its
first century. Six years later prices had fallen to half their previous levels
and unemployment in industrial areas reached 20 percent. New York City
was among the hardest hit. The urban problems Jefferson had seen in Europe were now affecting America. Horace Greeley, the young editor of the
literary magazine *New Yorker,* described the "filth, squalor, rags, dissipa-
tion, want, and misery" of those around him.[2] Greeley, recalling the farm
of his youth, began urging the city's poor to move to the country. Quickly
realizing the surrounding area did not contain enough land to accommodate the city's poor, he gradually expanded his call to "Go West."[3] The
vast land in the West could both provide farms for the impoverished city
dwellers and improve the lives of those who left and those who stayed.
Massachusetts Bay Colony leaders had espoused this idea two centuries
earlier, believing the West would draw off the East's discontented poor,
and this premise soon became accepted as truth. Frederick Jackson Turner
incorporated this "truth" of the "frontier" as America's "safety-valve" into
his "Frontier Thesis." (Subsequent scholarship disproved this, demonstrating that it was not the urban poor who migrated, but farmers seeking
better land.)

In 1841 Greeley merged the *New Yorker* with *The Log Cabin,* a political paper he created to support Whig candidates in the 1840 election, to form the weekly *Tribune.* The New York *Tribune's* distribution eventually exceeded two hundred thousand. Its readership has been estimated at more than one million, in a country of approximately thirty million. In the 1840s and 1850s the *Tribune* became America's "national newspaper." No other editor could match Greeley's influence, especially among farmers. Realizing that many urban poor lacked the skills and knowledge to become successful farmers, Greeley determined he would instruct them.

But farming in the 1840s differed greatly from Greeley's boyhood days in rural Vermont. Cash crops to feed the mills had replaced home-grown fruits and vegetables to feed the families. The farm wife tended a small garden that furnished fresh food for the family table, while her husband concentrated on growing cotton and wool for textiles, corn for meal and livestock feed, or hides for shoes and harnesses. Wheat soon replaced corn as the preferred crop. Being less bulky, wheat cost less to ship and arrived at the mill in better condition, and more people around the world ate wheat products than corn. With the conversion to cash crops, farming became a business, with all the attending considerations, including transportation availability and cost. Single crops were also more susceptible to blight or insects and quickly depleted the soil's nutrients. The farmer could move farther west seeking new and larger plots to till, but that might take him farther away from transportation. Greeley realized, however, that an educated farmer could stay on his farm, adding the needed fertilizers and enhancements to replenish his soil and increase his production, with the additional benefit of not having to move and start all over.

But Greeley understood that before he could instruct farmers, he must first learn this new farming himself. He also quickly found that the wisdom garnered by generations of New England farmers did not apply to conditions in the prairies of Illinois. While lamenting the scarcity of scholarly agricultural literature, Greeley read and recommended what was available. He suggested that a young farmer, armed with the latest literature and with knowledge of his own land, could choose the most suitable fertilizers and minerals. "Let us make the most of what we have, by diffusing, studying, discussing, criticizing, Liebig's *Agricultural Chemistry,* Dana's *Muck Manual,* Waring's *Elements,* and the books that each treat more especially of some department of the farmer's art," he wrote, "making ourselves familiar, first, with the principles, then the methods, of scientific, efficient, successful husbandry."

In 1853 Greeley bought a seventy-five-acre farm at Chappaqua, thirty-five miles from downtown New York. There he created his own "experimental station," trying many of his ideas before recommending them
to his readers. He experimented with "swamp muck, lime, salt, gypsum,
bone-dust, and artificial, as well as mineral, manures" to improve his soil.
He dug, blasted, and picked out rocks, built underground drainage systems, and practiced deep-plowing to increase production. He used between four and five thousand tons of rocks from his property to build a
barn that would still be standing long after he was gone.

Also in 1853, Greeley hired Solon Robinson as the *Tribune's* agricultural editor, a position Greeley continued to fill with the best men available. Robinson's weekly columns featured the latest scientific methods and
the newest equipment on the market. Greeley himself wrote many articles
on horticulture and veterinary medicine based on information he gleaned
from other writers and tidbits learned on his farm. The *Tribune* covered
everything from crop rotation to a steam-powered manure distribution
system. Greeley hoped to transform agriculture from a process of blindly
repeating crude traditional methods into a profession "as intellectual and
dignified as Physic or Law." He encouraged farmers to treat their labors
with the same respect a manufacturer or merchant gave his business.

In addition to instructing readers through the pages of his newspaper,
Greeley took his educational campaign to a national level. The influence
he enjoyed within the Whig party carried over into the new Republican
Party, which he helped create, and extended beyond his role as the editor
of his party's first leading newspaper. He exercised his power in both roles
to fight for farmers' causes, especially for an independent Department of
Agriculture and for agricultural colleges. Greeley believed the American
farmer, whose life's work required a thorough knowledge of the sciences,
needed a comprehensive curriculum from elementary school through college dedicated to the science of agriculture. Geology and chemistry, he
wrote, were "the natural bases of a sound, practical knowledge of things."
There were a few schools offering courses in agriculture, including the
Agricultural College of Michigan, the Peoples College of New York, and
Norwich Academy in Vermont. But Greeley decried the lack of colleges
for farmers; farming was, he said, the most indispensable of all professions, and agriculture was a science that deserved the same status as other
professions. Throughout the 1840s and 1850s Greeley laid the groundwork for Justin Morrill's landmark bill that created colleges emphasizing
agriculture.

In 1850, a Westerner, Illinois College Professor Jonathan Baldwin Turner, proposed a "University for the Industrial Classes" in every state to educate farmers and industrial workers. He urged farmers to pressure Congress to appropriate enough public land "to create and endow in the most liberal manner, a general system of popular Industrial education, more glorious in its design and more beneficent in its results than the world has ever seen before." Although the Illinois legislature sent Congress a set of resolutions encapsulating Professor Turner's ideas and asking that each state receive $500,000 worth of public land to "endow a system of industrial universities," Congress did not act on the resolutions. University of Illinois president Edmund J. James later claimed Turner and his supporters "selected" Morrill to introduce the Land-grant College Bill because he was from an older, Eastern state and would be more likely to succeed than a Westerner.[4]

When Justin Smith Morrill, a blacksmith's son, arrived in Congress in December 1855, he brought a lifelong interest in learning and education. Although largely self-taught, as were many mid-nineteenth-century American business and political leaders, Morrill was well versed in economics, finance, architecture, literature, and agriculture. He soon proved himself to be Congress's tariff and tax expert and made an invaluable contribution to the Union's success in the upcoming Civil War. But perhaps his greatest gift to the nation's future proved to be the land-grant colleges that continue to thrive today, 150 years later.

After introducing his bill Granting Lands for Agricultural Colleges on December 17, 1857, Morrill spoke in the House of Representatives on April 20, 1858, supporting the measure. He first considered its constitutionality. The federal government, he noted, spent millions for the benefit of commerce on railroads, lighthouses, coast surveys, harbor improvements, and support for the Navy and Naval Academy. Authors and inventors benefited from copyrights and patents. Large land grants had also boosted general education, "But all direct encouragement to agriculture has been rigidly withheld."

He next addressed the decline in American agriculture. Between 1840 and 1850, New England wheat production had dropped from 2,014,111 bushels to 1,090,132, while potato production shrank from 35,180,500 to 19,418,191 bushels. Southern states showed similar trends, with Virginia growing eighteen million fewer pounds of tobacco in 1850 than in 1840. Decreasing yields indicated "wide-spread deterioration of the soil" with proportionate loss of capital and wages. "Our country is growing debilitated, and we propagate the consumptive disease with all the energy of private enterprise and public patronage," Morrill declared, and he asked, "Does not our general system of agriculture foreshadow ultimate decay? If so, is it beyond our constitutional power and duty to provide an incidental remedy?"

Lack of knowledge and skill had caused this downward spiral, Morrill continued, and only the federal government could reverse the trend. Foreign governments aided agriculture and the results were impressive. Belgium's "once noted battle-fields" were now "equally noted model farms," which supported a population of 336 per square mile compared to Virginia's twenty-three people per square mile. Sparing no expense, France created botanical gardens, veterinary schools, five agricultural colleges, and nearly one hundred "inferior agricultural schools" that surpassed "all others in existence." England had several agricultural schools and colleges, but "jealousies of caste" kept the enrollment low. The United States, meanwhile, with ninety-five times the land of England and seventeen times that of Belgium, imported more than $100 million in agricultural products in 1857.

Agricultural colleges, Morrill continued, would not compete with literary colleges since each would serve separate needs. Farmers and "mechanics" needed specialized schools and literature "quite as much as the so-called learned professions." In agricultural colleges, farmers could learn the capability of soils and the benefits of various fertilizers, which grasses produced the best livestock and the most milk, deep plowing and drainage methods, remedies for crop diseases, and how to control insects. Tuition would be free, while the sale of crops could help defray expenses. (Although not specifically mentioned, educating the children of farmers and mechanics would also strengthen America's democracy by increasing the number of educated voters.)

The sale of public lands, lands that "should be considered a common fund for the use and benefit of all," would finance the colleges. Each state would receive twenty thousand acres of public land for each representative and senator. The government had previously awarded 45,109,879 acres to veterans. New states had received generous grants. Ten states and one territory had received 25,403,993 acres since 1850 to build railroads. By 1857, 67,736,572 acres had gone to states and territories for schools and universities. Morrill estimated under his bill approximately 5.8 million acres would go to agricultural colleges, leaving more than one billion acres of public land. In recommending the measure's passage, he urged, "Let it never be said we are 'the greatest and the meanest of mankind.'"

After delivering the speech that "was probably something better than my friends expected," Morrill overcame strong opposition from Southern Congressmen and guided his bill to passage in the House by a 105 to 100 vote. The bill then moved to the Senate, where Benjamin Wade of Ohio became its sponsor. Southerners, clinging to the safety of a narrow interpretation of the Constitution, bitterly opposed the measure. Clement Clay, of Alabama, called it "one of the most monstrous, iniquitous and dangerous measures which have ever been submitted to Congress." James Mason, of Virginia, labeled it "one of the most extraordinary engines of mischief," a misuse of federal property, and "an unconstitutional robbing of the Treasury for the purpose of bribing the States." Despite strong opposition from nearly all Southern and many Western senators, Wade pushed the bill to a vote. On February 7, 1857, the Senate passed the measure with two minor amendments, 25 to 22. The House then approved the amended version 148 to 95 on February 16 and sent it to President James Buchanan. Greeley fully supported Justin Morrill's bill, which, according to Greeley, passed even though "every Filibuster, Cuba-stealer and active Slavery Propagandist said Nay." When Buchanan vetoed the bill and publicly expressed doubts about its constitutionality, Greeley claimed the president had acted as a puppet of the slave owners, who opposed education for the workers.

Despite Buchanan's veto, Morrill knew his "College Land Bill" enjoyed widespread support among the American people. Thirteen states had instructed their representatives and senators to vote for the measure when it came up again. With Abraham Lincoln's election as president in 1860, prospects looked good. Pressing Civil War matters, however, took precedence. On December 16, 1861, Morrill introduced a revised version of his earlier bill. "Without excluding other scientific and classical studies," the colleges' curricula would include agriculture, mechanical arts [engineering], and, military tactics, a provision Morrill probably added inspired by recent Union defeats. Morrill also increased the land allotment from twenty to thirty thousand acres for each representative and senator.

Although Western states would greatly benefit from the proposed colleges, they opposed having public lands within their boundaries sold to build Eastern schools. They also argued that speculators would buy large tracts and let them sit idle while waiting for prices to rise. While the House Committee on Public Lands considered the measure, Morrill gave a copy to his friend "Old Ben" Wade and asked him to introduce it in the Senate. Wade presented the bill on May 2 and shepherded it through the upper house. Again, Westerners, led by Kansas Senator James Lane, resisted. Fearing that outsiders would claim all of Kansas' prime public lands before the state could reserve lands for schools, Lane sought to restrict the agricultural college land grants to the territories. Lane considered the bill the "most iniquitous" to the Western states of any measure ever introduced into Congress. "In it is contained the ruin of the State that I . . . represent." Henry Rice, of Minnesota, predicted that speculators would grab the best land, "blighting, like the locusts, every region which may attract them." Wade countered that the federal government had treated Western states generously, and he denied any state's special claim to federal lands within its boundaries. Iowa Senator James Harlan also refuted Lane's argument. Harlan pointed out even if all the land claimed came from Kansas, the state would still have immense acreage remaining. Lane then offered an amendment limiting the land claimed in any one state to one million acres. Wade accepted the proposal and the bill passed the Senate on June 10 by a 32-7 vote.

After the House Committee on Public Lands reported negatively on the bill, Morrill unsuccessfully tried to introduce a substitute measure. When the Senate version came to the House on June 17, Morrill told his colleagues everyone already understood the bill since it had been before Congress and the country for the preceding five years. After several attempts to amend or delay the bill failed, the House approved the "College Land Bill" 90 to 25. President Lincoln signed it into law on July 2, 1862. Horace Greeley was ecstatic. He called the measure an "augury of wide and lasting good" and claimed that if only five colleges resulted from the act, "it would be worth the years of struggle and the cost of administration."

Under the act, each state received thirty thousand acres of public land for each of its representatives and senators in Congress. In Western states, where public land still existed, public officials would select actual parcels of land. The state could either sell its allotment immediately or hold it until prices increased. States with no public lands received scrip, which they had to sell to assignees to prevent one state from owning land in another. Assignees then could redeem the scrip for actual parcels of land. The states would create a "perpetual fund" by investing the proceeds from the land or scrip sales in "stocks of the United States or of the States, or some other safe stocks, yielding not less than five per centum." The fund's capital would "remain forever undiminished." Income from the investments would serve as a "nucleus" for "the endowment, support, and maintenance of at least one college" in each state. States themselves had to finance the building of "libraries, laboratories, museums, workshops, gymnasiums, military halls and other educational appliances." Also, states had to agree to the law's provisions within two years and establish a college within five years.

Although several states, led by Iowa, Michigan, and Pennsylvania, quickly accepted the conditions of the Land-grant College Act and moved to create colleges, initial progress was slow. One reason was the flood of federal land that came onto the market simultaneously. Lincoln had approved a transcontinental railroad bill giving large tracts to the Union Pacific and Central Pacific Railroads on July 1. The Homestead Act, signed six weeks earlier, gave individuals 160 acres of public land to settle and develop. Eventually, claimants acquired 70 million acres of prairie farmland under the Homestead Act and another 130 million acres passed to builders of the transcontinental railroad. Veterans of the Mexican War and of various skirmishes against the Indians had already received warrants for more than 61 million acres. Eventually, the colleges received 17,430,000 acres.

Many states sold their scrip during this glutted market and received less than one dollar an acre. Cornell University, New York's land-grant institution, held its grant until the market improved and received $5,765,000, or $5.82 an acre. But only nine states received more than $1.25 an acre. Total proceeds reached $7.5 million. Furthermore, states often had little money for buildings since the bill passed during the Civil War. Also, because the new colleges had few teachers and limited curricula, very few students applied for courses in agriculture or mechanical arts.

Although progress was slow for all the land-grant colleges, Morrill remained steadfast in his faith and support. He helped incorporate Vermont's State Agricultural College in 1865, when it was merged with the private University of Vermont as The University of Vermont and State Agricultural College, and served many years as a trustee. In 1872 he proposed creating a permanent educational fund from the sale of public lands to help maintain the land-grant colleges. When this measure failed, he tried again, and again, and again. Between 1872 and 1890 Morrill brought forward seven bills to aid the land-grant colleges. In 1890 he argued an additional land-grant would not interfere with free homesteads, preemption, experiment stations, or future legislation governing railroads. The 1862 law had created forty-eight colleges that were "sending forth a large number of vigorous young men to scientific, agricultural, mechanical, educational, and other industrial careers." The previous law had "borne healthy and excellent fruit," but the colleges needed more money. This time Morrill carried the day. President Benjamin Harrison signed the second Land-grant Act into law on August 30, 1890.

This second act gave states an additional $15,000 a year initially for their land-grant institutions. This amount gradually increased to $25,000 a year. The second Land-grant College Act also mandated that colleges "where a distinction of race or color is made in the admission of students" would receive no money. But, simultaneously, it allowed "equal-but-separate" institutions. Only one land-grant had been designated for African Americans in the wake of Morrill Act of 1862, Alcorn State (then named Alcorn University) in 1871, but designation of land-grants for black students in Southern and border states swiftly followed the Morrill Act of 1890, creating the group of schools known collectively as the 1890 Institutions (see Carolyn Mahoney's chapter of this volume).

Even with the additional funding from the 1890 bill, Morrill was not content. In 1897 he failed in another attempt to win more money for the colleges. As late as November 1898, just one month before he died, Morrill was considering the best time to approach Congress for another increase. He believed he should wait until "the people have learned and appreciated the large number of soldiers and officers that were furnished by the Land Grant Colleges" in the Spanish-American War. Other efforts to strengthen and extend the power of the land-grant system Morrill had fathered were successful, however. In 1887, the Hatch Act had created the system of agricultural experiment stations, funded by the federal government and administered by land-grant colleges and universities throughout the nation, thus strengthening their capacity for applied research in the agricultural sciences. And sixteen years after Morrill's death, the Smith-Lever Act provided federal funding for cooperative extension services at the land-grant institutions, extending and enriching their service missions to working farmers and to rural communities.

In 1910, nearly fifty years after Lincoln signed the Land-grant College Act, Frederick Jackson Turner delivered Indiana University's commencement address, describing the contributions of the land-grant universities, which he called "state universities." Turner considered these universities, with free tuition and open to all, to be "democracy in the largest sense," reflecting the pioneer society and Jeffersonian democracy. These schools expanded scientific studies, especially applied sciences, moved away from the traditional curriculum, united vocational and college work, and developed agricultural, engineering, and business courses—"all under the ideal of service to democracy rather than of individual advancement alone." With the frontier's passing, the American democracy no longer had unlimited quantities of untouched resources. "Scientific farming must increase the yield of the field, scientific forestry must economize the woodlands, scientific experiment and construction by chemist, physicist, biologist and engineer must be applied to all of nature's forces in our complex modern society. The test tube and the microscope are needed rather than ax and rifle in this new ideal of conquest." The "state universities" must train the scientists to meet these demands and encourage their research. Turner also believed the land-grant universities, with curricula in law, politics, economics, and history, could safeguard democracy by supplying "from the ranks of democracy" public administrators, legislators, and judges, who could disinterestedly and intelligently "deal dispassionately with the problems of modern life, able to think for themselves, governed not by ignorance, by prejudice or by impulse, but by knowledge and reason and high-mindedness." To produce such leaders, "Those who investigate and teach within the university walls must respond to the injunction of the church, 'Sursum cord'—lift up the heart to high thinking and impartial search for the unsullied truth in the interests of all the people; this is the holy grail of the universities" (Turner 284–89).

Fifty-two years later, while commemorating the land-grant colleges' one hundredth anniversary, Allan Nevins called Lincoln's signing of Justin Morrill's bill "an immortal moment in the history of higher education in America." Nevins believed, "Great social changes are never effected by ideas alone, but they are never effected without them, and without passion behind the ideas. The most important idea in the genesis of the land-grant colleges and state universities was that of democracy, because it had behind it the most passionate feeling." American democracy, Nevins wrote, means "liberty of action and equality of opportunity" (Nevins, *The Origins*). The passionate idea behind the land-grant college movement was that democracy could not survive unless every man had the opportunity to pursue any occupation to which he aspired, without restriction. "The struggle for liberty when carried to its logical conclusion is always a struggle for equality, and education is the most potent weapon in this contest." A democratic society must be open, without caste lines, with members being free to move from occupation to occupation and from place to place. By the mid-nineteenth century, this freedom ensured that men, women, and children would continue streaming westward. Nevins saw Jeffersonian equality as the cornerstone of this westward movement, "the right of every person to an equitable chance in the world, to his innate human dignity, and his fair station before the law." Out of this national temperament arose the impetus for Morrill's Land-grant College Act, which Nevins considered "remarkable as a profession of faith in the future in the midst of civil war." The act coincided with the "vision of the families of bright children, springing up by the million over prairie, plain, and foothill, hungry with a New World appetite for knowledge, wisdom, and inspiration." In one hundred years, the Morrill Land-grant College Act had created seventy colleges and universities, which granted a majority of the higher degrees in the United States. Nevins concluded, "It has justly been said that 'they are now the most important sector of higher education in the country—nay, on the globe.'"

Today, fifty years after Nevins's assessment, the land-grant universities and their affiliated schools continue as "the most important sector of higher education" in the world. America's "revolution in education" strengthened our democratic nation by making college available to students for whom it would have otherwise been unachievable. The flexible entrance requirements, free tuition, expanded courses of study, and democratic atmosphere were unprecedented in universities in the United States or anywhere else in the world. Another early contribution was the training of high school teachers who would overcome the gap between elementary school and college preparatory training for most Americans. These revolutionary changes prompted existing universities to reconsider traditional methods and adopt new curricula to make themselves more relevant. For the first time, too, the new schools broke the sectarian control over higher education.

Today there are 110 land-grant institutions: 76 land-grant universities, including 18 historically black colleges, and 34 American Indian schools. More than 1.5 million students attended land-grant colleges and universities in 2009 (at the time of writing, the last year for which comprehensive enrollment data are available), including about 55,000 at the main campus of The Ohio State University, the largest, and 2,800 at Kentucky State University, the smallest of the original land-grant universities (White Earth Tribal and Community College with 113 students is the smallest of today's schools). The land-grant institutions have granted twenty million degrees, including one-third of all master's degrees and more than one-half of all doctorates awarded in the United States. The eighteen predominantly African American land-grant colleges and universities have awarded more than seven hundred thousand degrees. These universities have obviously strengthened American democracy.

While the Homestead and Transcontinental Railroad Acts seem hardly relevant to today's society, land-grant colleges and universities continue to strengthen our democracy by educating more and more of its citizens. Today's land-grant institutions, however, face challenges and changes not evident when Nevins wrote in 1962, but "the most important sector of higher education in the world" is fully capable of answering these challenges. As Justin Smith Morrill said in 1857, "We have schools to teach the art of manslaying and make masters of 'deep-throated engines' of war; and shall we not have schools to teach men the way to feed, clothe, and enlighten the great brotherhood of man?"

NOTES

1. Expanding citizenship rights is a consistent theme in American history.
2. This and subsequent Greeley quotations and information are found in Coy F. Cross II, *Go West, young man! Horace Greeley's Vision for America.*
3. Greeley's "West," and that of most nineteenth-century Americans, gradually moved from western New York and Pennsylvania to Ohio, Indiana, and Illinois. Not until the country had fulfilled its "Manifest Destiny" and spread to the Pacific did "the West" include the plains and areas beyond the Rockies.
4. This and subsequent quotes and information on Morrill and the Land-grant College Act are found in Coy F. Cross II, *Justin Smith Morrill: Father of the Land-grant Colleges.*

The 1890 Institutions in African American and American Life

CAROLYN R. MAHONEY

The Second Morrill Act and the Creation of the 1890 Institutions

Through the passage of the first Morrill Act of 1862 as well as other efforts, privately supported schools for blacks gradually gained acceptance, and by 1880 more than one hundred black colleges and universities had opened their doors in the South, in border states, and in Washington, D.C. The groundwork was laid for the establishment of the black land-grant college. But the Morrill Act of 1862, while affording the opportunity to Southern states to establish a second land-grant institution for the purpose of educating African Americans, had in fact only resulted in one such school: Alcorn Agricultural and Mechanical College, now Alcorn State University. In reality, the Southern states still balked at the idea of supporting land-grant institutions specifically designated for blacks. It was in this climate that Justin Morrill, now a U.S. senator (he had been a member of the House of Representatives when he sponsored the 1862 legislation that bears his name), introduced another land-grant measure in early 1890. After months of debate in both houses of Congress, failed votes, and reintroduction of the proposal with modifications and amendments, the measure was passed on August 19 and President Benjamin Harrison signed it on August 30 (*Leadership and Learning* 6–8).

This second Morrill Act did not provide a gift of land to the states. Instead, it authorized funding that would come from the sale of public lands: $15,000 to each state in 1890 and $1,000 annually for the next ten years until the maximum of $25,000 was reached (*Leadership and Learning* 8). The act also contained a provision that institutions practicing racial discrimination would not be eligible for the funding. The Southern states were given four alternatives for meeting this requirement: (1) to establish a black land-grant college under state control; (2) to designate an existing private college for blacks as the land-grant college; (3) to name an already existing state-supported black institution as land-grant; or (4) to take over a private black college as a state college. Under these stipulations, the 1890 land-grant institutions were established, and a new acronym took its place in the annals of higher education: the HBCUs (historically black colleges and universities) (Mayberry 46–47).

For nearly one hundred years after the Civil War, the HBCUs were the primary source of education for blacks. Most of these were normal schools that prepared students to be teachers, a real necessity at the time given the dearth of educated blacks. During these years, the following institutions were established: Lincoln University (1866); Alcorn State University (1871); South Carolina State University (1872); University of Arkansas, Pine Bluff (1873); Alabama A&M University (1875); Prairie View A&M University (1876); Southern University (1880); Tuskegee University (1881); Virginia State University (1882); Kentucky State University (1886); University of Maryland Eastern Shore (1886); Florida A&M University (1887); Delaware State University (1891); North Carolina A&T (1891); West Virginia State University (1891); Fort Valley State University (1895); Langston University (1897); and Tennessee State University (1909).

"Separate but equal" remained the presiding doctrine in the South until 1965, and so during that time period the 1890 institutions were the only means of offering the three-pronged land-grant services of instruction, research, and extension to African Americans. Their long-standing commitment to serving the needs of this population gave the HBCUs the opportunity to attract a cadre of exceptional educators, including author and orator Booker T. Washington and scientist George Washington Carver at Tuskegee University; poet Melvin B. Tolson at Langston University; John Mercer Langston, the first African American elected to Congress from Virginia, at Virginia State University; the Harvard-trained Harlem Renaissance writers Sterling Brown and Cecil A. Blue at Lincoln University; and physics professor John M. Hunter at Virginia State University, who is credited with teaching more blacks who earned doctorates in physics in the United States than any other professor. Through their efforts and those of others of their ilk, the 1890 institutions began to make significant contributions to African American life and, as they reached out through academic, research, and extension services, to American life in general.

The Educational Mission of the 1890 Institutions

Most of the schools that would eventually be designated as 1890 land-grant universities started out providing elementary and secondary education to the majority of the enrolled students. Because of the overriding need to provide basic education to this previously uneducated segment of American society, the institutions concentrated on teacher training and devoted themselves to a traditional curriculum: the classics, letters, humanities, and other aspects of the liberal arts. It was mainly after 1900 that these schools began offering curricula in the areas of agricultural and mechanical arts. From 1900 through the 1920s, the institutions struggled to establish collegiate programs leading to the bachelor's degree. Hampered by inadequate funding and the difficulty of attracting adequately trained teachers to their staffs, the black colleges nonetheless made significant strides in educating students. Without the resources to train them as scientists, engineers, and other specialists, the land-grant colleges concentrated on matriculating high-caliber teachers, with approximately 90 percent of all graduates entering this field (Christy and Williamson 4–5). The paucity of resources meant that a greater burden fell on the faculty and administrators of the 1890 institutions. One notable example of how black educators rose to the challenge occurred at what is now Alabama A&M, founded in 1875 by William Hooper Councill. When the annual state appropriation of $4,000 proved too meager to maintain the college, President Councill and his entire faculty contributed their salaries to keep the doors open (Christy and Williamson, 16).

Tuskegee University

In a similar vein, the story of Booker T. Washington is well known but worth recounting in the context of how African Americans worked and sacrificed so that the privilege of an education could be afforded to others of their race. Washington was born a slave in Virginia and moved with his family after emancipation to work in the salt furnaces and coal mines of West Virginia. Educated at Hampton Institute, he began a career as a teacher. At age twenty-five, he was selected by a three-man commission to open a school in Alabama. On July 4, 1881, in an old church and run-down shanty, he welcomed thirty students to Tuskegee Normal School. Throughout the early years of poor facilities and inadequate funding, Washington's vision kept the school alive. With the purchase of a nearby hundred-acre farm for $500, he laid the foundation for his model of a school where students lived and worked on campus (*Leadership and Learning* 22). To raise funds for his school, he traveled the country unceasingly, speaking to audiences comprising both blacks and whites, and soon became well known as an orator. In 1895, he was asked to speak at the opening of the Cotton States Exposition, a remarkable achievement at that time for a black man. In his Atlanta Compromise speech, he laid out his major thesis: that blacks should secure their constitutional rights through economic and moral advancement rather than through legal and political avenues. This conciliatory stance angered some blacks, among them W. E. B. DuBois, who feared that Washington's ideas would set back the fight for equal rights. Whites, as would be expected, approved of his views, and this gave Washington the support he needed to maintain his school ("Booker Taliaferro Washington"). When Booker T. Washington died in 1915, after thirty-four years of service to Tuskegee, the school had an endowment of nearly $2 million and property worth $1.5 million. It offered instruction in thirty-eight trades and professions in fifteen departments and employed 197 faculty members (*Leadership and Learning* 22). Washington's tenacity and foresight gave birth to one of the finest HBCUs in the nation.

Today the small school that began in a shanty is a world-class university with a student enrollment of nearly three thousand. It is the only HBCU with a fully accredited College of Veterinary Medicine and produces more than 75 percent of the African American veterinarians in the world. It is the only HBCU in the nation designated as the location for the National Center for Bioethics in Research and Health Care. Continuing the work of George Washington Carver, it supports a center for plant biotechnology research that trains U.S. scientists and students as well as scientists from Ghana, China, Nigeria, South Africa, Uganda, Egypt, and Tanzania. The College of Engineering, Architecture and Physical Sciences has been expanded to include the only aerospace engineering department at an HBCU, and the institution is a leading producer in the country of African American engineering graduates in chemical, electrical, and mechanical engineering. One of two centers funded by NASA to develop technology for growing food in space can be found at Tuskegee, and it is one of only eleven universities in the world funded and authorized by the W. K. Kellogg Foundation to establish and operate a Kellogg Conference Center, which is the technologically sophisticated hub of Continuing Education and Hospitality/Tourism Management Training. The Tuskegee story is one that exemplifies the powerful force that is education (http://www.tuskegee.edu).

Indeed, all of the 1890 institutions are models for the change that can be wrought in people's lives through the power of education. Their goal has always been to provide an educational experience that many black Americans would otherwise not have had. Some graduates' names are instantly recognizable: Oprah Winfrey, who attended Tennessee State University; Alex Haley, who attended Alcorn State; and Jesse Jackson, who attended North Carolina A&T. The Olympic athlete Wilma Rudolph and the singer Yolanda Adams attended Tennessee State. Civil rights activist Betty Shabazz and actor/comedian Keenan Ivory Wayans attended Tuskegee. A number of recent members of Congress pursued a higher education at 1890 institutions, including Rep. Corrine Brown, Democrat-FL, at Florida A&M University; Rep. James Clyburn, Democrat-SC, at South Carolina State University; Rep. Jesse Jackson Jr., Democrat-IL, at North Carolina A&T; Rep. Kendrick Meek, Democrat-FL, at Florida A&M University; Rep. Edolphus Towns, Democrat-NY, at North Carolina A&T University; and Rep. David Scott, Democrat-GA, at Florida A&M University. These alumni and many others have made remarkable contributions to society and the nation.

And then there are the hundreds of thousands of students served by the 1890 institutions who have achieved success simply by becoming college graduates, a goal that they have often been the first in their families to reach. The colleges and universities have a strong record of nurturing African American students and setting them on their paths to meaningful careers, as the Tuskegee story has illustrated. A snapshot of the other seventeen 1890 land-grant institutions reveals the wide-ranging educational opportunities available to students at these fine institutions.

Alabama A&M University

Alabama A&M University (AAMU) listed a total enrollment of 5,814 students for the Fall 2010 semester. AAMU students have a wide range of programs from which to select, including food science, communicative sciences and disorders, civil engineering, education, urban and regional planning, clinical psychology, and forestry. Alabama A&M is home to one of the largest graduate schools among HBCUs, with more than one thousand enrolled students. For those seeking the terminal degree, the institution offers four PhD programs: food science, physics, plant and soil science, and reading/literacy. AAMU is a top producer of African American PhDs in physics and is the nation's leading producer of African American PhDs in plant and soil science. The school proudly records that a Nobel Laureate has visited the campus every year since 1997, and that AAMU biotechnologists are making headway in the production of an "allergy-free" peanut, an accomplishment that will make a significant difference in the lives of millions of American children (http://www.aamu. edu*)*.

Alcorn University

With three locations in Mississippi, Alcorn State University serves approximately 4,300 full- and part-time undergraduate and graduate students. The Alcorn mission statement promises that it will prepare its graduates "to be well-rounded future leaders of high character and to be successful in the global marketplace of the 21st century." To foster this goal, the institution has seven schools that offer a number of majors. Undergraduates find a wide range of degree choices, from chemistry to music performance to nutrition and dietetics. Alcorn also has a strong record in graduate education, with nine degree programs to offer students: the Master of Science in Education; the Master of Arts in Teaching; the Master of Science in Agriculture; the Master of Science in Biology; the Education Specialist in Elementary Education; the Master of Science in Nursing; the Master of Science in Computer and Information Sciences; the Master of Business Administration; and the Master of Science in Workforce Education Leadership. This array of disciplines makes Alcorn graduates a powerful presence throughout the nation: they heal the sick, help the less fortunate, teach children, produce art and music, head thriving businesses, conduct research, work to save the environment, and help solve world hunger. Alcorn faculty stress that the institution's outstanding reputation for educating minority scientists and educators stems, in part, from a tradition of involving students in research (http://www.alcorn.edu).

University of Arkansas at Pine Bluff

Billing itself the "flagship of the Delta," the University of Arkansas at Pine Bluff (UAPB) pledges that students will find excellent career choices available at the institution, and this promise is borne out through undergraduate degree offerings in early childhood and other teacher education programs, regulatory science, aquaculture and fisheries, theatre and communication, political science, rehabilitative services, industrial technology, nursing, computer science, and a range of other degree programs. The top ten undergraduate majors at UAPB, by enrollment, are business administration, criminal justice studies, biology, industrial technology, early childhood education, psychology, computer science, human sciences, accounting, and health/physical education. Students who pursue graduate studies at UAPB have the following choices: Master of Education, Master of Arts in Teaching, Master of Science in Addiction Studies, Master of Science in Aquaculture Fisheries, and Master of Science in Agricultural Regulations. A Center of Excellence designate of the U.S. Department of Agriculture, the UAPB bachelor's degree program in regulatory science is the only one of its kind in the nation. This program is the product of an enabling partnership with national governmental agencies such as the U.S. Department of Agriculture and the U.S. Department of Transportation (http://www.uapb.edu).

Delaware State University

Delaware State University is a unique mixture of the past, present, and future. Situated on a historic plot of Delaware land, what began as a one hundred-acre campus is now a picturesque four hundred-acre campus that takes pride in its older buildings, including one that is a national historic landmark. Time capsules from nearly a century ago can still be unearthed. The old blends seamlessly with the new as research in the fields of medicine, military defense, agriculture, and other vital areas occurs on an ongoing basis. The institution also boasts satellite campuses in both Georgetown and Wilmington, four outdoor athletic fields, two farm properties, and the Airway Science Program, which maintains a fleet of planes and a base of operations at the Delaware Air Park in Cheswold. Reported enrollment in 2011 was slightly over 3,800. Students can choose from among fifty-six undergraduate degree programs, twenty-five master's degree programs, and five doctoral degree programs. Undergraduates have broad choices, including a career path in aviation management or professional pilot; agriculture and related sciences degrees, including food and nutritional sciences, wildlife management, and aquatic science; an array of options in the Department of Communications, such as broadcast journalism, public relations, and television production; the cutting-edge fields of cell/molecular/biotechnology sciences and forensic science; and the service-oriented career paths of community health and social work. Delaware State University's Vision Statement sets out its objective to be "renowned for a standard of academic excellence that prepares our graduates to become the first choice of employers in a global market and invigorates the economy and the culture of Delaware and the Mid-Atlantic Region" (http://www.desu.edu).

Florida A&M University

Florida A&M University has evolved from a humble beginning in 1887 as the State Normal College for Colored Students with fifteen students and two instructors to become known as an academic powerhouse in higher education. Currently FAMU has approximately thirteen thousand students and a faculty of approximately six hundred. The university has thirteen schools and colleges and one institute, which offer the following degrees: fifty-two bachelor's, twenty-seven master's, one specialist degree, and ten doctoral degrees in biomedical engineering, chemical engineering, civil engineering, electrical engineering, mechanical engineering, industrial engineering, pharmaceutical sciences, physics, educational leadership, entomology, and environmental science.

Accredited by the Commission on Colleges of the Southern Association of Colleges and Schools, Florida A&M is located in Tallahassee, the capital of Florida. The campus is situated on 423 acres with 156 buildings. The physical assets of Florida A&M University are valued at approximately $410 million. Florida A&M University, the Home of the Mighty Rattlers, is proud of its 125-year legacy that boasts of many significant accomplishments such as the following:

> Ranked No. 1 among public universities by the National Science Foundation (NSF) for producing African American graduates that go on to earn PhDs in science and engineering;

Awarded 36 percent of its graduate degrees to students in STEM
and health professions specified by the board of governors as
strategic areas of emphasis;

In September 2011: (1) *Washington Monthly* ranked FAMU
among the top hundred universities in the nation; (2) *The
Princeton Review* named FAMU among the best colleges
in the Southeast; (3) *Business Week* named FAMU one of
the country's "Most Innovative Colleges" in the area of
technology transfer; and (4) FAMU won its seventh national
title as the Championship Team for the 22nd Annual Honda
Campus All-Star Challenge.

Originally founded to meet the needs of the underrepresented and
underprivileged, Florida A&M continues to pursue its goal to educate
and train young men and women as qualified professionals who will become the leaders of tomorrow and who will serve the world by solving
complex issues that impact the quality of life for humanity.[1]

Fort Valley State University

Located in Fort Valley, Georgia, the seat of Peach County, Fort Valley
State University (FVSU) is one of Georgia's three public historically black
colleges and universities and Georgia's only 1890 land-grant school. From
humble beginnings more than a hundred years ago, FVSU now has more
than 3,500 students representing 130 of the state's 159 counties, thirty
states, and ten countries. The school proudly proclaims that it embraces
a history that weaves together African American culture with a commitment to personal and intellectual growth and a deep sense of community. The institution's acclaimed biology and chemistry departments send
more students of African descent to medical and dental programs than
any other Georgia state school. Another sterling feature of the school is
the Cooperative Developmental Energy Program, the nation's only program aimed at preparing minorities and women to pursue energy-related
disciplines. Students in the program earn two bachelor's degrees: one sci-
ence-related and one energy-related. The institution also offers the only
four-year veterinary technology degree program in the state of Georgia.
In addition, FVSU awards the Bachelor of Arts and the Bachelor of Science degrees in more than fifty majors, as well as graduate degrees in
education, counseling, public health, animal science, and biotechnology.

FVSU has contributed greatly to the state's agriculture over the years through its applied research and outreach programs. The mission of the Agricultural Research Station is to engage in scientific investigations that hold promise for generating new knowledge and technology that enhance the agricultural industry and the quality of life for residents of Georgia. Within this broader mission, emphasis is on enhancing small-scale agriculture and assisting the rural disadvantaged. FVSU is particularly known for its specialty plant biotechnology research and internationally reputed small ruminant research and outreach programs. Working jointly with the U.S. Department of Agriculture and the University of Georgia, FVSU's Cooperative Extension Service seeks to identify and develop educational programs for a diverse clientele that includes the rural disadvantaged, working homemakers, small/family and part-time farmers, lay community leaders, youth, small business owners, and other members of the general public in Georgia.

While relatively small, Fort Valley State University definitely drives economic growth in the area. Based on data gathered between July 1, 2009, and June 30, 2010, a report from the Selig Center for Economic Growth in the University of Georgia's Terry College of Business shows that FVSU had a $141 million economic impact on the state in fiscal year 2010, and generated 1,784 jobs. The school is understandably proud of its role in both the lives of its students and the broader economic and academic life of the state and nation (http://www.favu.edu).

Kentucky State University

Kentucky State University (KSU) began as an idea. In October 1885, leaders in Kentucky met to discuss issues critical to the social welfare of America and the state. One issue that stood out was the fact that Kentucky needed more normal schools to train African Americans to teach in black elementary schools. A subcommittee charged with devising a plan of action to meet this need created the State Normal School for Colored Persons. It submitted a resolution to the General Assembly in the spring of 1886, and the legislators authorized the school's creation in May of that year. Several cities bid for the right to be the site of the new school, but Frankfort, the state capitol, made the best offer: a monetary incentive and a parcel of land where the school could be built. When it opened in October 1887, there were three teachers, fifty-five students, and one building.

Nearly 125 years later, the school has changed from an institution that focused on training teachers to a comprehensive university with a variety of majors. Though KSU has maintained its liberal arts roots, students can also choose training in professional fields such as nursing and public administration. Another change has been in the population. The faculty, staff, and students are an ethnic mix, making KSU the most diverse public institution in the state. The institution is committed to maintaining its focus on service to African Americans, and thus KSU has made it an important part of its mission to collect and preserve Kentucky African American history, from university history to the contributions of African Americans throughout the state. This history and memorabilia are collected in the campus Center of Excellence for the Study of Kentucky African Americans.

KSU's Land Grant Program (LGP) focuses on the agricultural, educational, economic, and social problems of the people of the Commonwealth of Kentucky, especially limited resource persons and families. This is accomplished through LGP's three distinct areas: the Community Research Service, the Cooperative Extension Program, and the Aquaculture Research Center. A recently established Master of Science in Aquaculture/Aquatic Sciences has helped to establish aquaculture as KSU's premier program.

The location of the university in the state capital enables it to contribute to the training of state workers through its governmental services center. Students can participate in government internships and earn from three to twelve academic semester credit hours. The school also offers a supplementary internship program through which pre-law students can gain experience and earn academic credits while working as interns in the office of the Kentucky Attorney General. With more than 2,500 students, the school that was once an idea is now an integral part of the state's public university system (http://www.kysu.edu).

Langston University

Langston University was established in 1897 as the Colored Agricultural and Normal University in the all-black town of Langston, Oklahoma. In accordance with the legislation that created it, the school provided African Americans with an industrial and agricultural curriculum, a teachers' college, and a liberal arts curriculum, and it did so with less funding than many Oklahoma institutions of the time that pursued just one of these missions. In 1941, the school became Langston University, named, as was the town, in honor of John Mercer Langston, an African American educator and U.S. congressman from Virginia. After white colleges across the nation began accepting black students, Langston was faced with a sensitive issue when some Oklahoma politicians began questioning whether the school was still needed. Langston University weathered that particular storm, and in 1978 the State Regents for Higher Education assigned it an urban mission. The following year, the university opened offices in Oklahoma City and Tulsa. That same year, the professional programs of nursing and physical therapy were added to the curriculum. In 1984, the American Institute for Goat Research was established. The name was changed to E (Kika) de la Garza Institute for Goat Research in 1990, and today it is an internationally recognized agricultural research station. In 1989, Langston created the E. P. McCabe Honors Program, and soon began offering master's degrees in education and rehabilitation counseling and a doctoral degree in physical therapy. These new initiatives led to steady enrollment increases, including a sizable number of white students (http://digital.library.okstate.edu/encyclopedia/entries/L/LA021.html).

Today, approximately three thousand students call Langston University their academic home. They choose from degree programs as varied as child development, drafting and design technology, agribusiness, bilingual/multicultural education, health care administration, and rehabilitation counseling, among many others. With a rich and distinguished history as the state's only historically black institution of higher education, and as the westernmost HBCU in the nation, Langston University maintains its commitment to its African American roots (http://www.langston.edu).

Lincoln University

By the 1950s Lincoln University, the oldest of the 1890 land-grant schools, was the model of a black, segregated institution of that time. Students who came had the expectation of being taught by some of the best black academics in the nation, who held degrees awarded by some of the most prestigious universities throughout the United States, schools such as Harvard, Cornell, Chicago, and Columbia. But declining enrollments due in part to decreasing enrollment of military veterans and also to legal challenges to segregation that siphoned off students to other schools put Lincoln University's existence in peril. When the U.S. Supreme Court ruled in the case of *Brown v. the Board of Education of Topeka, Kansas*, in 1954, a new era began for the institution. Student enrollment doubled by the end of the 1950s, and one-third of the student population was white (Holland).

The Lincoln University of today has expanded its mission to embrace the needs of a broader population while remaining committed to its historic roots. Situated on 169 acres on a hilly prominence with a panoramic view of Jefferson City, the institution serves approximately 3,300 students, both undergraduate and graduate. Currently, white students comprise slightly over half of the student body, with the majority of these being commuter students from Jefferson City and surrounding towns. Lincoln students can choose from an array of undergraduate majors, including environmental science, agribusiness, civil engineering technology, political science, criminal justice, medical technology, and wellness. Those continuing their education can earn master's degrees in business administration, history and sociology, environmental science, and several fields of education. The educational specialist degree is also offered.

While it has changed considerably since its founding, Lincoln University continues to offer an exceptional education both to its historical base and to the broader clientele that has found it to be a perfect academic home (http://www.lincolnu.edu).

University of Maryland Eastern Shore

The University of Maryland Eastern Shore is a forward-looking institution located in Princess Anne, Maryland. Founded in 1886 through the beneficence of the Delaware Conference of the Methodist Episcopal Church, the school was established as the Delaware Conference Academy. When the state was faced with the directive of providing a land-grant school to which African Americans could be admitted, it assumed control of what was by then known as Princess Anne Academy and renamed it the Eastern Shore Branch of the Maryland Agricultural College. In 1926, the college passed into the complete control of the state. In 1970, the school became the University of Maryland Eastern Shore (UMES) and has since developed an academic program as impressive as any educational institution of its size in the eastern United States. Today, the university boasts a 742-acre campus, which includes a 350-acre research and teaching farm. It is nationally recognized for the beauty of its grounds. With a low student-to-faculty ratio, well-funded research programs, and a historic tradition of inclusion, UMES is a strong engine for growth and development in the area, responding to student needs, local needs, and global concerns.

Over recent years, UMES has added seventeen new degree-granting programs to its academic roster. The more than 4,400 students who call UMES their academic home can choose from major programs leading to the BA and BS degrees in twenty-six disciplines in the arts and sciences, professional studies, and agricultural sciences, as well as thirteen teaching degrees and eight pre-professional programs. Students seeking a graduate degree have the following fields of choice: At the PhD level, educational leadership, food science and technology, organizational leadership; marine-estuarine and environmental sciences at the MS and PhD levels; toxicology at the MS and PhD levels; and the MS in applied computer science, chemistry, food and agricultural sciences, guidance and counseling, physical education, and special education. Professional doctoral degrees are offered in physical therapy and in pharmacy. UMES is the only four-year institution on the Eastern Shore that offers both undergraduate and graduate degrees in computer science. This field, as well as the fields of hospitality management, aviation sciences, engineering and law enforcement, is especially beneficial to the area, particularly since graduates of UMES often choose to remain on the Eastern Shore, finding jobs in their chosen fields and adding to the region's economic and ethnic diversity. In this respect as in many others, the University of Maryland Eastern Shore continues to look toward the current and future needs of the community and the state (http://www.umes.edu).

North Carolina A&T University

With the passage of the Morrill Act of 1890, the General Assembly of North Carolina wasted no time in mandating a college for African Americans within the state university system. First established as the Agricultural and Mechanical College for the Colored Race and operated in Raleigh as an annex to Shaw University, the school quickly found a permanent home when a group of Greensboro citizens came together to donate land and initial funding for the first building. Today, North

Carolina A&T University (NCA&T) is situated on two hundred acres in Greensboro. With a student enrollment of more than ten thousand and a workforce of 2,170, the institution is an academic and economic force in North Carolina. The students who matriculate at the university can do so in any of 117 undergraduate degree programs, in more than fifty master's degree programs, and in doctoral programs in mechanical, electrical, and industrial engineering; energy and environmental systems; and leadership studies.

North Carolina A&T has many points of pride. It graduates the largest number in the nation of African American engineers at the undergraduate, master's, and doctoral levels. It is home to the largest number of psychology undergraduates in the nation. Through its nationally accredited AACSB School of Business and Economics, it is a top producer of African American certified public accountants. In keeping with its heritage, it is home to the largest agricultural school among HBCUs, and it is the second largest producer of minority agricultural graduates.

But for all its educational might, NCA&T retains the family feel of a traditional HBCU. The student-to-faculty ratio is sixteen to one, and 63 percent of undergraduate classes have fewer than thirty students in them. Eighty-nine percent of new freshmen and 41 percent of all undergraduates live on campus. In a 2008 survey, 74 percent of seniors reported tutoring or teaching other students, and 80 percent of seniors participated in community or volunteer work. The "Aggie" model is clearly one that has proven to be successful (http://www.ncat.edu).

Prairie View A&M University

The Reconstruction Period after the Civil War was a time in which political and economic special interest groups aggressively lobbied the federal government in their attempt to shape the culture of the vanquished Southern states. Prairie View A&M University had its beginnings during this time. The Texas Constitution of 1876 pledged to provide separate schools for whites and blacks, and also pledged to establish an agricultural and mechanical college. A consequence of these provisions was the establishment of Alta Vista Agricultural and Mechanical College of Texas for Colored Youth in August of that year. Land was purchased from the Alta Vista Plantation for this school, and eight African American men, the first of their race to enroll in a state-supported college in Texas, began their studies there in March 1878. The name "Prairie View" was first applied to the school through an 1879 legislative act, and in 1973 it became Prairie View A&M University.

From that first class of eight, Prairie View's enrollment now exceeds eight thousand, including more than two thousand graduate students. These students come from throughout the United States as well as from many foreign countries. During the university's 130-year history, it has awarded some 46,000 academic degrees. Today it has established a reputation for producing engineers, nurses, and educators, among other professions. With a roster of baccalaureate degrees in fifty academic majors, thirty-seven master's degrees, and four doctoral programs, the university is a comprehensive public institution of higher education. The main campus remains in Prairie View, which is located approximately forty miles northwest of Houston. The College of Nursing facility is located in the Texas Medical Center in Houston. Specialized programs and services in juvenile justice; architecture; teacher education; social work; and the food, agricultural, and natural resource sciences benefit Prairie View A&M's target service area, which includes the Texas Gulf Coast Region, the commercial area known as the Northwest Houston Corridor, and urban Texas centers (http://www.pvamu.edu).

South Carolina State University

From its struggle since its founding in 1896 as the state's sole public college for black youth, South Carolina State University in Orangeburg has overcome obstacles and made enormous strides. Support from various sources helped the school survive the Depression. During the 1950s and 1960s, hundreds of S.C. State students took part in various civil rights demonstrations; many were arrested. The year 1968 proved a deadly one on campus, as it did elsewhere in the nation. Three young men were slain and twenty-seven were wounded by state highway patrolmen in what became known as the Orangeburg Massacre.

Although S.C. State has been open to white students since 1966, it has retained its mission and character as a historically black institution with the result that it is, today, ranked third in the nation in graduating minorities with the doctor of education degree. Its nearly five thousand students major in a wide range of programs, including agribusiness, accounting, art, English, drama, physics, and political science. Its impressive list of "only's" includes the following:

> The only undergraduate environmental science field station in the nation;
>
> The only undergraduate degree program in nuclear engineering in South Carolina;
>
> The only master of science degree in transportation in South Carolina;
>
> The only master of business administration degree with a concentration in agribusiness in South Carolina;
>
> The only doctor of education degree focusing on education administration in South Carolina; and
>
> The only HBCU in the country with an interdisciplinary Art Museum and Planetarium in one facility.

Although small, its economic impact in the state is considerable. Of its approximately thirty thousand alumni, more than eighteen thousand live in South Carolina and collectively earn an estimated $207 million in additional income as a result of education and degrees earned at S.C. State. The university supports more than 1,500 jobs and has a $152.5 million impact in the Orangeburg community, and a statewide impact of $181.5 million. The school also prides itself on a number of outstanding alumni, including eight college presidents; more than two thousand minority officers in the U.S. Army, surpassing West Point, and fourteen General Officers; six members of the current South Carolina General Assembly; and James E. Clyburn, Majority Whip for the 111th Congress.

S.C. State is currently ranked #1 in Social Mobility by *The Washington Monthly,* a ranking it also achieved in 2006, 2007, and 2009; and it is ranked #49 among HBCUs by *Black Enterprise Magazine.* It is truly a small but mighty powerhouse (http://www.scsu.edu).

Southern University and A&M College

Southern University and A&M College traces its origins to 1880 in New Orleans, when a group of black politicians petitioned the state legislature to establish a school for African Americans. The result was Southern

University, which was founded that same year and first opened to students in March 1881, on Calliope Street in New Orleans. With the passage of the Morrill Act of 1890, the school was reorganized as a land-grant institution, with separate divisions for agriculture and mechanical arts. Southern remained in New Orleans until 1912, when a legislative act authorized its move to Baton Rouge, where it reopened in 1914. During the 1970s, a major reorganizational change occurred, and the Southern University System, with its own Board of Supervisors, was established. This system, still in effect today, consists of Southern University and Agricultural & Mechanical College at Baton Rouge, Southern University Law Center, Southern University at New Orleans, Southern University at Shreveport, and the Southern University Agricultural Research and Extension Center. The approximately eight thousand students who enroll each year can choose from bachelor's degree programs in forty-two areas, master's degree programs in nineteen areas, five doctoral programs, and two associate degrees.

Southern University has developed a set of values based on the French and Creole concept of "lagniappe," meaning "something extra." "Lagniappe," as Southern has adopted it, incorporates these values: leadership, accountability, giving, nurturing, integrity, accessibility, pride, patience, and excellence. For the Southern family of administrators, faculty, staff, and students, these values reflect the role that the university plays in both the Greater Baton Rouge community and the world at large (http://www.subr.edu).

Tennessee State University

For more than a dozen years, Tennessee State University (TSU) has been listed in *U.S. News and World Report's* "Guide to America's Best Colleges." Now a comprehensive, urban, land-grant university, Tennessee State was founded in 1912 in Nashville as a normal school, one of three authorized by the Tennessee State General Assembly in 1909. The institution became a four-year teachers' college in 1922, gaining the capacity to grant bachelor's degrees. In 1979, it merged with the University of Tennessee at Nashville to become Tennessee State University, offering more than forty-five bachelor's degree programs, twenty-four master's degree options, and seven doctoral degrees.

TSU can point with pride to a number of facts: (1) its exceptional marching band is internationally known as the "Aristocrat of Bands"; (2) it is home to one of the best forensic debate teams in the nation; (3) it counts media mogul Oprah Winfrey, Olympic athlete Wilma Rudolph, Johns Hopkins cardiac surgeon Dr. Levi Watkins, and cell phone microchip inventor Jesse Russell among its distinguished alumni; (4) in 1999, researchers at TSU Center for Automated Space Science were the first to discover a planet outside our solar system; and (5) it graduates the highest number of African American bachelor's degree holders in agriculture, agriculture operations, and agriculture-related sciences.

Currently, nearly 6,500 undergraduates and 1,900 graduate students from forty-six states and forty-five countries call TSU their academic home. They have an exceptionally wide range of majors from which to choose, many of which reflect today's highly specialized and technological job market, including aeronautical technology, applied geospatial info systems, e-business technology, cardio-respiratory care sciences, and urban policy and planning. Graduate students can seek advanced degrees in a multitude of areas, including agriculture and consumer sciences, arts and sciences, education, public service and urban affairs, and health sciences. As TSU's Mission Statement promises students: "Your future drives our mission" (http://www.tnstate.edu).

Virginia State University

Founded in 1882 as the Virginia Normal and Collegiate Institute, Virginia State University (VSU) was the first fully state-supported four-year institution of higher learning for African Americans in the United States. Today, its student population of 5,600 benefits from personal attention by the faculty and staff of VSU. As a result, in 2008 *U.S. News and World Report* named the university the top public master's-level HBCU in America for the second consecutive year. Situated atop a rolling landscape overlooking the Appomattox River in Chesterfield County, the 236-acre main campus is home to more than fifty buildings, including sixteen dormitories and seventeen classroom buildings.

Students who matriculate at VSU can choose from among fifty-two baccalaureate and master's degree programs and a Certificate of Advanced Study within five schools: the School of Agriculture; the School of

Business; the School of Engineering, Science and Technology; the School of Liberal Arts and Education; and the School of Graduate Studies, Research and Outreach. Since 2008, students also have the option to pursue a PhD program in health psychology, the only one of its type in the state.

In 2006, VSU inaugurated Low Income Families with Talented Students (LIFTS), a financial aid program that meets 100 percent of a qualifying student's financial need by providing 75 percent through scholarships and grants and limiting debt through student loans to 25 percent of VSU's in-state cost of attendance over four years, regardless of state residency. LIFTS is the first program of its kind among HBCUs (http://www.vsu.edu).

West Virginia State University

At the time that West Virginia State University (WVSU) was founded in 1890 as one of the seventeen land-grant institutions authorized by Congress under the Second Morrill Act, West Virginia was one of the states that maintained a segregated educational system. The school was established in Institute, West Virginia, eight miles from Charleston, as West Virginia Colored Institute, offering the equivalent of a high school education, vocational training, and teacher preparation. In 1915, it began to offer college degrees. In 1929, the name was changed to West Virginia State College. With the U.S. Supreme Court's 1954 landmark decision outlawing school segregation, the college rapidly converted to an integrated institution serving a predominantly white, commuting, older student population. This shift occurred due in part to demographics and in part to a concerted effort to reverse an enrollment decline that had begun in the early 1950s. Integration achieved the desired effect, with enrollment eventually quadrupling. Around the same time, a decision by the West Virginia Board of Education compelled the school to surrender its land-grant status, the only one of the 1890 institutions to do so. Only after a twelve-year effort was this status restored, by an Act of Congress, in 2001.

During the 1970s, a community college component was initiated, and recently, with approval to offer graduate courses, university status was conferred on the school. Although the racial proportions of the student body, faculty, and staff have changed dramatically since WSVU's inception, it still emphasizes diversity and its tradition as a historically black college. Its mission statement guarantees that it has "evolved into a fully accessible, racially integrated, and multi-generational institution"; that it is "a living laboratory of human relations"; and that it offers "a vibrant community in which those who work, teach, live, and learn do so in an environment that reflects the diversity of America." The approximately four thousand students who live and learn in this milieu currently come from forty-three states and the District of Columbia as well as from seven other countries. They can select from seventy-eight areas of study leading to a bachelor's and, in three of those areas, a master's degree. The nineteen-to-one student-to-teacher ratio ensures that students receive the personal attention for which HBCUs are known (http://www.wvstateu.edu).

The Breadth and Depth of the 1890 Institutions

The academic impact of the seventeen 1890 land-grant universities and Tuskegee University (which has operated throughout its distinguished history as a de facto land-grant because in 1891 the State of Alabama designated Alabama A&M as the state's 1890 land-grant institution) is indeed substantial. For more than 120 years, these institutions have opened their doors both to the underserved and underrepresented and to those who have sought the kind of education that can only be found at such service-oriented institutions. Their graduates influence every facet of American life and society, from education through politics, health care, the arts, agriculture, science, the military, and so much more. This influence extends beyond the boundaries of the nation and into the world at large. If education were all that the 1890 land-grant universities excelled in, they would be considered an unqualified success. But their range extends far beyond the educational value they provide, into research and the extension programs that reach those who are disadvantaged and most in need of the kinds of services that the 1890s are so able to supply.

Funding for Research at the 1890 Land-Grant Institutions

The first publicly funded research at the 1890 institutions occurred one year after passage of the Hatch Act when a branch experiment station was established at Prairie View A&M with the objective of "designing experimental and demonstration projects designed to improve instruction on campus and production practices among farmers" (Mayberry 92). In 1897, Alabama established an experiment station at Tuskegee under the direction of George Washington Carver, and in 1937 an agricultural branch experiment station was established under an arrangement with Virginia Polytechnic Institute and State University, the 1862 land-grant university in Virginia. Carver began with an annual appropriation of $1,500 that was supplemented by philanthropy and funding from Tuskegee. It was only after enactment of Public Law 89-106 on August 4, 1965, seventy-five years after the 1890 Morrill Act became law, that most of the historically black land-grant universities began receiving financial support for agricultural research. This important legislation authorized the United States Department of Agriculture (USDA) to fund research at institutions that had previously been deemed ineligible for such support.

In September 1966, Dr. George Mehren, Assistant Secretary for USDA, requested that the National Academy of Sciences develop a formula for distribution of the $283,000 allocated for sixteen campuses. Tuskegee and West Virginia State University did not receive this funding. In FY 1967 the funds were distributed equally at a level of $17,658.50 per campus. According to the formula developed, each institution received a base allocation of $10,000, plus an equitable fraction of the balance that ranged from two to ten percent. This resulted in a range of allocations from $12,413 to $22,424 that continued through 1971. Under new legislation that occurred in 1972, base funding increased to $100,000, resulting in a range of total funding per university from $126,960 to $653,430. Although Tuskegee had been excluded from the provisions of PL 89-106 passed in 1965, the institution was included in the 1972 legislation after the 1890 land-grants argued strongly for its inclusion and voluntarily reduced their allocations by one-sixteenth. Total funding for research rose from $283,000 in 1967 to $8.6 million in 1972. These funds were provided as five-year grants that were administered by the 1862 institution in the state. Direct funding to the 1890 institutions began with the passage of Section 1445 of Public Law 95-113, the Food and Agriculture Act of 1977. With enactment of this new federal law, funding under Public Law 89-106 was terminated. The 1977 legislation allowed 1890 universities to become fully incorporated into the United States land-grant system and authorized permanent funding for the 1890 land-grant universities. Section 1445 stipulated that funding levels for research were to be not less than 15 percent of the total appropriations of the 1862 institutions. The level of authorization for research funding of the 1890 institutions and

Tuskegee increased to 25 percent with passage of the 2002 farm bill and 30 percent with passage of the 2008 farm bill (Brooks).

In 1971, the Association of Research Coordinators was formed in conjunction with the Cooperative State Research Extension and Education Service (CSREES) of the United States Department of Agriculture. This name was changed in 1978 to the Association of Research Directors. This association allowed an official avenue of representation of the 1890s through the National Experiment Station Committee on Organization and Policy, which was part of the National Association of State Universities and Land-grant Colleges (NASULGC). In March 2009, NASULGC became the Association of Public and Land-grant Universities (APLU). Advocacy efforts of this body, along with changing attitudes toward the black land-grant institutions, have played significant roles in recent successes in obtaining the before-mentioned federal funding.

The 1890 land-grant universities are today recognized by APLU as one of the five regions (Northeast, Southern, North Central, Western, and 1890s regions). Each region has an executive director who is instrumental in many of the most important functions of the regions. Today the Association of Research Directors (ARD) represents the federation of the eighteen 1890 land-grant universities. The mission of ARD is to "provide visionary and enlightened leadership to member institutions as they continuously address issues impacting their ability to accomplish the food and agricultural research challenges facing the state, the nation and world-at-large" (http://www.umes.edu/ard/Default.aspx?id=11342).

Areas of Research at the 1890 Institutions

Dr. Carolyn Brooks, the executive director for the Association of Research Directors (ARD), recently surveyed the 1890 institutions and requested information on what they considered their strongest areas of research. Results of the survey showed these areas to be (1) water quality and quantity, (2) aquaculture science and fisheries, (3) specialty crops/horticulture, (4) environmental sustainability, (5) animal and plant genomics, (6) urban forestry, (7) small ruminant initiatives, (8) small farms and rural development, (9) food science/safety, (10) nutrition for wellness, and (11) renewable energy.

On September 28, 2010, members of the Experiment Station Section (EES), the State Agricultural Experiment Station (SAES), and the

Association of Research Directors (ARD) met for the ESS/SAES/ARD Annual Meeting and Workshop, held in Nashville, Tennessee. The following examples of research currently being performed at each of the 1890 institutions were included in a slide presentation by Dr. Orlando McMeans (McMeans):

University of Arkansas, Pine Bluff

1. Micropropagation of pecans for large scale multiplication
2. Studying the *Arabidopsis* genome for detoxification of heavy metals and mycotoxins
3. Evaluating rice plants engineered to express isoflavone synthase (for health benefits)

Fort Valley State University

1. Georgia Small Ruminant Research and Extension Center (GSRREC)
2. Southern Consortium for Small Ruminant Parasite Control (SCSRPC), an international research group from twenty institutions
3. Screening for medicinal plants and for rapid biomass production

Lincoln University

1. Environmental stewardship: remediation of heavy metals in soils and air quality studies related to greenhouse gas fluxes in various ecosystems
2. Aquaculture: developing genetic lines of bluegill for commercial production
3. Small ruminant production: anthelmintic effects of herbal mixtures

Southern University

1. Nanotechnology application in forest health management

2. Assessing plants in restoration of urban ecosystems
3. Studying value-added, nutritionally functional crops that could have nutraceutical value
4. Economics of rearing cattle and goats together

North Carolina A&T University

1. Hydrothermal treatment and biological conversion of biomass for biofuels production (i.e., animal wastes and aquatic plants)
2. Improving the immune systems in poultry to enhance food safety without drugs or medication
3. Isolation and characterization of food grade *Bifidobacterium* strains for probiotic formulation
4. Economic assessment of changes in trade arrangements, bio-terrorism threats, and renewable fuels requirements on the U.S. grain and oilseed sector

University of Maryland Eastern Shore

1. Sustainable agriculture for managing soil and water contamination from poultry farms
2. Molecular characterization and predictive modeling of *Salmonella spp.* from processed poultry; and prevalence, growth, survival, and control of *Listeria* in blue crabs
3. Utilization of seaweeds as functional foods
4. Studying millets, sudangrass, and switchgrass for conversion to biofuel

Kentucky State University

1. Integration of freshwater prawn nursery and grow-out systems into diversified farm systems
2. Development of pawpaw and primocane fruiting blackberries as niche crops in Kentucky and other states
3. Evaluation of three stocking rates, and alternative forages for meat goat production in Kentucky

Virginia State University

1. Developing biologically based strategies for insect pest management
2. Diversifying cropping systems to enhance agricultural profitability
3. Preventing the transfer of food-borne pathogens to specialty foods
4. Developing sustainable small ruminant production systems

West Virginia State University

1. Utilizing anaerobic digestion for converting agricultural residues and other waste biomass into bioenergy
2. Applying microbial ecology and genomics methods to understand how microorganisms mediate environmentally important processes, such as carbon cycling
3. Developing DNA markers and genetic mapping techniques for quality and yield improvement in vegetables

Alcorn State University

1. Environmental intervention on childhood obesity of preschoolers
2. Nanostructured materials synthesis, chemical sensor development
3. Development of specialty sweet potato

Delaware State University

1. Center for Integrated Biological and Environmental Research
2. The center is home to the DSU Plant Molecular Genetics and Genomics Research Program
3. Main focus of collaboration aims to better understand the mechanisms of disease resistance in beans and so contribute to the production of disease resistant varieties

Tennessee State University

1. Nursery: Otis L. Floyd Nursery Research Center is dedicated to the improvement of the Tennessee nursery crop industry
2. Animal Science: Goat breeding to improve health, reproduction, growth, carcass traits, and anti-microbial resistance
3. Production of leaner and more profitable poultry through the identification of genes that are associated with excessive fat deposition

Prairie View A&M University

1. Biocontrol of animal and plant invader species in pasture and cropping systems of the Texas Gulf Coast Prairie
2. Ecological systems approaches to cropping and pasture enterprises in Southeast Central Texas

Alabama A&M University

1. Plant tissue culture and genetic transformation, genetic engineering, molecular biology and immunology program
2. Biotic and abiotic controls on soil microbial enzyme production, turnover, and in-situ activities
3. Evaluation of alternative feedstock for sustainable biofuel production in an agro-forestry system
4. Biological weed and disease management and soil health for sustainable vegetable production

Langston University

1. Langston's American Institute for Goat Research (AIGR) focuses on angora, meat, and cashmere goats, nutrition studies on high-producing dairy goats, value-added products from goat products

2. Aquaculture Program: research and extension work on phyto-plankton has provided information and techniques to fish producers to help them reduce the incidences of off-flavors in their catfish and hence increase the market value

South Carolina State University

1. SCSU is collaborating in a multidisciplinary, multistate program to investigate the causes of obesity among youth in "An Integrated Approach to Prevention of Obesity in High Risk Families." SCSU is focusing on obesity issues among children in South Carolina, particularly from African American families. This investigation also aims at identifying the crucial behaviors practiced among the resilient low income families in the same obesogenic environments.

Florida A&M University

1. Viticulture and small fruit research related to Florida grapes and small fruits
2. Biological control research for developing ecologically based solutions to pest problems affecting agriculture, natural resources, and human health
3. Bioenergy research to uncover renewable and more sustainable forms of energy and biofuels, educate young bioengineers, and aid limited-resource farmers

Tuskegee University

1. Developing marker genes for sweet potato, peanut, cocoyam, yam, and Frafra potato
2. Developing edible vaccines (sweet potato and peanut): *Cholera enterotoxin* epitope gene, rabies glycoprotein genes
3. Developing nutritious, disease resistant, and environmentally adaptable high yielding crop plants
4. Developed crop growing systems for NASA space application

Clearly, the research being conducted at the 1890 institutions has far-reaching implications for affecting the lives and well-being of all U.S. citizens as well as for residents of foreign countries. From the various projects focused on increasing the nutrient value of crops to projects designed to test control of agricultural pests; from investigations into causes and prevention of obesity to assessment of bioterrorism threats; from development of new energy systems to increasing nutritional value for small ruminants; from developing crop growing systems for application in space to developing vaccines: the 1890 institutions are making significant strides in bettering the lives not only of African Americans, their historical and target population, but of people in the United States and the world over.

The Role of Extension at the 1890 Institutions

Hampton and Tuskegee Institutes were the pioneers of extension activities in the historically black land-grant institutions. Informal efforts began before there was any public funding available. Hampton Institute, one of the few 1890s that received some of the money following the enactment of the Morrill Act of 1862, taught the agricultural sciences to students and encouraged graduates to return to their communities to educate neighbors and improve community life. Booker T. Washington, a graduate of Hampton, made this philosophy a bedrock of the founding of Tuskegee Institute in 1881. Former students as well as faculty served as informal extension agents by traveling to rural communities and visiting farmers and their families at churches, on the farms, and in the homes. Their mission was to promote self-help and improve the standard of living. The first annual extension conference was held at Tuskegee in 1892 with more than four hundred farmers, teachers, and ministers attending. Extension efforts were enhanced when George Washington Carver was hired by Tuskegee in 1896. As one of the most distinguished agricultural scientists in the United States, Carver worked with farmers to promote crop rotations to improve soil quality and crop production. Carver initiated the Moveable School through development of plans for the Jessup Agricultural Wagon. This wagon began operating in 1906 and carried farm implements, dairy equipment, seed, and other items to farmers in the surrounding area.

Seaman A. Knapp (often called the father of extension) was in charge of farmers' demonstration work for the USDA. Knapp was so impressed with the Jessup Wagon that he worked to secure funding to hire Thomas M. Campbell, a former Tuskegee student, to operate the wagon. Campbell became the first black extension agent upon his employment in 1906. Shortly thereafter, John B. Pierce was appointed as the first black farm demonstration agent in Virginia and the second in the nation, after Thomas Campbell (*Leadership and Learning* 84–87; *The Journal of Extension*).

Public funding for extension began with passage of the Smith-Lever Act of 1914. This act, however, made no provision for sharing these funds with the historically black land-grant institutions. The funds were distributed to the states, which were given the authority as to how they were to be distributed. The majority of states did not make these available to the 1890 institutions; by 1972 only four of these institutions had received extension funding (Wilson, Hartman, and Vander 11; *Leadership and Learning* 84).

Passage of Public Law 89-106 in 1972 allowed the 1890 universities to begin receiving federal funds for extension. These funds were administered through the 1862 schools, under the supervision of their directors of extension, because the federal legislation mandated that there should only be one extension program per state. Decisions regarding hiring, firing, compensation, travel, equipment, supplies, and other matters were vested in the 1862 institutions. Total funding for the 1890s was $4 million in 1972 and increased to $6 million in 1976 (*Leadership and Learning* 87).

The Food and Agricultural Act of 1977 provided the first authorization for direct funding to the 1890 land-grant institutions and set the level of funding at 4 percent of the total appropriations that occurred annually for Smith-Lever funds. Direct funding gave administrative control of extension programs to the 1890 institutions, though the requirement for cooperation with the 1862s continued so that there would be a unified cooperative extension program within each state. The percentage of funding was increased in 1982 to 5.5 percent and to 6 percent of the total appropriations of Smith-Lever beginning in 1983. The Farm Security and Rural Investment Act of 2002 (Public Law 107-171) changed the authorization level to 15 percent, and the Food Conservation and Energy Act of 2008 (Public Law 110-246) changed the authorization level to 20 percent (*Leadership and Learning* 88).

Cooperative Extension Today

The mission of 1890 extension today as described on the Association of Extension Administrators' Web site is to assist diverse audiences, with emphasis on those who have limited social and economic resources, to improve their access to positive opportunities through outreach education. This has been accomplished through agricultural extension programs in both rural and urban areas that encourage more efficient production techniques through sustainable farming and gardening practices. Also, many of the 1890 institutions have programs that work extensively with youth in the poorest regions of the states and in locations where opportunities for advancement are very limited. Many programs teach students how to prepare for college and how to improve professionalism; others help young African Americans set goals and teach them how to achieve those goals (http://www.1890aea.org).

On November 13, 2010, L. Washington Lyons, the executive director of the Association of Extension Administrators, presented information regarding the current state of extension at the APLU Annual Meeting in Dallas, Texas, as follows:

> *Nutrition, Diet and Health:* The major areas of extension under this category include food safety, nutrition education to decrease obesity, improved knowledge of how to choose the best foods to purchase, and promotion of health literacy;
>
> *Agricultural Sustainability:* The major categories of outreach in this area are (1) agricultural diversification emphasizing small-scale production of special crops (fruits and vegetables, etc.); (2) small ruminant production; (3) aquaculture production in cages, ponds, and indoor systems; (4) organic agriculture; (5) value-added products and niche markets; (6) farm financial management emphasizing how to operate a viable business; (7) training on risk management; (8) how to market agricultural products; and (9) rural development;
>
> *Community and Family Sustainability:* There are numerous programs in the 1890s on leadership development, parenting education, family resource management, 4-H and youth development, caregiving programs, and community development;

Natural Resources and Environment: Projects include the
following: improving water quality, general improvement
of environmental quality, conservation management, agro
forestry/woodlot management, protection of wetlands, and
recycling waste products;

Others: A sample of other extension areas includes Department
of Defense partnerships such as those addressing issues with
military families; and Department of Energy partnerships to
include energy conservation and alternative energy.

A Sampling of the Variety of Extension Programs Currently Ongoing at the 1890 Institutions

The 1890 institutions employ both vision and creativity in the conceptualization and implementation of extension programs. There are far too
many excellent programs to include them all here, but a brief sampling
serves to illustrate the depth and variety of offerings. Through the T-
TEAM (Texas Teens Exploring Entrepreneurial Minds) project at Prairie
View A&M and through SIFE (Students in Free Enterprise) at Kentucky
State, significant numbers of African American and Hispanic middle
school students learn the value of money using basic business and money
management skills. At North Carolina A&T, the "mini-society" program
uses an experienced-based approach to teach youth, ages eight to twelve,
entrepreneurial concepts.

Lincoln University has implemented a "Men on Business" college assurance program that works with inner city youth to improve professionalism and decrease their high school dropout rates. Currently, 100 percent
of students in this program have graduated from high school. The societal
implications of this type of program are profound: inner city high school
dropouts frequently end up as members of gangs and often face incarcera-
tion. Alabama A&M University provides the "Yes I Can" curriculum to
eighth graders. This is a six-week program that has almost two thousand
participants from ten schools and is designed to increase the number of
students who will complete high school and enroll in vocational or four
year colleges. The Ladies and Gentlemen's Club was formed by Delaware
State University to improve student success in passing mandatory state
tests and to improve attitudes and behaviors so that students can become

responsible members of society. More than ten thousand members report that they are better prepared for these tests and for life after completing this program. South Carolina State University has improved 4-H participation with after-school enrichment programs. Prairie View A&M has initiated the Teen Leadership Connection, another after-school program in which more than fifteen inner city clubs have been formed. Virginia State University provides high school students with firsthand knowledge of how to measure water quality and how the quality levels impact the Chesapeake Bay area. Many urban and even many rural students have little concept of the source of their food and how it moves from field to fork. Extension programs have therefore been developed to educate students about agriculture. At Lincoln University and Prairie View A&M University, students have age-appropriate, hands-on learning opportunities, including working in community gardens. North Carolina A&T State University works with kindergarteners through the twelfth grade in the "Discover Agriculture" program that teaches children about plants and animals through participation in farm demonstrations.

These are just a few examples of extension programs that have had significant impacts on thousands in terms of business development, decreased school dropout rates, and increased levels of acceptance into universities around the country.[2]

The 1890 Institutions: Significant Contributors to Society

The many thousands of individuals who have earned bachelor's, master's, and other advanced degrees; the numerous areas that have been impacted and advanced through the research being conducted at 1890 institutions; the agriculture, natural resource, health, and education needs that are met through extension efforts: for all of these, our nation owes a debt to eighteen schools that all, in varying ways, overcame obstacles and persevered to become the vibrant and indispensable institutions that they are today. Through their academic programs, through research, and through the extension services that reach both their historical populations and other underserved societal groups, the 1890 institutions have made and continue to make significant contributions to the lives of African Americans and others.

NOTES

1. Compiled by Marian B. Gibbons, Director, Office of Communications, College of Agriculture, Florida A&M University, September 12, 2011. E-mail: marian.gibbons@famu.edu.
2. See Web sites for each institution for more information on Extension programs.

The Modern Public University

Its Land-Grant Heritage, Its Land-Grant Horizon

E. GORDON GEE

The land-grant university is the social conscience of American higher education. As the principled paradigm of what colleges and universities should be in a nation that cherishes equality, democracy, and opportunity for all, the land-grant institution has defined and modeled the values that all of our country's great public universities hold dear.

The storied history of the land-grant is traceable to the tenacity of one individual with a vision of how things should be, and could be. Vermont Congressman Justin Morrill believed that America's colleges were failing to provide the kind of education needed by the nation's farmers and industrial workers, and he was convinced that their productivity—and so, their lives—could be improved through the teaching of practical subjects that would enhance their skills.

When Morrill introduced his land-grant bill into Congress in 1857, education in America was a wide open proving ground. At the time of Morrill's bill, Horace Mann, Henry Barnard, Bronson Alcott, and countless other less well-known education reformers were laboring to ensure that, starting with their era, schools would be free and coeducational. They wanted to develop statewide systems of education, to establish laws that would make school attendance compulsory, and to expand the curriculum to include vocational tracks. These efforts to increase opportunities for all children and create bonds among an increasingly diverse population were radical notions at the time. But the moment for such innovations was right, and they forever changed the nature of schooling in this country.

It was at this point that Justin Morrill introduced his unprecedented legislation to fund educational institutions by granting federally controlled land to the states for the establishment of "land-grant colleges." These institutions were to offer programs in agriculture, science, engineering, and home economics as well as traditional academic subjects. Morrill's 1857 bill was passed by Congress despite opposition from Southern legislators, who viewed it as a violation of states' rights. In the end, however, these legislators carried the day because the bill was vetoed by President James Buchanan on the grounds that it was contrary to the policy of the federal government, which up to then had left control of education to the states. Undaunted, Morrill resubmitted his bill in 1861. The secession of the Southern states from the Union and the advent of a new president guaranteed its success this time. The Morrill Act would set in motion the most signal, durable, and far-reaching of the many nineteenth-century reforms in higher education.

When President Abraham Lincoln signed the Morrill Act in 1862, higher education was still very much the exclusive domain of the few, the white, the male, the wealthy, and, by and large, those living in cities. But Lincoln was looking to the future and was determined to make good on the ideals of human equality set forth in the Declaration of Independence. Born to illiterate parents on the frontier, the president knew that the democratic promise of "We, the People" depended on an educated electorate capable of self-government. And he understood that making higher education available to the so-called industrial classes was his fractured nation's best choice for peace, democracy, growth, and prosperity.

In the years after the Civil War, an industrializing America found itself in need of a new kind of workforce. Highly trained professionals—in engineering, agriculture, forestry, public health, home economics—were increasingly required to respond to society's ordinary but very real needs. If it created a need and a place for these new professionals, however, industrialization at the same time created a considerable class of disadvantaged workers for whom the American dream of unlimited opportunities seemed unrealizable.

For such workers—indeed, for all citizens in search of advanced learning—the Morrill Act democratized American higher education, effectively re-charting its course. Establishing land-grant institutions in every state proved critical in extending educational opportunity beyond the wealthy, the well-connected, and the urban. As they continue to do today, the land-grant colleges and universities expanded access and opportunity to those whose parents had never considered the possibility of a college education; to those who, earlier, could scarcely imagine a better life; to those of great ability, regardless of means. The Morrill Act set the country on an accelerated path to realizing its founding promise to create a meritocracy based not on wealth or family connections but on ability, determination, and effort.

The intent of the act has never been compromised. On the contrary, a second Morrill Act was passed in 1890, requiring states either to show that race was not a criterion for admission to their existing land-grant institution or else to designate a separate land-grant institution for persons of color. Among the latter are a number of today's fine historically black colleges and universities. Then, just over one hundred years later, by act of Congress, twenty-nine Native American tribally controlled colleges and universities, collectively known as the 1994 Land-grant Institutions, were given land-grant status. Their addition brings our nation's total number of land-grant institutions to 105. These 105 institutions embody the enduring spirit of this country with its democratic idealism, overriding faith in people, and conviction that a community is more than the sum of its individual members. This is the heritage of the Morrill Act.

It is scarcely surprising, then, that our land-grant institutions have been a wellspring of this country's prosperity, innovative spirit, and ability to sustain democracy through the enlightened participation of an educated citizenry. Founded, as we have seen, in the finest tradition of optimism and ethical values, these institutions remain the guardians of Morrill's and Lincoln's extraordinary vision.

Paradoxically, they are also stewards of the rise of America's great public universities—paradoxically because public universities in this country predate their land-grant successors by nearly a hundred years. Our public institutions can trace their roots to the late eighteenth century, when the sale of lands in the Northwest Territory provided support for free public education at all levels. After the Revolutionary War, American leaders persuaded President Thomas Jefferson that the young nation needed a military academy to train new officers. True to his notion that "In matters of style, swim with the current. In matters of principle, stand like a rock," Jefferson signed the legislation founding the United States Military Academy at West Point only after he was assured that the academy's student body would represent a democratic society (Jefferson).

Public education, then, has been essential in shaping this country from its earliest struggling days. Born in the Age of Enlightenment, the United States is firmly rooted in notions about freedom, self-governance, and opportunity. Our nation's founders knew that the full expression of the American mind and spirit could be realized only if education were made broadly available to the people of the new republic. If the authority of this fledgling democracy were truly to reside with its people, then the people needed the skills to think, to reason, to debate, and to act in pursuit of the common good.

By 1820—when Justin Morrill was ten years old and Abraham Lincoln eleven—a dozen state universities had been established. By the fall of 2009, according to the *Digest of Education Statistics,* there were nearly 1,700 degree-granting public institutions of higher education in this country, including research and doctoral universities, master's and baccalaureate institutions, and two-year colleges and technical schools (National Center for Education Statistics Table 5). Now a public college or university is within the economic reach and geographic proximity of every citizen. And he or she can choose from a buffet of curricular possibilities, depending on interest and need. Morrill's and Lincoln's vision has been realized. College is no longer the privilege of a rarefied elite but the prerogative of the prepared.

From its idealistic beginnings, American higher education has matured into a powerful and positive presence throughout the nation and the world. Our great public universities are recognized as model communities of learning and unencumbered thought, crucibles of basic and applied research and creative expression, independent sources of moral authority, institutions committed to the public good, and agents of opportunity.

That reputation has much to do with the land-grant roots of many of those schools. This is especially true of the land-grant vision of the university's social role. Because all of America's public institutions have come to share this vision, our public colleges and universities today are the front door to the American dream that seemed so threatened at the end of the nineteenth century.

It is important to remember that an inherent principle of the land-grant institution was that students would return home after receiving their degrees and thus be able to make their hometowns better places. While that is still the idea, hometowns are now all over the globe. The nation's land-grant institutions, indeed all colleges and universities, now must train their students not simply to go home, but to go wherever their calling takes them and to lead along paths that will take all of us beyond the routine, the expected, and the easy.

Our students, when they leave us, must be prepared to negotiate successfully in a world that will bombard them with more information, more perspectives, more everything than we can imagine, even today. With the instant availability of information via satellite TV, with instant messaging and data management on their smartphones, which also give them instant access to just about anybody anywhere anytime, our students must operate in world at once more knowable than ever before, and more difficult to sort out. Add Twitter, Facebook, YouTube, and Google+ to that picture, and you have a world that is wired to demand instant assimilation, instant interpretation, and instant decision making. It is a world that is more global, more interconnected, and more interdependent.

The best way to prepare these Millennial Generation students to be leaders in today's and tomorrow's world is to ensure that American higher education is based in having a passion for learning and ideas; in valuing a more civil and democratic future; in understanding and respecting differences; in recognizing and building on commonalities; and in holding sacred the right to stand up for one's own beliefs—and the need to stand up for those of others. Our land-grant institutions were founded on these principles, principles that now have fused with the fabric of every great American public university.

For three decades I have been privileged to lead great universities, both public and private. In that time I have come to understand the university as a narrative. It is a story unbounded by time or place. It is a story about validating teaching and learning, about fostering creativity and real-world solutions to unyielding problems. What makes the university's story unique is its ability to make a difference for the future and its power to be a relentless force for progress in a world that has yet to be fully imagined.

Holden Thorp, chancellor of the University of North Carolina at Chapel Hill, has declared that our major universities are the "crown jewels" of this nation. He has also noted, however, that these crown jewels could be used to better effect. Chancellor Thorp and his co-author Buck Goldstein make this clear in their book *Engines of Innovation*. They are convinced that universities have a unique capacity to solve problems. Where else, they ask, can you find a collection of spectacularly talented people working across such broad lines of inquiry? These are our problem solvers, those with an urgent curiosity and a resolute commitment to progress. These are people who collaborate, who imagine, who create, and who are not afraid to fail. Imagination today, it might be said, is what steel was 120 years ago—the building block of progress.

In the nineteenth century that witnessed both the Morrill Act and industrialization, the great fortunes of the world were forged by muscle and sweat in mills and factories. Today, at an ever accelerating pace, the great fortunes of the world are amassed from products of the mind. If smokestacks were once the signposts of prosperity, now it is college bell towers that signify that ours is an era when ideas are the catalysts of progress.

The very notion of progress, of course, presumes that there is always more to be done, more room to improve, more lives to be nurtured and made whole. While the educational horizon (like all horizons) is ever expanding and ever out of reach, those of us who have committed our lives to higher education must not lose sight of the point at the far edge of our line of vision. The lesson and legacy of the public university is to push forward toward that point as aggressively as possible.

The success and speed of our march toward the horizon will depend on how we adapt to the conditions we find as we make our way. The ability to adapt is a law of nature and of human endeavors, including those of colleges and universities. G. K. Chesterton once remarked that tradition is the democracy of the dead (Chesterton). If, for some, challenges to the traditional ways of doing things are unsettling, our public colleges and universities thrive on such challenges. They are accustomed to evolving in the pursuit of new ideas, all the while adapting to external and internal forces such as burgeoning new populations of students, especially after World War II and the enactment of the G.I. Bill; curricular overhauls to keep current with student and workplace demands; and now the globalization of education, thanks to the Internet, distance learning, and unparalleled study abroad opportunities. The nation's public institutions have always risen to these challenges and more in order to meet the shifting needs of their students and the world into which they graduate. The truly great institutions of today and tomorrow will constantly move forward, adapting with greater and greater facility to a world that changes ever more rapidly.

As our institutions look toward the horizon, their paths will be determined by their thinkers' big, bold ideas, the epiphanies generated by relentless inquiry, careful research, and exhaustive examination. Those epiphanies, of course, often spring from ambiguity. This means that true creativity requires the elimination of the boundaries and assumptions we impose on ourselves. Big, bold ideas come only to thinkers who are unfettered by the past, nimble in the present, and driven toward the future. Nurturing those qualities in their thinkers requires colleges and universities that are prepared to go beyond the answers that have always been given and the boundaries that have always been respected. This, of course, is the calling of fine universities everywhere: to foster and support new theories, new approaches, new applications, and new solutions; to create, advance, and apply knowledge; to pioneer the discoveries and innovations that change—and save—lives. This is the particular calling, however, of America's great public universities. Why? Because their core missions of teaching, producing new knowledge, and serving the public are considered a sacrosanct social compact.

In carrying out that compact and carrying on with their courageous and innovative work, our researchers often come head to head with what have come to be known as "wicked" problems. In 1973, Horst Rittel and Melvin Webber, both urban planners at the University of California at Berkeley, authored a landmark article for the journal *Policy Sciences*. In "Dilemmas in a General Theory of Planning," Rittel and Webber define two kinds of problems: tame problems, or those with a solution that can be objectively evaluated as correct or incorrect, and wicked problems, which do not yield to traditional linear analytic approaches. Unlike tame problems, wicked problems are complex and long-term. Their solutions, according to Rittel and Webber, are not true or false, but better or worse. Every wicked problem is essentially unique, they maintain, and can be considered a symptom of another wicked problem (Rittel and Webber 160).

Grappling with so-called wicked problems has required institutions to recognize that their solutions, however uncertain, unpredictable, and partial, do not always lie within the tidy boundaries of traditional scholarly disciplines. New discoveries and breakthroughs are increasingly found at the intersections of disciplinary inquiry rather than in the rigid silos of traditional disciplines. Modern scholarship has life-changing capacity. There is power in taking on wicked problems. But that must be done, as Chancellor Thorp insists, with multidisciplinary teams. Spurred on by their social compact with our nation, America's great public universities expect to take up this task—and are prepared to do so. With their breadth and complexity, they can readily combine seemingly disparate areas of academic focus. And with their obligation and dedication to the public good, these institutions must and will bring the fruits of their multidisciplinary research to bear on pressing global problems.

We are all too well aware that these problems are numerous and growing. Food safety and security, poverty and health care, energy, water supplies, threats to the environment, and peacekeeping are only some of them. In his book *High Noon*, J. F. Rischard lists what he believes are the twenty most crucial global issues facing us today. "How well we deal with them over the next 20 years," he writes, "will determine how well the planet fares over the next generations" (65). Rischard separates these issues into three groups: sharing our planet (these are issues involving what he calls the global commons—global warming, biodiversity fisheries depletion, and so on); sharing our humanities (or issues requiring a global commitment, such as education for all, the digital divide, and natural disaster prevention and mitigation); and sharing our rule book (which he believes concerns the need for a global regulatory approach to biotechnology rules, intellectual property rights, and e-commerce regulation). These, certainly, are wicked problems. Rischard concludes that we must bring imagination and a different type of thinking to bear on these messy and ornery issues. He also points out the need for some really fast thinking. Many of our global issues—environmental challenges, infectious diseases, food supplies—require urgent remedies.

Who, if not America's great public colleges and universities, should imagine and develop responses to these wicked problems in whose resolution every human being has a stake? At Ohio State, for example, our experts are working on computer chips that can absorb their own heat and turn it into power, and on semiconductors that can use the spin of electrons to read and write data. They are working on natural and targeted controls against crop-eating insects. They are investigating what is causing abrupt climate change, whether there will be sufficient quantities of fresh water worldwide, and how climate change and water resources will be impacted by fossil fuel combustion. They are developing improved mechanisms for the detection of food pathogens, and they are coming up with new diagnostic tools, therapies, and vaccines for human and animal diseases, including those resulting from bioterrorism and natural hazards. They are helping to create stability in the world by partnering to draft the constitutions of newly sovereign nations.

At the same time, our scholars are unlocking the archaeological secrets of ancient Greece and uncovering the cultural history of American cities. Still others are writing film and music scores and discovering new insights into texts written in some forty languages and dating from the earliest times to today. This year, our entire campus is engaging in a year-long conversation that will focus on the core ethical, political, social, and economic issues related to immigration.

Writing in 1904, the fifth president of The Ohio State University, William Oxley Thompson, addressed the mission of the land-grant colleges for the U. S. Department of Agriculture, Office of Experiment Stations. In his article President Thompson notes that Justin Morrill's statute "evidently brings in the new conception of what we now term higher education. It evidently carries with it the doctrine that education other than classical and scientific, in the general conception of the word, is to be regarded as of equal importance with education at that time in vogue" (Thompson 92). He goes on to say that the primary focus of the land-grant institution was to be "agriculture and the mechanic arts." Importantly, however, Thompson also states the following: "The aim of the education provided for in the Morrill Act was the liberal as well as the practical education of the industrial classes . . . .[S]o without excluding [the traditional literary form of education] we intend to promote the liberal education of the industrial classes" (93). If, as Thompson points out, the sciences related to agriculture and the mechanic arts were to be "the chief subjects of instruction and investigation" (92) at the land-grant institution, the Morrill Act did not ignore the importance of the liberal arts.

So, Ohio State, like other great universities, is turning its sights on wicked problems. But it is not turning its back on those areas of scholarly endeavor that give us treasured glimpses into our human core, that open windows on creativity, and that reveal new truths to students who come to us likely never having seen such discoveries with their own eyes. This is the proud legacy of the land-grant institution. We embrace it, and we treasure the enormous contributions made in agriculture, engineering, medicine, veterinary sciences, and so many other fields of study. They are rich and strong precisely because they are grounded by the arts and humanities and the social sciences. Indeed, it was the clarion call of Justin Morrill and Abraham Lincoln to expand our reach and extend our value; to improve our communities now both local and global; to enrich the lives of those we hold dear as well as those we will never know; to expand possibilities for students, researchers, and everyone who looks to us for answers and solutions humanistic as well as scientific.

In the mid-1990s, or about the time of the establishment of the 1994 Land-grant Institutions, I chaired the Kellogg Commission on the Future of State and Land-grant Universities. The Kellogg Commission report affirms the role of public universities in sustaining democracy, building civic partnerships, and promoting community-based learning. The report also calls on us to "bring the resources and expertise at our institutions to bear on community, state, national, and international problems" (Kellogg Commission 10). This call for applied solutions and enhanced community engagement is a striking affirmation that our public colleges and universities have never been more critical to the citizens of this country—and the entire world.

Much has been said and written about the future of higher education in the United States, especially public higher education. A quick check on the Internet reveals that there are 152,000,000 possible Web sites of information on the topic. Countless voices are speaking out on how we can keep our institutions vital and contributory in today's version of a troubled economy; on how we can maintain our poise in the maelstrom of a national dialog that is both narrow and caustic; and on how we can most expeditiously and effectively tackle the wicked problems.

There is a simple answer to that cacophony of questions—though it is not an easy one. To accomplish what they must for their students, their states, and this nation, America's public colleges and universities must take it upon themselves to change the tone of our national conversation. They must seek higher ground by returning to their first principles. To connect and extend the original ideals of the land-grant institutions to the modern era, we whose business it is to mind the mighty engines of public universities must reimagine, reinvent, even reconceptualize the university, not merely rethinking what we do, but, more fundamentally, rethinking what we think, rethinking what the American university is and what it is capable of achieving.

In my office at Ohio State, amidst all the Scarlet and Gray memorabilia and the photos and other reminders of many fulfilling years dedicated to education, in a large frame in the line of sight of all my guests is a quotation that serves as my personal cautionary tale for the future. The quote is not from Plato, Thomas Aquinas, or John Dewey. Instead, the philosopher in question is a person with a good deal more hands-on experience in solving problems and leading people. There on an easel, looming over the conference table, inserting itself in the proceedings of every day, printed in a large font on an otherwise blank canvas, are the words of General Eric Shinseki. "If you don't like change, you're going to like irrelevance even less" (Peters epigraph).

How do our institutions of higher education escape irrelevance? They are, after all, repositories of human achievement, sanctuaries for the human spirit, and incubators of human aspiration. They assure civic, cultural, and technological advancement and foster intellectual curiosity. They sustain civil public discourse, hone appreciation for others and others' ideas, and, of course, inform and educate those who will follow us on this earth. These contributions, if unarguably vital, are insufficient insulation against irrelevance. That safeguard will come only if our great public institutions use their collective position of strength to become true agents of change in this country, to be recognized as the engines of intellectual ferment, economic development, and social, cultural, and artistic vitality.

This brings us back to our land-grant heritage and its mandates of expanding and improving what we know and what we are capable of doing and how we impart knowledge and skills. This is the physics of academic momentum that flows from the university to our students, to our research partners, to our civic partners, to all our constituents, and to the communities and workplaces they inhabit. We must move boldly forward, believing in and acting on the enduring principles of the past and the promise of the future. This is crucial to our country's future and to our local, national, and global economy. The surest way to guarantee the ongoing relevance of our great public colleges and universities is for these institutions to rekindle the passion for the land-grant ideals of Morrill and Lincoln.

This means that our colleges and universities must seek new ways to leverage human talents and expertise and bring their enormous resources to bear on solving urgent real-world problems. They must reach out more aggressively to ensure that those of ability who are born into modest means have access to the opportunities uniquely provided by a college education. They must expand the toolkit they provide their graduates. As they refine students' abilities to think, to reason, to write, and to understand others, they should make no apologies for also working to ensure that their graduates have the skills they will need to thrive. They must seek out ways to enhance their neighborhoods and schools, to conduct research for the public good, and to fuel our nation's economic prosperity. They must invent new funding models. Although the economy has altered the American landscape to a degree unseen in our lifetimes, our notion of what is expected of higher education continues to evolve. Let me say unequivocally that we must make our case for investment in the University (note the capital "U") by moral force, the moral force that comes from our thinkers' instrumental acts to feed the hungry, develop clean energies, cure disease, and teach our students how to think critically and act compassionately. Finally, our colleges and universities must do their utmost to sustain democratic values, insist on ethical conduct, and press for open and respectful dialog in our national discussions.

There is no question that higher education can transform individual lives and bring remedies to global problems of all kinds. The responsibility for effecting this transformation is borne by all institutions of higher learning, and the need to do so is urgent. In the percentage of the population with college degrees, the United States now ranks twelfth among thirty-six developed countries around the world (Lee and Rawls). The gap is growing, even as President Obama is calling for our country to once again reclaim its place at the top of that list. What is more, a telling and troubling fact has emerged from a recent College Board study. Students from the lowest-income families are eight times less likely to earn bachelor's degrees than the highest-income students (Lee and Rawls). The previous figures, already dismal, had indicated that such students were five times less likely to attain a college degree. These are sober facts that point to trends moving in the wrong direction.

Now is not the moment to take timid steps, cling to tired dogma, or stay within our comfort zones. What is needed is a full-scale recommitment to our system of public higher education and a no less wholehearted recommitment to the compact between our public colleges and universities and the communities they serve. The animating principle that has carried millions of Americans to universities and that moved previous generations to build those universities in the first place was a relentless belief in the future. All of public higher education in this country builds upon the same core values. We are all part of the same lineage. But with the words of Justin Morrill and Abraham Lincoln as touchstones, America's public colleges and universities must take it upon themselves to lead in creating a new epoch in this country and revitalizing a nation where the mind and the imagination flourish, where promises are kept, and where the American dream can be realized.

Commitments

Enhancing the Public Purposes and Outcomes of Public Higher Education

MARK G. YUDOF AND CAITLIN CALLAGHAN

The hot, humid summer of 1862 marked a perilous season for President Abraham Lincoln. Twenty-four thousand Union and Confederate casualties had littered the battlefields at Shiloh mere months before. Within a matter of weeks, the even bloodier Antietam would provide a macabre summer bookend. General McClellan, stripped of his supreme command and sulking in Virginia, was mired with his troops in the humiliating Peninsula Campaign. European diplomats were whispering that the South might prevail, and their sovereigns inclined their heads toward Richmond.

In the midst of this crucible, on July 2, the president signed a piece of legislation that, though it had little to do with the war effort, over the long arc of history would arguably alter the country's future as powerfully as any great Civil War battle: the Morrill Act.

The Morrill Act would provide the fulcrum on which the United States would pivot from a divided, underdeveloped society into a vigorously diverse, competitive, and advanced one in which mass education—the bedrock of both national and individual progress—is now the norm, not the exception. The great public research universities that arose from the Act became engines of opportunity and innovation that accelerated the nation's drive to industrial preeminence and, in large measure, still drive our nation's economy. Most significantly, these universities created generations of educated citizens—many of whom, because of socioeco-nomic background, gender, or race would not otherwise have been eligible for the college education that is our country's truest and greatest equalizer.

Understanding the magnitude of the Morrill Act's significance can be difficult—even for seasoned veterans of public universities—so it might help to pause for a moment and briefly consider a few of the other mile-stones in the history of American higher education.

This country has always had wonderful private colleges and univer-sities. The establishment of Harvard College in 1636 marked the New World's first foray into higher education, while the 1876 opening of The Johns Hopkins University introduced a new university model—one that nurtured and promoted graduate education and research as well as under-graduate education—that would be replicated by both private and public universities worldwide.

This country has also long held a commitment to public education. When John Adams drafted the 1780 Constitution of the Commonwealth of Massachusetts, he charged the state legislature with the stewardship of public schools. A few years later, the nascent Congress of the Confed-eration of the United States passed the Northwest Ordinance of 1787, which set aside land for public schools in prospective townships west of the Alleghenies.

The commitment to public grammar schools soon included universi-ties. Thomas Jefferson founded a publicly supported University of Virgin-ia in 1819, and identified public service as one of its missions. The Morrill Act was later followed by the 1887 Hatch Act, which instituted federal funding for agricultural research stations affiliated with universities. And in the twentieth century, California's 1960 Master Plan for Higher Edu-cation—a three-tiered system that guarantees a place in a state university or community college to every qualified Californian—stands as one of this country's greatest achievements for higher education.

Still, even when contextualized with these milestones, the Morrill Act stands out—for its genesis as well as for its legacy. Together with the Homestead Act and Transcontinental Railroad Act, which were signed in the same bleak summer, the Morrill Act ultimately formed a critical component of Lincoln's broader strategic vision for a free postwar United States. Given the magnitude of the fratricidal conflict that the president faced in the summer of 1862, it may not be immediately obvious why he felt compelled to include "land-grant" universities and colleges in this vi-sion. Lincoln himself had never attended college; neither had many of his fellow politicians. Nor did the infrastructure necessary to produce college-ready students exist at the time—even accounting for the many students who entered college in their early teenage years, as of 1860 "the United States possessed only 243 high schools outside Massachusetts, or about sixteen for each million people" (Nevins, *The State Universities and Democracy* 39).

Yet in mid-nineteenth-century America a growing and pervasive hunger seemed to exist for institutions of higher learning. As Jonathan Cole notes, in 1800 the United States was home to twenty-five colleges; by 1861, that number had grown to 182 (15). By 1862, broad Civil War mobilization had done little to dampen not only the tireless efforts of Vermont Congressman Justin Morrill, but also those of the Northern "farm organizations, labor unions, newspapers, [clergy], groups of educators, and a wide variety of reformers" that pushed for the Morrill Act's passage (Nevins, *The Origins* 3). Perhaps this enthusiasm may be explained in part by—as Lincoln himself stated in his 1859 "Discoveries and Inventions" lecture—"the curious fact that a new country is most favorably [suited] to the emancipation of thought, and [to] the consequent advancement of civilization and the arts."[1]

It was in the spirit of this "emancipation of thought" that the Morrill Act engendered the multitude of great public research universities we know today. True, in the decades immediately following the Civil War these full-fledged institutions still lay in the future. The founding faculties, legislators, and presidents of these universities faced an often Sisyphean battle of several years duration: for funding and other resources; for faculty, staff, and students; and even for a clear sense of institutional purpose. But the twentieth century was still young when Edwin Slosson included five public research universities, four of them land-grants, in his seminal text *Great American Universities*.[2] And as of 2011, six American public research universities—and seven land-grants—rank in the top twenty of the Shanghai Jiao Tong Academic Ranking of World Universities.[3]

Today, however, we are living in a time in which the spirit of the Morrill Act is under threat. Over the last several years, as the state legislatures charged with supporting these great public research universities have cut funding, many of these institutions have struggled to maintain the quality lauded by evaluators ranging from Slosson to Shanghai Jiao Tong. In the past decade alone, thirty of the nation's fifty state governments have slashed core funding for their public higher education institutions—core funding for which they have been responsible since Lincoln's time. From

Minnesota to Arizona, from Michigan to Pennsylvania to Florida, all across the country public university presidents are being forced to look for new ways to keep their institutions viable.

As we reflect on this painful disinvestment, both in our own state of California and around the country, it seems to us to be the result of an acute societal shift—the American public at large no longer sees public universities as integral to an advanced, healthy, more complete America. The spirit of Lincoln's "emancipation of thought" is difficult to find in the talking points of current legislators, much less in any "letters to the editor" from our fellow taxpayers. And this shift begs the following question: How did we go from viewing public universities as critical to our societal advancement—so critical, in fact, that it was worthy of Lincoln's endorsement during the Civil War—to viewing them as less essential?

To begin finding an answer, we must consider the idea of the commonweal, a somewhat archaic term for what we now call the commonwealth—the notion that individuals and groups come together for the public good, whether to raise a schoolhouse or to win a war. For generations, Americans have united behind the concept of the "public good," and the fruits of this unity range from battlefield victories to a broadly educated citizenry. Undoubtedly, belief in this concept helped our country advance after the Civil War, and it has been the impetus behind any upward arc in American education, civil rights, social services, and environmental protection.

However, there are also, in broad, general economic terms, "public goods" and "private goods." "Public goods," such as a public water system or a public park, are nonrival in consumption, and difficult to exclude in benefit. In other words, we all contribute something, and in return we generally all get tap water and a nice place to walk on Sunday afternoons.

Many goods are actually mixed in nature. They are hybrids, or public-private goods. For example, private mediators that work within a state court system are hybrids. In fact, these hybrids actually serve the "public good"—a private mediator might save both taxpayers and litigants hundreds of thousands of dollars in litigation costs, and expedite dispute resolution. Hybrid goods have existed for generations. The transcontinental railroad, which Lincoln signed into existence almost simultaneously with the Morrill Act, was built by both government bonds and private rail companies. The twentieth-century private aerospace industry grew in response to President Kennedy's call to go to the moon. And historically these hybrids have maintained a good balance between public and private interests.

In the last few decades, a clear privatization trend has driven American policy in all segments of our society, and it is tipping the balance of many hybrid goods toward "private." Several factors—efficiency, ideology, distrust of government—determine this trend. Still, widespread privatization also indicates a shift in our understanding of what the "public good" means—and helps illuminate why we now see public universities as incidental to this concept.

For example, consider the book *Social Statics,* by the British philosopher Herbert Spencer. Many years ago, one might have felt incredulous, just as Supreme Court Justice Oliver Wendell Holmes Jr. did, when reading Spencer's argument that the postal service, among other institutions, be fully privatized. "That which benefits the community as a whole," he wrote, "it will [become] the private interest of some part of the community to accomplish" (Spencer Part III, Chapter XXIX). A private postal service would probably have sounded both extreme and potentially problematic. Today, however, the U.S. Postal Service no longer receives a direct public subsidy—and it has not since 1983. And while the USPS still benefits from a legally protected monopoly on mailbox delivery, many people today do use private "postal services" such as UPS and FedEx.

There is plenty more evidence of a movement toward Spencer's ideology across the American landscape. In 2008 in Afghanistan, 69 percent of the Pentagon's forces were private contractors—the highest percentage in the history of U.S. conflict, and a nearly 40 percent increase since the Korean War (Schwartz, "Training the Military" 2).[4] Of these private contractors, only 14 percent were U.S. citizens (Schwartz, "Department of Defense Contractors" 11). In early 2011, NASA awarded $270 million outright to private American aerospace companies (Siciloff). Unable to replace its aging shuttle fleet—which now resides in museums and hangars—the agency hopes that private rockets and crew capsules will continue taking American astronauts to space. At the same time, in the research world, government funding of research and development (R&D) as a function of GDP has declined by 60 percent in the last forty years. In fact, as the national academies reported in 2010, "U.S. consumers [now] spend significantly more on potato chips than the government devotes to energy R&D" (National Academies Committee, *Rising Above the Gathering Storm Revisited* 6). Similarly, the rest of the world used to envy America's infrastructure, which was largely financed with public money. But now we invest only 2 percent of our GDP in it—a fraction relative to China's 9 percent, and the European Union's 5 percent (Kerry). And while China's high percentage reflects its intent to overcome an enormous infrastructure deficit, that figure will still probably level out at a higher percentage than that of the United States in the next several years.

Public universities, in contrast to some of these examples, have always been hybrid goods. There are private returns unique to the individuals who consume the particular good and who pay a price representing a portion of the total cost. Plus, there are benefits that flow to the entire polity— in the form of economic growth, cultural transmission, more democratic participation, health care, higher tax revenues, fewer incarcerations, and reduced welfare payments. Put simply, public universities are hybrid goods that appropriately receive taxpayer support as well as tuition support from students.

And yet the balance between taxpayer support and tuition support has also shifted over the last few decades. For example, in California in 1990–91 the state government spent $16,720 on each University of California student's education, while students paid a tuition amount of $2,680 (the total per student expenditure was $21,370). By 2010–11, however, the state's contribution had decreased by about 55 percent, in inflation-adjusted dollars, to $8,220 per student; tuition that same year was $7,230. Even more significantly, the total per student expenditure in 2010–11 dropped to $17,510—a direct result of the drop in state funding, and 18 percent less than what was spent on students in 1990–91 ("The Facts: UC Budget Basics").

In the past, the balance between taxpayer support and tuition support swung toward the former for some important reasons. Building upon the mandate of the Morrill Act, twentieth-century state governments and public research universities developed an extraordinary compact. In return for financial support from taxpayers, universities agreed to keep tuition low and to provide access for students from a broad range of economic backgrounds. They would also train graduate and professional students, promote arts and culture, help solve problems in the community, and perform groundbreaking research.

They made this compact because they understood—as did President Lincoln and the congressional legislators led by Representative Morrill—that a well-educated population is a necessary condition for broader economic prosperity, cultural growth, and informed democracy. In fact,

President Yudof's predecessor at the University of Minnesota, President James Lewis Morrill—aptly named for this essay, but alas, no relative of the Vermont representative—may have best articulated this invaluable correlation: "Democracy, it has been said, 'is based upon the conviction that there are extraordinary possibilities in ordinary people'—and the development of these extraordinary possibilities is the very reason and purpose of the state university. To underwrite the ongoing of their state university is the surest investment that the people of any state can make in their own future" (James Lewis Morrill 136).

To quote another predecessor, former University of California president Clark Kerr, "The best investment that any society makes is in the education of its young people, and this shouldn't basically be looked upon myopically as a 'cost'; it should be looked upon as the best investment that any society can make" (*The Gold and the Blue* 320). These are not mere platitudes but, rather, summaries of a rich symbiosis—the University of California, for example, *is* California, and vice versa. Our university educates qualified Californians from across all socioeconomic backgrounds (40 percent of our students are Pell grant recipients, and four of our campuses, Berkeley, UCLA, Davis, and San Diego, *each* enroll more Pell grant recipients than the entire Ivy League combined); it has been served by fifty-six Nobel laureates, in fields ranging from literature to physics; it develops more patents than any other university in the nation, and it has for the last seventeen straight years; and its hospitals not only train one in every two California doctors, but also treat more than four million patients a year. In other words, for generations our university truly has been, to paraphrase the former presidents, the "surest" and "best" investment in the future of California—and it has paid dividends.

Nationwide, many Americans experienced the extraordinary nature of the state government-public university compact, as well as the "extraordinary possibilities in ordinary people," after World War II, when the public-private balance of these universities actually tipped farther toward "public." The GI Bill gave thousands of returning soldiers access to higher education. Big initiatives such as Pell grants and California's Master Plan for Higher Education formalized a sense of ownership and willingness to support public universities.

That's all changing now. And the reason is that more and more Americans no longer believe the compact is important.

Part of this phenomenon can be explained by demographics. In the early 1960s, 57 percent of American families had children under the age of eighteen. In 2010, that number hovered around 46 percent (U.S. Census Bureau). In concert with that figure, American senior citizens now receive more than seven times the amount of federal benefits that American children do (Kirp).

Part of it can also be explained by the belief that those receiving a college education should have some skin in the game. Many people rightfully observe that public university students only pay a portion of the cost of their education. To see this borne out, you only have to glance at the online comment string for any major newspaper's article on state university tuition increases. For example, "I DO NOT MIND at all how much you complain to the school about the fees," wrote one online commentator on the *Los Angeles Times* article "Students ask Regents to Reject Proposed UC Tuition Hike" on July 14, 2011. "That is your RIGHT in a free country. . . . What I DO MIND, is when you think taxpayers should have to subsidize YOUR education. This is YOUR education, not ours, if you do not think you can get employment in your field of study to pay back the costs of getting that degree, then maybe you need to re-think your choices . . . .First lesson is free, DO NOT expect others to fund your life" (Gordon, Online Comment, 7:53am 15 July 2011). "Quit Whining!!!!!!" another chimed in. "This issue of college education affordability has been talked about for centuries. . . . Students do NOT want to pay a fraction of a percent of what it costs to educate them. . . . They Whine!!!!! Yes, as a student too, I whined. Once I got a good job, I realized what a bargain college education is" (Gordon, Online Comment, 5:58pm 14 July 2011). Another added, "It is not moral to tax those who are not in school to fund your lavish lifestyle, drinking on Friday's [*sic*], going mountain climbing in the gym, and taking useless courses like 'women's studies.' If you believe that it justifies the cost in your life, then you are more than welcome to pay for it out of your own pocket" (Gordon, Online Comment, 11:37am 14 July 2011).

Of course, anyone who wades into an online comment string should be inoculated first, but you get the point. The perception, as reflected in these comments, that only students should be responsible for their educations—and the frequent implication that much, if not all, of these educations is frivolous—tends to crop up prominently in commentary on student fees. But when it comes to undergraduate education, many cross-subsidies exist, and it is not always easy to assess who pays for what. Great research universities, for example, incur additional expenses. Hiring, retaining, and supporting faculty who are creators of knowledge right-fully costs more than compensating those who just transmit the accepted wisdom; or, as Penn State's Roger Geiger aptly summarizes, "[T]he elite public university is defined by faculty as well as undergraduate learning" (Geiger, "Expert and Elite" 29). Any conversation about the expense of a public education, therefore, must be framed by the critical link between the university's research and teaching—and that link ultimately inures to the benefit of undergraduates.

As a result, even though 73 percent of all undergraduate students in the United States attend public universities and community colleges (National Center for Education Statistics, Table 201), factors such as shifting demographics and perspectives—in addition to the increasing value of a college degree—help explain why these degrees really look like private goods to those who do not have students in their families. A college graduate's earning potential is greater than that of someone who only attended high school. And the general perception seems to be: "Why should I, when I'm struggling to make ends meet, subsidize your kid's future Lexus by giving tax dollars to higher ed?"

Legislators grasp this perception. They recognize that many voters identify college degrees as private goods, so they direct state funding elsewhere. Furthermore, they realize that a public research university dedicated to quality will do whatever is necessary to maintain it, including compensating for absent state funds through tuition increases. Thus, what we are seeing in public higher education is not actually so much an informed turn to privatization as it is a substantial reduction in public support. But it is not a seamless transition. The decline in state support for public universities creates some big problems, and, ultimately, these problems have an impact on everyone in our society—at a net loss for the "public good."

First, the privatization that occurs because of this decline can create a system of haves and have-nots within the same state university. Private industry, with an eye toward a specialized workforce and strong profits, might fund several engineering chairs, but it rarely earmarks support for the Medieval Studies program. A prosperous alumna may justifiably donate to the business school that launched her career, but the undergraduate library may suffer for funds. These examples might sound trivial to non-students. But when we compromise the overall quality of a public university, the many functions it performs in the broader community—the hospitals it operates, or the agricultural programs it manages—all suffer too.

Second, privatization has distributional consequences among the consumers of education. Even with scholarships, full pricing limits access for many families. And when students from less affluent families do find ways to attend, their educations can suffer from the demands of part-time or full-time work, the pressure to graduate on time, and the strain of growing student loan debt.

And third—and most important in the larger scheme—privatization further weakens both public understanding of these universities' society-wide value and, consequently, public commitment to these institutions. In other words, the further we privatize, the less society sees public universities as integral to the public good; and the less society sees public universities as integral to the public good, the further public universities privatize. This self-perpetuating spiral reinforces the belief that only the immediate, direct beneficiaries—students and their families—should pay. If private industry kicks in the difference, then so much the better.

Let us add one more complication to the mix—the public funding that we regularly allocate to specific functions at *both* public and private universities. For example, Americans direct billions of tax dollars every year to both nonprofit and for-profit private universities through measures such as federal research funding, Pell grants, and tax breaks.

In fact, tax dollars to private institutions have increased steadily over the last decade. Since 1999–2000, federal, state, and local appropriations to both not-for-profit (National Center for Education Statistics, Table 366) and for-profit private degree-granting institutions (National Center for Education Statistics, Table 368) have grown consistently. Private universities, in particular elite private research universities, receive hundreds of millions of dollars in federal research grants (some of which is reflected in government appropriations figures). As Harvard's Office of the Vice Provost for Research notes, the university's "largest single source for research funding is the federal government, with more than $612 million of federally funded research in FY 2010" (Harvard University Web site). The year before, in 2009, Johns Hopkins ranked first of all American universities in federally financed research spending with nearly $1.6 billion—more than double that of the University of Washington, which ranked second. (Federally financed research spending for all ten UC campuses in 2009 was about $2.4 billion.)[5]

Similarly, as the *Chronicle of Higher Education* reported in 2010, 50 percent of all students enrolled at for-profit schools receive Pell grants. To contextualize this statistic, consider that in the fall of 2010, 39 percent of University of California undergraduates system-wide received Pell grants, the highest percentage in the university's history (University of California Newsroom), while at Harvard in the 2008–09 academic year only 6.5 percent of undergraduate students received them.[6] In fact, nationwide the top six institutional recipients of Pell grant revenue are for-profit degree-granting schools, beginning with The University of Phoenix. And, as the *Chronicle* notes, while for-profit schools may educate only about 6 percent of the total number of undergraduate students in the United States, roughly 20 percent of all Pell grant recipients across the country attend these for-profit institutions ("For-Profit Colleges Capitalize on Pell Grant Revenue").

This is not to say that tax dollars should not fund research at private universities, or that lower income students at *any* institution do not deserve Pell grants. The point instead is that despite the widespread and increasing identification of college degrees as "private goods," public funding for higher education actually has not been cut off—it has just been decimated as it pertains to the core missions of public universities. The contrast of targeted investments in the comprehensive sphere of higher education with the dwindling support for public universities' core funding—which pays for instructors and subsidizes tuition—is troubling. And as President Yudof has noted in the past, these targeted investments begin to look like ornaments hung on a tree that has begun to wither from lack of water.

Still, the salve for this dwindling support is not tuition increases and private funding—these revenue sources cannot and should not constitute the entire funding base of public universities. Were they to become so, public universities would see a radical alteration in their mission, which is ultimately a service mission: public universities transform not only society but also, crucially, individuals who otherwise might not have opportunities. In other words, the public nature of public universities cannot be strictly measured in dollars; instead, it is measured in whom they serve and whom they teach.

Let us provide an example. Earl Warren—governor of California and Chief Justice of the U.S. Supreme Court—came from a working-class, immigrant family in Bakersfield, California. His immigrant father joked that he was "too poor to have a middle name" (Newton 16). No one in Earl Warren's family had a college degree. And yet, because the University of California accepted students from all socioeconomic backgrounds, Warren graduated from UC Berkeley. For the rest of his life, he credited the university with shaping his incredible career—a career that also transformed American society.

From time to time, President Yudof goes out and visits California high schools to meet the new Earl Warrens of this state. They are in towns such as Watsonville and Fresno and Monrovia. Just like Warren, they are mostly working class, and mostly from immigrant families. But their names are more likely to be Ernesto or Elena than Earl. And they are bent on achieving dreams just as lofty as his—dreams that will ultimately benefit all of us, too. And just like Warren, they know that their ticket is a college education.

Juxtaposed with their dreams is their home state—California, which lays bare the discrepancy between this country's vibrant private sector and its withering public one. California has a $2 trillion economy, the eighth largest in the world. California's state government, in contrast, has a $26 billion budget deficit. When Californians drive from LAX to UCLA, or down Route 101 in Silicon Valley, they pass a proliferation of new office complexes and shopping malls. And they are sharing the potholed road with all the employee shuttle buses for thriving companies such as Google and Apple and Microsoft. The point is that it is not California's economy that is broken—it is the state's political processes. A state such as California, blessed with natural resources, brainpower, and a powerful economic engine, ought to be able to figure out how to fund its public higher education system properly, fill potholes, take care of the disadvantaged, *and* keep the criminals locked away in jail. And yet, budget cycle after budget cycle, California seems unable or unwilling to bring home a state budget that meets its societal obligations.

The best check against this political brokenness is a public university like the University of California. Its service mission is to provide an excellent, affordable education to all qualified students. Its research aids both industry and state objectives in disciplines that range from agricultural practice to high-performance computing. And, crucially, the university educates the future leaders who will one day drive California's private sector, and it educates the future leaders who will one day reform California's public one.

In order to preserve these missions, public universities must be able to depend on a three-part funding base—a base of student-family contribution, private support, and public funding. Additionally, they may need to be able to depend on an expanded federal role in higher education. The Morrill Act itself demonstrated that the federal and state governments do not come to one another as strangers. Finding a right fit for the federal government in what has been the exclusive domain of the states will not be easy, but, as noted with regard to Pell grants and federal research funding, Washington already does much in this arena.

An expanded federal role could ease one of the biggest problems currently facing public universities: capacity, or the infrastructure and instructional firepower essential to providing a quality education. As our country grows and further diversifies, more students, not fewer, must be served, and growing capacity will be crucial. But given laggard state support, pursuing increased capacity will be a tricky proposition on most public campuses. Squeeze in too many students, and overcrowding begins to threaten quality. Raise prices to underwrite the growth, and the hopes and dreams of those who cannot foot the bill will be thwarted.

As a result, what we would propose, on the eve of the Morrill Act's sesquicentennial, is a new national higher education compact—one that we firmly believe is critical for public universities in the twenty-first century:

These universities should look at their operations with a "private" sensibility. They should establish realistic priorities, eliminate weak programs, adopt money-saving Internet technology services, and aggressively reduce waste.

At the same time, state governments should rededicate themselves to supporting these universities' core functions, not least because core functions will probably never get enough from private sources.

And if and when the federal government does begin to contribute in some way to core costs, a mechanism must be put in place to ensure that states do not treat the federal funding stream as an opportunity to disinvest even further in the institutions.

Most importantly, by implementing this compact we would demonstrate—at a national level—a public commitment to, and understanding of, these universities' societal value.

President Yudof is fond of saying that the University of California gave its state, to quote Wallace Stegner, "a society to match its scenery" (38). We believe the same may be said of all of our nation's public universities. They might be hybrids, but they exist *for* the public good, and it is our responsibility—our moral imperative—to leave these universities better than we received them. The Ernestos and Elenas deserve no less than Earl Warren, or the baby boomers, or our current students.

The Morrill Act became law at a bleak, violently divisive time in this nation's history—one in which higher education probably appeared frivolous and irrelevant next to a traumatic internecine conflict. Today we recognize the Act as critical to the rejuvenation and reconciliation our country so desperately needed at the Civil War's conclusion. The Act provided Confederate states with their own land-grant universities once they rejoined the Union. At the University of California, former Confederate scientists and brothers Joseph and John Le Conte served—to the institution's everlasting gain—as instrumental and beloved founding faculty in the university's initial years, for a brief period of which John also served as acting president. The university even asked, to some controversy, former General George McClellan to serve as its first president (he declined).

The early years of the twenty-first century—notable for their new, breathtakingly high benchmarks in state retreat from higher education funding—mark our own perilous season. The long-held vision of a better educated, more competitive, more complete American society—the "public good" writ large—has grown dimmer. And it will not brighten again unless we as a commonwealth appeal to our better angels and find a way to ensure the quality and expand the capacity of what became one of Lincoln's most important legacies: the nation's public research universities.

NOTES

Significant portions of a keynote speech delivered by President Yudof at the annual meeting of the American Law Institute on May 17, 2011, are incorporated in this essay. This speech was published in the American Law Institute's pamphlet, Remarks and Addresses at the 88th Annual Meeting, May 16th–18th, 2011.

1. Basler, vol. III, 363. NB "emancipation" is spelled "imancipation" in the original. With thanks to Dr. Daniel Howe for directing us to this speech.

2. Slosson profiled fourteen universities in total: Harvard, Yale, Princeton, Stanford, California, Michigan, Wisconsin, Minnesota, Illinois, Cornell, University of Pennsylvania, Johns Hopkins, University of Chicago, and Columbia (Slosson).

3. 2011 Academic Ranking of World Universities, http://www.shanghairanking.com/ARWU2011.html. The six public universities: UC Berkeley; UC Los Angeles; UC San Diego; University of Washington; UC San Francisco; University of Wisconsin-Madison. The seven land-grants: MIT; UC Berkeley; UC Los Angeles; Cornell University; UC San Diego; UC San Francisco; University of Wisconsin-Madison.

4. Schwartz, "Department of Defense Contractors" 9. As of March 2011, the percentage of contractors had dropped to 48 percent, and the percentage of contractors who are American citizens had risen to 23 percent (see page 11).

5. "Some Universities Increased Internal Spending." See the searchable table for federally financed research spending rank by institution.

6. "Percentages of Pell Recipients Stay Steady at Wealthy Colleges." See the interactive graph.

Challenges to Viability and Sustainability

Public Funding, Tuition, College Costs, and Affordability

DAVID E. SHULENBURGER

Overview

This chapter examines the viability of public research universities and challenges to that viability. The discussion opens with an enumeration of many of the profound accomplishments of public universities, for without knowledge of historic successes a focus on present challenges would likely seem unjustifiably negative. We are fortunate that public research universities remain strong institutions, contributing mightily to their states, the nation, and the world.

The primary challenge to future viability arises from the substantial decline in real, per student state funding, which has fallen more than 15 percent from the levels achieved in the late 1980s. Total real per student funding has remained roughly constant only because tuition has been raised to offset state funding reductions, but of course this substitution of charges to students for state funding is not without negative consequences. While public research universities have experienced declining funding, their private research university competitors have enjoyed real, per student funding increases as their revenues from both tuition and private giving have greatly exceeded those of the publics. The result is that public research universities today pay faculty more than 20 percent less than private universities (a decline from a position of near parity in the 1970s), have leaner instructional staffs, and are attracting students with lower SAT scores.

Nonetheless, graduates of public universities experience success after graduation. Indeed, recent research is presented that demonstrates that the return on investment for earning degrees from public universities is greater than that at private universities and that employers express preference for employing public university graduates. Today public research universities have held constant their share of total postsecondary enrollment and, given the growth in that population, have enrolled a steadily increasing number of students. Similarly, public research universities continue to receive about 62 percent of all federally awarded research grants, up from the 57 percent level of the late 1970s.

But the present positive situation is threatened. The higher education market is a competitive one, and for public research universities paying lower salaries to faculty and having fewer resources for scholarships and student support and for libraries and computing than private competitors represent threats that cannot be ignored. Were it not for the skillful management of public universities that has kept real educational expenditure per student constant for the last twenty years, dire effects would be more apparent today. But if state funding continues to decline in real terms and the funding disparities between public and private universities continue to increase, the future will tell a different and more negative tale. A bright future for public research universities must include increased revenue from state and private giving and increasingly wise use of those resources by public university leaders.

The Baseline: Incomparable Contribution
to Students and Society

Two streams have merged to produce today's public research university. The first is the well-known land-grant stream that flows from the Morrill Acts of 1862 and 1890. The purpose of the Morrill Acts was to create in each state

> at least one college where the leading object shall be, without excluding other scientific and classical studies and including

military tactics, to teach such branches of learning as are related to agriculture and the mechanic arts, in such manner as the legislatures of the States may respectively prescribe, in order to promote the liberal and practical education of the industrial classes on the several pursuits and professions in life.

While the progenitor organization from which the Association of Public and Land-grant Universities (APLU) arose included only land-grant universities, the APLU of 2011 includes seventy-four "land-grants" and 114 additional universities, the second stream of non-land-grant public research universities. Together, all 188 member universities have come to orient themselves to the APLU mission statement declaring in part that the historic mission of public higher education is

to offer access, opportunity, and a quality education to all who can benefit from the experience; to discover and develop the new technologies that will keep the nation competitive and safe; to produce a skilled workforce that meets America's needs and to provide new knowledge to citizens throughout their lifetimes; to contribute to the nation's national defense and security needs; and to support the advances in the sciences, arts, and humanities so vital to the cultural and social progress of this nation.

Since passage of the first Morrill Act 150 years ago, the United States has depended on public research universities to:

Educate 85 percent of undergraduate students and 70 percent of graduate students enrolled in *all* research universities;

Produce more than 50 percent of the doctorates granted in the United States in eleven of thirteen national needs categories—including 92 percent of doctoral degrees in agriculture, nearly 90 percent in natural resources and conservation, and 60 to 80 percent in computer and information sciences, engineering, foreign languages and linguistics, mathematics and statistics, physical sciences, and security;[1]

Serve as the primary route to a research university degree for minority students—more than eight hundred thousand of the almost one million minority students enrolled in research universities are at public universities, including Hispanic Serving Institutions, Tribal Colleges, and 1890 institutions;

Offer distinct opportunities for minority Americans through the seventeen 1890 institutions and Tuskegee University. While enrollment is open to all students, 81.5 percent of their enrollment (85,000 students) is African American;

Perform about 60 percent of the nation's federally funded academic research—some $19.3 billion in 2008—and nearly two-thirds of all academic research, totaling more than $34 billion annually. The 1890s universities are all research universities and, while small in enrollment and faculty, produce about $185 million of research annually;

Serve as an engine for the economy. According to the Association of University Technology Managers, research at public universities in fiscal year 2008 led to:

> 358 start-up companies,
> 2,891 new technology licenses (16,555 are actively in force),
> 6,460 applications for new patents, and
> 1,791 patents.

The 1862 and 1890s land-grant universities and the additional public research universities combine the capacity for innovation of highly qualified faculty interested in investigating phenomena and problems of both basic and applied natures with the education of both graduate and undergraduate students. That combination generates synergy that enriches both education and research. It also fuels a dynamic outreach effort that dramatically improves agricultural and business productivity. While the challenges facing these universities are broader than those extant 150 years ago, public research universities are as relevant and valuable today as in 1862 or 1962 when the Act's one-hundredth anniversary was celebrated.

Challenges to Public Research Universities: Falling State Appropriations

These great public institutions are challenged today on many fronts. Perhaps chief among the challenges is the reduction over time in state

Figure I. Real State Appropriations to Higher Education per FTE (2010 Constant Dollars)

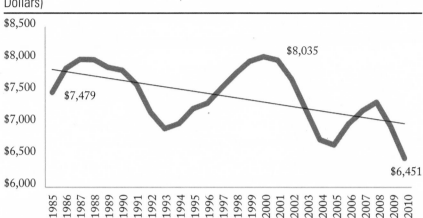

Source: Computed from data collected by State Higher Education Executive Officers, *State Higher Education Finance* (hereafter *SHEF*). Accessed May 2011.

appropriations per full-time equivalent (FTE) student. Figure I shows appropriations for all levels of public postsecondary education. From $7,479 in 1985, real appropriations per FTE student were reduced to $6,451 in 2010, a reduction of 13.7 percent.

State legislators frequently contend that their total appropriations for higher education generally increase from year to year. Figure II demonstrates that those contentions are not accurate. Real appropriations (shown here in constant 2010 dollars) do have an upward trend over time but demonstrate cyclical variability, declining in recessionary periods and increasing more rapidly during relative prosperity. Their increase from $54.11 billion in 1985 to $74.95 billion in 2010, an increase of 38.5 percent, is impressive. But the appropriations per FTE student shown in Figure I are products of both total appropriations and changes in FTE enrollment over time.

As Figure II demonstrates, FTE enrollment at all levels of postsecondary education grew steadily from 7.23 million in 1985 to 11.62 million in 2010, an increase of 60.7 percent. Total appropriations increases of 38.5 percent and FTE enrollment increases of a much larger 60.7 percent resulted in the reduction in per FTE appropriations shown in Figure I. Thus, legislators are right to congratulate themselves for increasing appropriations for higher education over time; unfortunately, their increases

Figure II. Growth in Total Real State Appropriations for Higher Education (in billions) and Growth in net Enrollment (in millions)

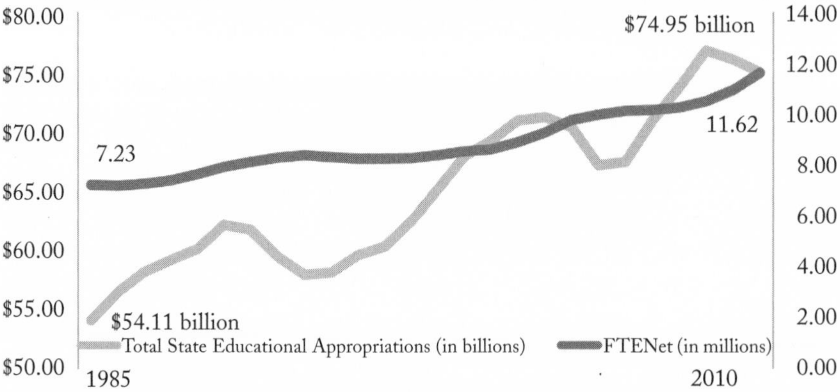

Source: Computed from data collected by State Higher Education Executive Officers, *SHEF*. Accessed May 2011.

were overwhelmed by the demand for access to public higher education of millions of additional citizens.

It does not follow that declines in state appropriations per student lead to reductions in per FTE educational revenue. As Figure III demonstrates, "total educational revenue"[2] (here defined as the sum of appropriations and net tuition)[3] increased modestly from \$9,753 in 1985 to \$10,772 in 2010, an increase of \$1,019 or 10.4 percent over twenty-five years. This increase represents a compounded annual growth rate of .4 percent per year over the entire period. Thus, total revenue per student in real terms has been nearly constant. As we shall see later, this contrasts sharply with the private, not-for-profit sector of higher education. Public higher education's nearly constant revenue is the result of the decline in per FTE appropriations by state legislatures and an increase in net tuition revenue from \$2,274 to \$4,321 during the 1985 to 2010 period.

In 1985, the National Association of State Universities and Land-grant Colleges, or NASULGC (APLU's name until 2008), assembled an ad hoc Committee on the Future of State Universities, which persuaded a group of scholar-leaders to put their best thinking about the future into a book titled simply *The Future of State Universities* (Koepplin and Wilson). Duward Long's chapter on "Financing in the Year 2000" had as its first assumption, "[B]oth society and individuals benefit from higher education

Figure III: Public Higher Education Real Educational Revenue per FTE (2010 constant dollars)

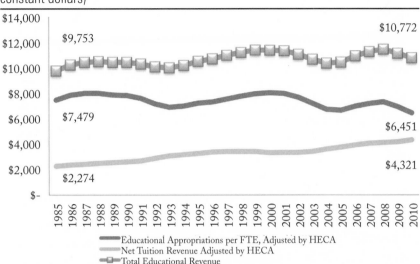

Source: Computed from data collected by State Higher Education Executive Officers, *SHEF*. Accessed May 2011.[4]

and that the benefit, while unquantified and unquantifiable, is sufficient to justify investment of public funds by a variety of subsidies for the higher education industry, public and private." While Long based his chapter on this assumption, he observed that the balance was shifting and the magnitude of private benefits from education was beginning to erode the willingness of governments to support higher education (Long 210–11).

The proportion of public university revenue arising from state appropriation has continued to decline, from 77 percent in 1985 to 60 percent in 2010 (shown in Figure IV) as tuition grew from 23 percent to 40 percent of higher education educational revenue. Whether the shift in responsibility for funding higher education from the state to the student has been due to the shift toward private benefits flowing from higher education that Long posited or has resulted from other motivators, such a shift is unmistakable.

Public university leaders do not believe that the distribution of educational costs should shift to the point that the student bears the majority of the cost. A 2011 Pew Research Center poll found that 57 percent of public university presidents felt that the largest share of a student's college

Figure IV: Appropriations and Net Tuition as a Percent of Educational Revenue in Public Higher Education

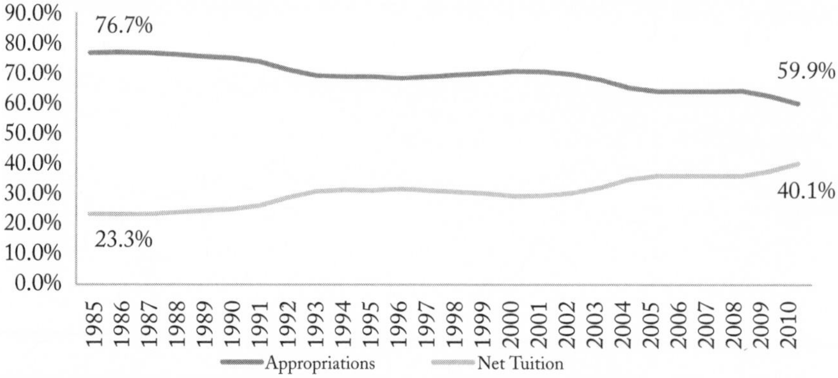

Source: Computed from data collected by State Higher Education Executive Officers, *SHEF.* Accessed May 2011.

expenses should be borne by state and local governments, a sharp contrast with the 84 percent of private university presidents who felt that students or their families should bear the largest share of expenses (Pew Research Center, answers to question 27).

The public is somewhat more accepting of the shift of costs toward the student, though sentiment varies by demographic group. Pew's companion poll of the public found that only 22 percent of white respondents believed that the state or federal government should bear the largest share of college costs; minority respondents largely placed much more responsibility on government, with 47 percent of blacks and 52 percent of Hispanics expressing the belief that responsibility for bearing the largest share of higher education funding should belong to the government (Pew Research Center 42).

Public/Private Benefits of Higher Education

Professor Walter McMahon of the University of Illinois published in 2009 an exhaustive review of the returns on investment in higher education and concluded, based on the ratio of private to public returns, that "48% of the cost [of higher education] should be borne privately and 52% publicly" (326). McMahon continues, "If the roughly 50% of total investment costs in higher education that are foregone earnings at most public institutions are included in total costs, as they should be, then 76% of the total costs currently are being borne privately and 24% publicly" (326).

The private benefit of higher education continues to grow. Sandy Baum and Jennifer Ma's "Education Pays, The Benefits of Higher Education for Individuals and Society" demonstrates not only the existence of an earnings premium associated with various levels of higher education but the dramatic growth of that premium over the last decades. Those with degrees are more likely to have pensions and health insurance and are more likely to be employed. New research has found that even the ultimate private benefit, increased life span, in recent years has come only to those who obtain college degrees (Meara, Richards, and Cutler).

But the impact of a college degree has significant neighborhood effects (the effects of the education on society that go beyond the impacts that education has on the students who receive it) that Baum and Ma also identify. Important among them is Enrico Moretti's research findings that increases in the proportion of college degree holders in a given population lead to significant wage increases for those who do not hold college degrees (Baum and Ma 17). Consistent with Friedman's *The World is Flat*, which maintains that we cannot insulate ourselves from international competition, Moretti's findings illustrate why public subsidy that serves to increase the proportion of the population with college degrees is good for all of us. Baum and Ma add a data-rich catalogue of public benefit: reduced poverty; reduced public assistance expenditure; improved health (including a reduced propensity to smoke); greater cognitive skill development of children living with educated parents; increased willingness to volunteer, to give blood, to vote, and even to understand the opinions of others.

The private benefits of higher education are not distributed evenly; some benefit more than others. Across gender and race/ethnic groups, however, the benefits from obtaining higher education are uniformly positive and large (Baum and Ma 12). Higher education remains the most certain path to social and economic mobility, but those from lower-income families participate proportionately less in higher education than those from higher-income families. A major public-good agenda must be to bring participation rates of these individuals up to those of the total population.

Economic returns to those who obtain degrees in fields such as education and social sciences are generally lower than to degree holders in fields such as business, engineering, science, and math (Thomas 280). Given the national need for those educated in low-paying fields such as public school education and social welfare, the country does not now have, and is unlikely in the future to have, sufficient numbers of students educated in these areas unless it provides considerable subsidy to students who specialize in them or, alternatively, acts to push wages for those professions upward. The private goods incentive to obtain degrees in these disciplinary areas is weak.

Nearly every public college/university president is engaged in the effort to persuade states and the federal government to fund a larger proportion of university budgets. Unfortunately, the pursuit of greater state subsidy generally has not been successful; the proportion of higher education paid for by the states continues to decline. In addition, federal appropriations that might hold down tuition hikes increasingly are targeted to students and not to institutions; hence, they are not available to subsidize essential institutional operations. Efforts to secure more resources from all levels of government must and will continue. In a nation that is now falling behind many countries it formerly led in competitiveness, federal legislators ignore the public goods nature of higher education at our peril because it is investment in education that is most likely to reverse this situation. States that do not promote and fund vital public universities are similarly uncompetitive in attracting and retaining firms that contribute to the states' economies. Because both graduate and undergraduate education retains much of a public goods character, it is clearly appropriate that governments at both levels provide substantial subsidy for it.

Challenges to Public Research Universities: Private Universities Surge Ahead in Resource Acquisition

A second major problem confronting public higher education is its financing relative to private higher education.[5] Figures V and VI compare average per FTE revenue sources typically used to finance educational activities of public and private research universities. The data are normalized on a per FTE student basis to facilitate comparison because the median public research university has 26,301 full-time equivalent students while its private counterpart has only 11,657 (Desrochers, Lenihan, and Wellman; IPEDS). Grant and contract and auxiliary and clinical/hospital revenues are excluded so that the focus can be primarily on revenues from which the financing of most educational activity flows.

Figure V. Average Public Research University (PU) Per FTE Educational Revenue Sources

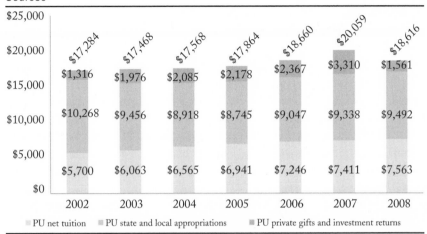

Source: Desrochers, Lenihan, and Wellman, Delta Cost Project, *Trends in College Spending 1998–2008,* 2011 Table a, 44, 45.

Figure VI. Average Private Research University (PR) per FTE Educational Revenue Sources

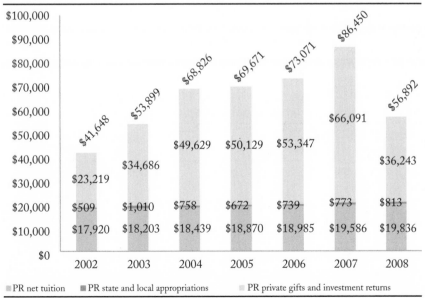

Source: Desrochers, Lenihan, and Wellman, Delta Cost Project, *Trends in College Spending 1998–2008,* Table a, 44, 45.

A clear difference between public and private is the much smaller amount of tuition and private gift and investment return revenue per student in public universities and the far larger amount of state and local appropriated revenue. The sum of the revenues available from these three sources typically used to finance educational activities, moreover, is vastly different. The financial advantage of the private research university, which was $24,364 *per student* in 2002, grew to an enormous $66,391 per student in 2007 and declined to $38,276 in 2008 when stock market values fell sharply. These differential revenue figures stand in sharp contrast to the total per student public university revenues of $17,284, $20,059, and $18,616 in the respective years. The differential of revenue between the public and private universities is more than the total educational revenue of the publics in each year.

As Table I shows, total education revenue for private research universities began the 2002 to 2008 period with 2.4 times the educational revenue per student of the average public research university and rose to a revenue multiple of 4.3 before falling back to 3.1 times the available resource per student in 2008. The private research university advantage in net tuition ranged from a multiple of 2.6 to 3.1. The overwhelming advantage for the privates throughout the period was in the Gift and Investment income category, ranging from 17.6 to 23.8 times the amount per student of the publics. Note that in 2008, when there were sharp stock market reversals and endowment portfolios fell dramatically in value, the

Table I: Ratios of Average per Student Private Research University Funding to per Student Public Research University Funding

Expenditure Categories	2002	2003	2004	2005	2006	2007	2008
Net Tuition Income	3.14	3.02	2.81	2.72	2.62	2.64	2.62
Private Gifts and Investment Returns	17.64	17.55	23.80	23.02	22.54	19.97	23.22
State and Local Appropriations	0.05	0.11	0.08	0.08	0.08	0.08	0.09
Total Educational Resources	2.41	3.09	3.92	3.90	3.92	4.31	3.06

Source: Desrochers, Lenihan, and Wellman, Delta Cost Project, *Trends in College Spending, 1998–2008,* Table a, 44 and 45.

ratio of private to public endowment returns remained near its high point as public university endowments fell apace with privates.

Net tuition ratios as represented in Table I are derived from the average tuition figures for each of the university categories. Because the averages can be skewed by distributions that diverge from the normal, averages sometimes are not the best representative statistics. Tables II and III supply data for "list" tuitions and endowment totals per FTE student at the median, maximum, and minimum levels.[6] While much variation in tuition and endowment levels is evident, the levels of both at private research universities exceed those at public research universities regardless of whether they are measured at the median, minimum, or maximum levels. Note that list tuition at the median private very high research university is 4.7 times that of its public counterpart and the lowest tuition at the private very high research universities is 8.6 times that of the lowest public counterpart. Tuition discounting (the reduction of tuition charges by application of institutionally funded financial aid) represents a larger percentage of list tuition at private very high research universities, but a central difference between all such private and public universities is the far heavier dependence of private universities on tuition revenue as a funding source. The relative stability of the ratio of net tuition in private research universities to that in publics, shown in Table I, illustrates the heightened importance of tuition as a revenue source over time for both public and private universities.

Just as with tuition, the per FTE student endowment assets advantage of private research universities is robust whether evaluated at the median, highest, or lowest deciles. While the most poorly endowed of the private research universities have only $6,785 in endowment assets per student, that amount is about 3.25 times the $2,084 per student held by their public counterparts. The wealthiest, with nearly one million dollars, surpass their public counterparts by an overwhelming amount.

Market values of endowment resources have rebounded from the 2009 trough for both public and private universities but state appropriations to public universities continue to fall. Since gift, endowment, and investment revenue made up 73 percent of the median private research university per student revenue (in 2006) but only 12.6 percent of that of the median public, the precipitous market decline in endowment values that began in 2008 undoubtedly had the more pronounced effect on expenditures from endowment income streams in private institutions (Delta Cost Project IPEDS Data).

Table II: List Tuition 2009-10

University Category	Median Tuition	Highest Tuition	Lowest Tuition
Private Very High Research University (PR VH)	$38,679	$41,316	$32,057
Private High Research University (PR H)	$31,890	$41,655	$4,290
Private Masters University (PR M)	$23,101	$38,820	$4,428
Public Very High Research University (PU VH)	$8,191	$14,416	$3,707
Public High Research University (PU H)	$6,947	$13,554	$1,320
Public Masters University (PU M)	$5,998	$12,750	$2,008

Source: Computed from the Integrated Postsecondary Education Data System, IPEDS. Accessed May 2011.

Table III: Endowment Assets per FTE Student, 2008-09

University Category	Median	Highest Decile	Lowest Decile
PR Doctoral	$53,300	$927,321	$6,785
PR Masters	$9,530	$53,863	$904
PU Doctoral	$11,920	$73,676	$2,084
PU Masters	$1,950	$11,132	$406

Source: *Trends in College Pricing 2010,* Downloads http://trends.collegeboard.org/ college_pricing/downloads Abstracted from Figure 14. Original data source: National Association of College and University Business Officers, NACUBO.

Similarly, the market rebound since spring 2009 has had the greatest relative positive effect on spending in some of the private universities. The severe endowment decline (average of 18.7% in 2009) was just sufficient to take endowment levels back to where they were toward the end of 2006 as endowment values fell on average 18.1 percent in 2008 but grew by 17.2 percent in 2007 and 15.3 percent in 2006.[7] As we go to press (March 2012) the Dow Jones Industrial Average stands near 13,100, far above its March 9, 2009, trough value of 6,547 and about 8 percent lower than its all-time high reached on October 9, 2007 (DJIA). Endowment expenditure practices of universities, public and private, have become more conservative, but the relative levels of endowments have been restored nearly to previous highs.

Differences in Educational Expenditures

Such large and persistent differences in revenues per student inevitably translate into differences in education-related expenditures per student. The differences in expenditure are especially large in the instructional expenditure category; very high private research universities spend 4.25 times more per student than public very high research universities. The differences in expenditures between public and private counterparts for student services and academic support are smaller but are directionally the same. Private universities simply spend more per student in all categories than do public universities.

I do not make these income, asset, and spending comparisons to argue that public research universities should be funded on par with private universities; rather, I seek to demonstrate that a very large and rapidly growing funding disparity has developed. In an internationally competitive market for the human, intellectual, and physical resources needed to produce high quality research and education, a funding disparity of the current magnitude not only destabilizes the equilibrium that has long

Figure VII. 2008-09 Median per FTE Expenditures by Category and Institution Type

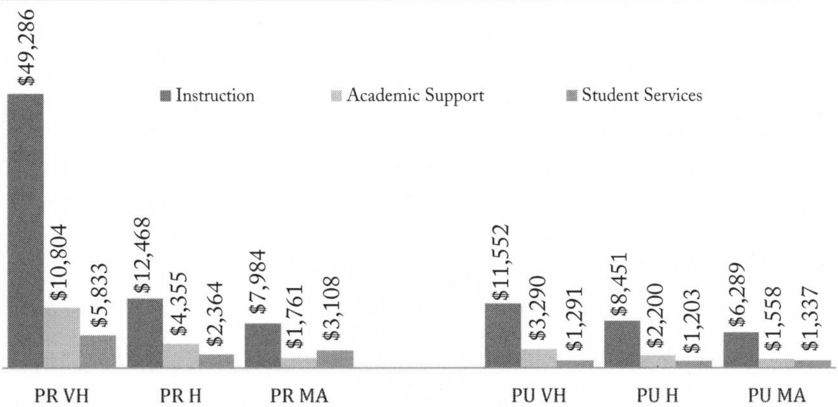

Source: Computed from IPEDS. Accessed May 2011.

existed between U.S. public and private universities, but could put public research universities at a competitive disadvantage.

Relative Declines in Faculty Salaries

The large and growing public/private research university divides in faculty salary, teaching load, and student selectivity were first illuminated by the work of Thomas Kane and Peter Orszag in 2003.[8] In areas such as faculty salaries, where parity between very high public and private research universities was achieved in the 1970s, a 15 to 20 percent salary gap now exists.[9]

Figure VIII starkly illustrates the competitive disadvantage in recruiting and retaining faculty that has developed for public universities relative to their private counterparts over the last twenty years. A large and increasing faculty pay gap has opened over the last three decades and is increasing in size. Public research universities paid assistant and associate professors nearly on par with their private counterparts in 1970 but by 2008–09 the publics had on average fallen more than seventeen percentage points behind the privates.

A study by F. King Alexander also concluded that salaries at public and private research universities have moved from being roughly equal in 1980 to more than a 20 percent advantage at the private universities by 1998 (120). In addition, he discovered that fringe benefits are less generous at public universities and do not serve to reduce the compensation gap (127). An interesting facet of Alexander's analysis is his calculation of the "noncompetitive" salary ranking of the twenty least competitive public universities.

In 2003, Cindy Zoghi examined the decline in relative salaries for the 1975 to 1994 period. She found that the public university decline in relative salaries was not offset by broadly defined amenities, including intangible job attributes or more traditional fringe benefits. In other words, the relative decline is in total compensation, not simply in wage levels. Zoghi observed that "Changes in the level of amenities over time do not explain the relative wage trends observed" (56). Her summary conclusion is also a warning: "Unless public faculty are somehow compensated for this loss of income . . . those who can find positions in higher-paying private institutions will do so, and the public university will only be able to recruit and retain lower-quality faculty" (56).

Figure VIII. Average 9-month Salaries of Full-time Faculty in Various Carnegie Categories as a Ratio of those in Private Doctoral Universities

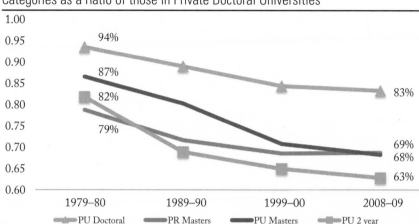

Source: National Center for Educational Statistics, NCES, *The Condition of Education 2010,* Indicator 44.

Relative Declines in Faculty/Student Ratios

Unfortunately, the total faculty disadvantage is only partially reflected in faculty salaries. The ratio of faculty to students at public universities has increased from 6.6 per 100 students in 1976 to 7.3 but the faculty/student ratio increased from 8.3 to 8.7 at private universities during that same period. While both private and public universities used a portion of their resources to increase the key faculty to student ratio, private universities maintained their advantage over the thirty years and now have a 20 percent advantage over their public counterparts. Similarly, it appears that public universities have fallen behind as they purchase fewer inputs than their private counterparts in the academic support and student services areas, as well as in instruction (see Figure VII above). Given that these two categories of expenditures are constituted by standard competitive market commodities, public universities are at a double disadvantage as they are able to purchase fewer of these commodities (at approximately the same competitive market unit price paid by private universities) and they pay less to their employees who must use smaller quantities of commodities as they deliver educational services to students.

Figure IX. Ratio of Instructional Staff per 100 Students at Public and Private Universities

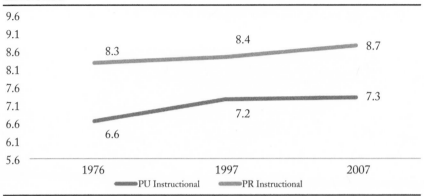

Source: NCES, *Digest of Education Statistics 2009,* Table 244.

Relative Declines in Competitiveness for Top SAT Scoring Students

As a final measure of relative competitiveness, consider the differences in the measured quality of freshmen who choose to attend public research universities as compared to private research universities. Table IV demonstrates the decline in SAT scores at public research universities from 1986 to 2000 using Kane and Orszag's work and from 2001 to 2007 using IPEDS reporting. (I acknowledge that using SAT scores to measure student academic ability is limited and exceedingly narrow; however, at this point it is the only available metric that can be used for national comparisons across institutions.)

First, the SAT scores of students at public very high research universities are significantly lower than those at private very high research universities in both critical reading and math at the 25th and 75th percentiles of entering freshmen students. Second, the differential between the public and private university entering student SAT scores has grown since 1986 in each of the four categories. The only positive indicator for public research universities is that the SAT-Math differential did not widen for the 2001–07 sub-period at the 25th percentile level.

Noteworthy are the differences in the levels of the 75th percentile of the students at the private very high universities and at their public

Table IV: Change In SAT Scores of Entering Freshmen 1986 to 2007

	Public Very High Research Universities 2001	Private Very High Research Universities 2001	Public Very High Research Universities 2007	Private Very High Research University 2007	Relative Gain of Private Over Public Universities 2001-2007*	Relative Gain 1998 to 2000 matched selectivity group of Public and Private Institutions**
SAT Critical Reading 25th Percentile	516	626	517 (55th percentile of all students)***	638 (87th percentile of all students)***	11	12-18
SAT Critical Reading 75th Percentile	627	719	632 (85th percentile of all students)***	736 (98th percentile of all students)***	12	12-13
SAT Math 25th Percentile	537	652	544 (58th percentile of all students)***	659 (88th percentile of all students)***	0	16-23
SAT Math 75th Percentile	649	737	657 (87th percentile of all students)***	752 (97th percentile of all students)***	7	17-23

Source: *Computed from IPEDS; **from Kane and Orszag, Brookings Institution, September 2003, 12; ***from SAT Percentile Ranks, College Board.

counterparts. The SAT math score for the private university students is 752 and the critical thinking score is 736. The corresponding public university student scores at the 75th percentile are 657 and 632. The SAT scores of students at the private universities are not far from the maximum score of 800, but the privates continue to widen the gap over the publics. In this very narrow tail of the distribution, the competition is for the very best students, but still the privates succeed in widening their advantage.

The Higher Education Research Institute's periodic survey of college faculty finds that university faculty perceptions correspond with the data presented in Table IV. In the 2005 survey, only 37 percent of public university faculty felt that "most students are well-prepared academically," in sharp contrast to the 67 percent of private university faculty who agreed with that statement. At the other extreme, 33 percent of public university faculty agreed that "most of the students I teach lack the basic skills for college level work," while 16 percent of their private university counterparts agreed (Higher Education Research Institute).

In our paper, "University Tuition, Consumer Choice and Affordability," Peter McPherson and I reflected on the growing preference for private over public higher education:

> One often hears the contention that attending a prestigious private university is worth the large price differential between it and a public university. During the last two years, applications to prestigious private universities have skyrocketed far beyond the rate of growth of high school graduates or of applications to public universities, apparently reflecting the applicants' belief that obtaining a degree from such a school confers benefits that more than justify the higher cost and that will last a lifetime.[10] A recent Gallup Poll found that 40.9 percent of respondents believed quality was higher at private universities, 36.5 percent believed that public and private universities were equal in quality, while only 3.7 percent believed quality was higher at public universities (Selingo). (McPherson and Schulenberger 62)

That academically more able students gravitate toward private universities is confirmation that these beliefs are being converted into action.

What we report here is the differential choice of students earning higher scores on the SAT to attend private universities. We infer their reasons from opinion research such as that cited above. It is worth repeating that there are not robust research findings to support the conclusions that improved learning or lifetime earnings and opportunities are associated with graduating from a private research university rather than a public one. Nevertheless, perceptions acted upon clearly impact reality.

The Impact of Public/Private Higher Education on Learning, Earnings, and Job Prospects

Does it matter which college a student attends? Do students learn more at one type of institution than another? Do employment prospects upon graduation vary by type of undergraduate institution attended? Do lifetime earnings vary by type of university attended?

The Cooperative Institutional Research Program (CIRP) has tracked the attitudes of incoming college freshmen for thirty-five years and has observed very large increases in the proportion of students who say they selected a specific college because of quality or outcome factors. About their 2007 survey results they conclude, "These data indicate that incoming college students might be reacting to the national debates on measuring the quality of college education and accountability by weighting related factors more heavily in their admissions decisions" (Prior, Hurtado, Sharkness, and Corn 12). The 2007 compilation of CIRP campus surveys further supports the notion that today's students are aware that they are buying a bundle when they choose to attend a specific college. Table V lists the top seven reasons given for selecting a given university, all of which relate to different attributes of the bundle that appealed to the students. Note that price is an argument of significance for some students

Table V: Top Reasons Noted as Very Important in Selecting College Attended

	All	*Men*	*Women*
College has a very good academic reputation	63.0%	57.2%	67.6%
Graduates get good jobs	51.9%	47.3%	55.6%
A visit to the campus	40.4%	34.4%	45.2%
Was offered financial assistance	39.4%	34.8%	43.1%
Wanted to go to a school about the size of this college	38.9%	31.4%	45.0%
College has a good reputation for its social activities	37.1%	35.2%	38.6%
The cost of attending	36.8%	32.7%	40.1%

Source: Prior, Hurtado, Sharkness, and Corn 30.

but, more frequently, other parts of the bundle persuade the potential student.

During recent years, applications for admission to prestigious private universities have skyrocketed far beyond the rate of growth of high school graduates or of applications to public universities, apparently reflecting the applicants' beliefs that obtaining a degree from such a school confers on the degree recipients benefits that more than justify the higher cost and that will last a lifetime. What is the nature of evidence concerning the differences in learning, earnings, or labor market prospects between research and non-research universities and between public and private institutions of both types?

Learning Differences

Within the community of research universities one often hears the argument that the undergraduate studying in a research institution receives a superior education to the undergraduate studying in a university in which the faculty is not engaged in research. The rationale generally provided is that the student in the former benefits because her education is informed by faculty who are current in the literature, who know the latest research findings, and who themselves are contributing to that research and writing the textbooks rather than teaching from texts written by others. Those favoring the non-research university education experience contend that the opposite is true, that the research university undergraduate is neglected by faculty because faculty spend time in the lab rather than the classroom and often relegate undergraduate teaching to graduate students who themselves are occupied with pursuit of their own degrees rather than with creating the optimal learning environment for their students. Whether the higher tuition at the research university is "worth it" largely hangs on which of the arguments, if either, is correct.

Unfortunately, we know little about differences in learning across Carnegie types. APLU and the American Association of State Colleges and Universities (AASCU) launched the Voluntary System of Accountability (VSA) in 2006 to begin to measure and document differences in learning. The universities agreeing to be part of VSA bound themselves to rigorously measure value-added-to-learning outcomes using specified tests of learning and techniques of measurement, in part to resolve controversy over such impact.[11] At this writing the VSA effort is entering into the fourth year of its value-added measurement trial. Evaluation of the trials may help develop understanding of the causes of differences in learning patterns across public universities. Such understanding should be a basis for university improvement.

A major study of learning on college campuses published in 2011, *Academically Adrift*, found significant differences in learning across the twenty-four institutions in its sample but concluded that the institutions in which students had the largest learning gains were the ones in which "students reported higher incidences of behaviors that are beneficial for learning" (Arum and Roksa 114–17). Essentially, their finding is that the learning differences discovered were more strongly associated with individual student behaviors than institutional differences.

This is a potentially fruitful area for continued study. If we grow to understand the causes of learning differences among universities, we will gain the ability to improve learning in all universities. Until research demonstrates otherwise, claims that some institutions or groupings of institutions based on types of governance produce greater learning outcomes than others simply are not supported.

Earnings and Labor Market Entry Differences

A companion contention is that attending a prestigious private research university is worth the large price differential between it and a public university because career earnings of private university graduates are more than sufficient to offset their higher tuition. Arguments to support such opinions take varied forms: for example, that the higher faculty salaries in private research universities permit them to hire excellent faculty; that they hire faculty who care more about good teaching because students are paying so much to attend; that the support provided by such schools to their students ensures that they learn and, therefore, employers are willing to pay a premium to hire their graduates. Some contend that students at such universities develop a network of associates from the children of wealth and status that disproportionately attend the schools and that association with such classmates will provide them opportunity advantages throughout life or that graduation from such schools signals to employers differences in productivity and earnings; thus, the higher wages paid to them become based on the signal rather than on their productivity. The former contentions are market-based and suggest that higher productivity is created by attendance and that productivity is rewarded in the market. The latter contentions are inherently non–market based, suggesting that microeconomic fundamentals are not at work in the labor market.[12]

Some of the older research literature finds that private, prestigious universities convey earnings benefits on graduates, but co-variation of student characteristics with institution type, indebtedness levels of students, and restriction of the results to full-time employed graduates make the findings less than definitive. The common finding is that variation of future earnings within a university's graduates is far greater than variation in earnings across universities (McMahon 293). That is to say, the data tend to show that a given student does not change lifetime earnings prospects when she earns a bachelor's degree from a high-quality private college rather than a high-quality public college. More recently, carefully controlled academic studies have been made of the impact of college quality on lifetime earnings. They generally find (as does the study authored by Zhang that is described in the exhibit below) that when entering test scores, family income, etc., are controlled for, college quality (however defined) or public/private governance makes little difference in earnings (Zhang 871–98).

A 2011 study by Stacy Dale and Alan B. Kruger ("Estimating the Return to College Selectivity") updating their 2002 article ("Estimating the Payoff") produces striking results. It is notable because it is the first study to utilize earnings data from federal administrative sources (Social Security Administration) rather than self-reported earnings data. In addition, earnings of graduates were tracked over a prolonged period and were not simply snapshots of an arbitrary period of time after graduation. For the cohort of students attending in 1976, earnings were tracked from 1983 to 2007; for the cohort of students in 1989, earnings were tracked through 2007. When the authors adjust for student high school GPA, SAT scores, and the SAT score averages of the colleges that the students applied to but did not attend, their "estimates of return to college selectivity . . . generally are indistinguishable from zero" ("Estimating the Return to College Selectivity"). Since private research universities tend to be more selective than their public counterparts, their findings essentially are that private university graduates do not enjoy an earnings premium. Interestingly, the data from administrative sources used in their 2011 study produced essentially the same results as did the self-reported earnings data used in their 2002 study.

Table VI: Benefits—Public vs. Private University

Earnings impacts by university quality/governance	
Middle-quality, public	9.2%
Middle-quality, private	10.6%
High-quality, public	18.0%
High-quality, private	17.5%

Source: Zhang.

Dale and Kruger's findings are bolstered by those from a 2010 study by PayScale: "Public schools proved to be far better value overall, at least for in-state students. Because of the lower costs paid by in-state students—$82,301 compared with $126,933 for out-of-state students at public institutions and $170,219 for students at private schools—they enjoyed the best net annualized ROI: 9.7 percent. . . . Private schools yielded a net annualized return of 9.1 percent" (Di Meglio). The unique strength of the PayScale methodology is that it considers not only earnings but also the cost of obtaining the education.[13] That cost includes both the tuition rate and the average number of years taken by graduates of a given university to earn their degrees.

The PayScale study has two principal weaknesses. First, the tuition data utilized in it is list tuition and not net tuition. Because discount rates vary considerably by college, it is difficult to generalize about the net effect of the use of list tuition instead of net tuition.[14] The second weakness of the PayScale study is that the earnings data utilized are self-reported. Self-reported data are, by definition, not independently verified. The similar findings from the 2002 and 2011 Dale and Kruger studies that used both self-reported and administrative earnings data, however, suggest that the PayScale results from self-reported data should not be dismissed lightly. On the other hand, Dale and Kruger's studies had controls that assured that the sample was relatively unbiased, whereas the PayScale study's sample consisted of those who sought out the firm's services; the biases imparted to the results of the PayScale study because of this means of sample selection are unknown. On the other hand, the fact that the PayScale sample is large, including about one thousand alumni per each of 554 schools, adds some credibility.

Striking are the PayScale data for the top twenty-five universities ranked by return on investment (Table VII). Twenty of those twenty-five

Table VII: PayScale's Ranking of Universities by Net Return on Investment

Rank	University	Governance	Net ROI
1	Georgia Tech	Public	14.2%
2	Brigham Young	Private	14.1%
3	University of Virginia	Public	14.1%
4	William and Mary	Public	13.6%
5	Col. School of Mines	Public	13.6%
6	Virginia Polytechnic Institute	Public	13.1%
7	U. of Michigan	Public	13.1%
8	UC Los Angeles	Public	13.1%
9	UC Berkeley	Public	13.1%
10	UNC Chapel Hill	Public	13%
11	U. of Florida	Public	13%
12	Cal Poly	Public	12.9%
13	Texas A&M	Public	12.7%
14	James Madison	Public	12.6%
15	U. of Delaware	Public	12.6%
16	UC San Diego	Public	12.6%
17	Cal Tech	Private	12.6%
18	MIT	Private	12.6%
19	Harvey Mudd	Private	12.5%
20	Harvard	Private	12.5%
21	NC State	Public	12.4%
22	Binghamton	Public	12.4%
23	Missouri Science and Technology	Public	12.4%
24	Purdue	Public	12.4%
25	University of Illinois	Public	12.4%

Source: Computed from Web site made available in Di Meglio, http://www.business-week.com/bschools/content/jun2010/bs20100618_385280.

are public universities and only five are private. Di Meglio places emphasis on the eighty-eight universities that exceeded a benchmark of 11 percent ROI because "over the past 30 years, the S&P 500 Index averaged about 11 percent a year." Sixty-four of those eighty-eight schools meeting or exceeding this ROI benchmark are public universities; twenty-four are private. Clearly, the PayScale study is consistent with both Zhang's and Dale and Kruger's findings that earnings of graduates of private universities do not exceed those of public universities.

Note that no unbiased national data base exists that tracks university graduates throughout their careers from which a university might gather

Table VIII: Top Twenty Universities Preferred by Recruiters

Rank	University	Rank	University
1	Penn State	11	Brigham Young
2	Texas A&M	12	Ohio State
3	U. of Illinois	13	Virginia Tech
4	Purdue	14	Cornell
5	Arizona State	15	UC Berkeley
6	U. of Michigan	16	U. of Wisconsin
7	Georgia Tech	17	UCLA
8	U. of Maryland	18	Texas Tech
9	U. Of Florida	19	NC State
10	Carnegie Mellon	19	U. of Virginia

Source: *Wall Street Journal,* http://online.wsj.com/article/SB1000142405274870455410 4575435563989873060.html.

data to support claims of superior earning or career success for its graduates. Data bases that do exist suffer from potential bias because they are made up of responses from graduates who voluntarily self-report that data. The Spelling's Commission 2006 call for development of a National Unit Record System was directed at creating an unbiased data base that could be used for documenting such claims (Commission on the Future of Higher Education), but such a development appears unlikely in the short run since both the House and Senate versions of the 2008 Higher Education Opportunity Act contain language prohibiting the Department of Education from creating data systems that track students over time, including a student unit record system.

Efforts to link state data bases that use objective employer-reported earnings into a single national data base are under way (Ewell and Boeke). If those efforts succeed, an objective, nationwide data base on earnings will exist. Unfortunately, the earnings of many graduates would still be excluded from such a data base, for instance, the self-employed and those working abroad.

A 2010 *Wall Street Journal* poll of top corporate recruiters concluded, "State universities have become the favorite of companies recruiting new hires because their big student populations and focus on teaching practical skills give the companies more bang for their recruiting buck." The top twenty schools preferred by the recruiters are listed in Table VIII. Only three private universities appears on this top twenty list. All seventeen public universities are research universities.

What is the Competitive Position
of Public Universities Today?

The short answer is that public four-year higher education is doing very well, at least in comparison to four-year private higher education. Figure X, which examines all higher education except the for-profit sector, shows that four-year public universities lost about 12 percent of their enrollment market share while private higher education lost about 20 percent of market share over time and that two-year public colleges have gained enrollment market share at the expense of both sectors.

Figure XI broadens the examination to all of higher education, including the public, private, not-for-profit, and for-profit sectors. In this expanded market context, public four-year higher education lost 19 percent of its market share while private four-year higher education lost about 31 percent. The gainers are two-year public colleges, which increased their share by 65 percent, and for-profits, which increased their share from essentially zero in the mid-1960s to 10 percent in 2009. (Note: The U.S. Department of Education does not report data on for-profit enrollments prior to 1967 so a small portion of the private university enrollment share prior to 1967 actually consists of for-profit enrollments.)

While the public four-year reduction in market share has been less than that of private counterparts, little comfort could be taken if the size

Figure X. Distribution of Full-time Equivalent Enrollments Across Post Secondary Education Excluding the For-Profit Sector

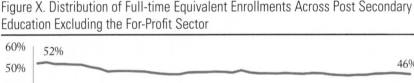
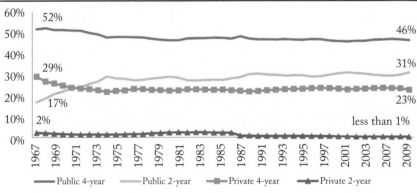

Source: *Digest of Education Statistics 2010,* Table 226.

Figure XI. Distribution of Full-time Equivalent Enrollments across all Post Secondary Education

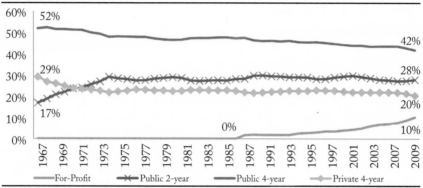

Source: *Digest of Education Statistics 2010,* Table 226.

Figure XII. Full-time US Enrollment in Higher Education

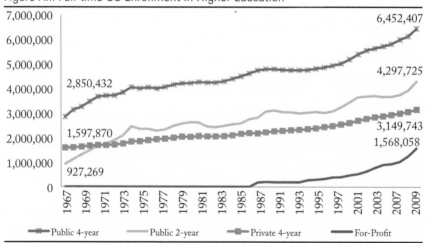

Source: *Digest of Education Statistics 2010,* Table 226.

of the market were declining or stable. But as Figure XII shows, the market has been increasing in size at a significant rate. All four of the major sectors exhibited significant FTE enrollment growth. Thus, even though public four-year higher education lost 19 percent of its market share in the 1967–2009 period, it gained 3.6 million FTE students. Private four-year higher education lost 31 percent of its market share but gained 1.55

million FTE. The loss of enrollment share to community colleges and to for-profit colleges is at least partially because these two newer entrants into the higher education market attracted new sets of students into the market for higher education. Thus, the gains experienced by these two sets of entrants may not be entirely at the cost of public and private four-year colleges and universities.

It is not clear whether the meteoric rise of for-profit enrollment will continue. Dramatic declines in applications for enrollment at some major for-profit institutions in the 40 to 50 percent range occurred in early 2011 as the Education Department carefully (and publicly) scrutinized the questionable tactics many for-profits had used to build enrollment and the for-profits in response took various actions that may make their business practices more acceptable (Marklein). Most agree, however, that community college enrollment growth will continue to grow at least apace with that of four-year higher education (Kasper 19–20).

Are Costs "Out of Control"?

Concerns about future enrollment in research universities, both public and private, often center on what is characterized as their "out of control" costs, a view frequently expressed by legislators and trustees. Consider the 2003 statement of a prominent legislator reported by *The New York Times* in an article on public university tuition increases: "Colleges and universities have not shown a willingness to contain costs," he said and committed to introduce legislation to withdraw federal money from big tuition raisers (Anderson, "Public College Tuition Increases").

What are the facts? Figure XIII clearly demonstrates that public and private universities have increased tuition at rates considerably in excess of the 2.46 percent compounded rate of inflation in the 1996 to 2010 period. But while this increase reflects list price increase, it does not reflect increase in cost of delivering education for all of the types of institutions. *Price* changes are what consumers experience while *cost* changes are directly experienced by producers.[15] As the discussion above explained, much tuition increase behavior of public universities has been driven by their attempt to offset revenue reductions in state appropriations.

To get at cost increases one has to disaggregate the various activities in which universities engage and examine expenditures per FTE student in those expenditure categories associated with the provision of education.

Figure XIII. Compounded Annual Growth Rate of Nominal Median Tution 1996–97 to 2009–10

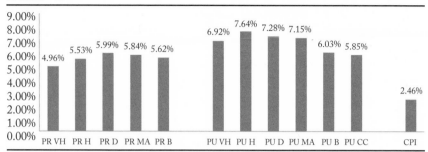

Source: IPEDS, accessed May 2011.

Figure XIV. Increase in Real Education and Related Expenses Per FTE

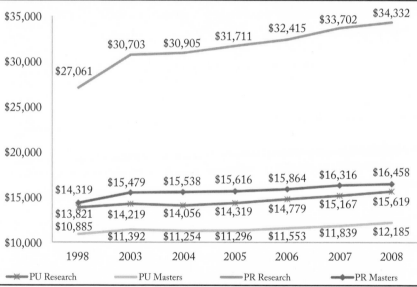

Source: *Trends in College Spending 1998–2008*, Delta Cost Project, 2009, 46–47.

Jane Wellman of the Delta Cost Project collects those items into a single factor that she calls Education and Related Expenses, that is, the "full cost of education." That category includes "100% of reported expenditure on instruction and student services, as well as the instruction share of costs for 'general support, administration, and maintenance' including academic support, institutional support and operations and maintenance" (*Trends in College Spending 1999–2009* 43). Figure XIV displays data on public and private masters and research universities.

Evident is not only the significant difference in cost between public and private research universities, but a quantum difference in the rate of real cost increase in private research universities relative to each of the other categories. Private research universities had real cost per FTE increase at a 2.41 percent compounded annual rate in the 1998–2008 period whereas public research universities experienced an annual increase of 1.23 percent, roughly half the private rate. As the data clearly illustrate, public higher education has the cost of education under control to a far greater degree than private research universities.

Has Tuition Increased to a Level that College Has Become Unaffordable?

Are we at a point at which tuition has become so high that higher education is unaffordable? There are many different ways to answer this question, but here we will consider only one perspective, the degree to which a year's tuition at median higher education institutions fits into the budget of median households. The average discount rates for private (33%), public (18%), and community colleges (11%) are used to convert tuition to average discounted tuition in Figure XV (College Board Advocacy and Policy Center).

Is college affordable? The percentages in Figure XV do not provide answers for every family, but they do reveal that both list and discounted tuitions at public higher education institutions are no more than 16 percent of median family income, an amount for which many families could budget. Clearly public universities and colleges are more affordable than private ones.

But will the trajectory of tuition be one that will soon reverse this pattern of affordability? To answer that question, one has to consider the full set of factors that affect affordability. Colleges discount tuition and award financial aid in other forms, the federal government awards Pell grants and provides tax credits for qualifying families, and states make various kinds of awards to offset tuition. When all of these are taken into account, the cost of college is put into proper perspective, as is the trend of tuition. Surprisingly, the College Board finds that net tuition has been falling at

Figure XV. Median Tuition as a Percent of Median Family Income

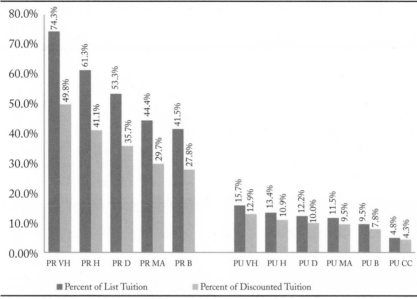

Source: Median Tuition Data from IPEDS accessed May 2011. Median Household Income ($52,029 in 2008), US Census Bureau, USA Quick Facts http://quickfacts. census.gov/qfd/states/00000.html.

Figure XVI. College Board's Estimation of Real Net Tuition

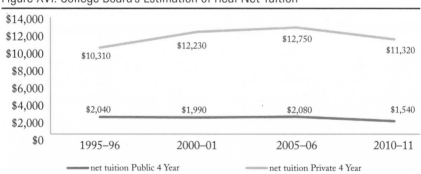

Source: The College Board, *Trends in College Pricing 2010,* Data Table for Figure 7.

public universities since 1995–96 and at private universities since 2000–01. Figure XVI shows the net tuition trend to be downward!

Will this continue to be the case? That is a matter of public choice. Pell grants and income tax deductibility of college expense for some have been the primary federal contributors to this trend line. With the state of the federal budget, can these contributions continue? Universities have rapidly added to both need-based and merit aid as their real state appropriations per FTE student have dwindled. Can this continue? Will states begin to reverse the twenty-plus-year decline in appropriations per FTE and relieve the upward pressure on public university tuition?

A Brief Note on Research Competitiveness

While the focus of this chapter is on the ability of public research universities to continue to offer strong undergraduate, graduate, and professional programs, a brief consideration of their ability to remain competitive in research is warranted.

Figure XVII makes clear that the share of research done by public universities, both of the total and of federally funded research, has

Figure XVII. US Public/Private University Shares of Federal and Total Research Funding

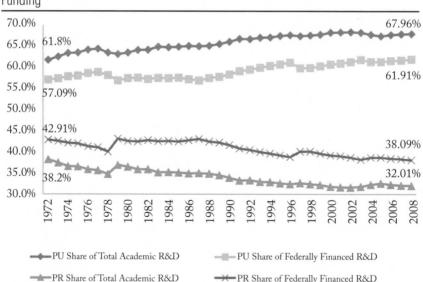

Source: Calculated from *NSF Federal Funds for R&D* (various years) http://www.nsf.gov/statistics/fedfunds/.

increased over time. Neither the decline in real state appropriations per FTE student nor the relatively greater success of private universities in obtaining tuition and endowment funding has diminished the competitive ability of public research universities. Despite the relative decline in faculty compensation and relative increase in teaching workload, public research university faculties continue to expand the share of research done by their universities.

Many are concerned about the ability of public universities to maintain, much less increase, this research share into the future given the relative diminishment of their resources. APLU president Peter McPherson summarized the reasons for concern about the future in his *Recommendations to the NRC Committee on Research Universities,* so I will not repeat those arguments and reasoning here.

Concluding Comments

Clearly, the last twenty-five years have been difficult for public universities. States have reduced real appropriations, and public universities have offset these declines with tuition increases. While public universities had to be quite judicious in managing costs, private universities were not so constrained. While they did not have substantial state appropriations to lose, private universities did have control over tuition and increased it substantially above the rates that their public counterparts charged. Private universities' substantially larger endowments grew rapidly (with a major reversal in 2008–09 that is now nearly restored). The net result is that private research universities now have substantially greater resources than public research universities, and they use those resources to pay faculty better, make more faculty available to students, and provide greater amounts of both student and academic support.

Yet despite the competitive reversals, public universities continue to fulfill their missions in an admirable fashion. They remain attractive to students and annually increase the numbers of students that they serve both absolutely and relative to their private counterparts. They have remained relatively attractively priced to students and provide a bargain educational alternative for students. Research has not demonstrated differences in learning outcomes based on university governance. The graduates of public universities continue to enjoy at least as much success in the labor market as the graduates of private universities. And public universities continue to increase their share of all university research, remaining highly competitive for federally funded research grants.

But the cloud of funding disadvantage relative to their private counterparts remains and is growing darker over time. Some suggest that the model of public funding that has brought public research universities this far is broken. Consider the argument of Paul Courant, James Duderstadt, and Edie Goldenberg:

> The model of state-based support of graduate training made sense when university expertise was closely tied to local natural-resource bases like agriculture, manufacturing, and mining. But today's university expertise has implications far beyond state boundaries. Highly trained and skilled labor has become more mobile and innovation more globally distributed. Many of the benefits from graduate training—like the benefits of research—are public goods that provide only limited returns to the states in which they are located. The bulk of the benefits are realized beyond state boundaries.

Only more direct federal funding of public universities, especially of graduate education and research, is likely to correct the problem they identify.

Others argue that the state appropriations and tuition-funded model of public universities is broken and predict success only for those public universities that become "a hybrid . . . a university that functions in the public interest and (traditionally) with public support, though with enough private money to insulate itself from political influence" (Berrett). This hybrid is, of course, a cross between the heavily endowed private university and the public university of today.

I am cautiously optimistic about the future of public research universities. Their contributions are so significant to the economic and cultural competitiveness of the states that fund them and to the welfare of their citizens that I cannot believe that state governments will forever let them wither. Similarly, the nation's competitiveness crucially depends on the research and innovation these universities produce; this fact produces a powerful reason for the needed federal investment. I am also cautiously optimistic that for-profit universities will be properly regulated so that the quantity of public resources allocated to their students properly reflects the educational value they produce.

But most of all I have faith in the faculty, administrative leaders, and governing boards of public research universities. They have demonstrated over time the ability to adapt to their environments such that their universities collectively thrive and serve their students and communities well. Not all their innovations are productive, but unproductive innovations naturally die out. The productive ones are seized on by other universities, imitated, and improved upon. So long as our several hundred public research universities are free to be creative, I am optimistic that they will continue to flourish. This does not diminish their need for greater governmental and philanthropic support; it does ensure that when such support is forthcoming, it will be used wisely.

NOTES

This chapter extends, updates, and draws heavily from the texts of papers I co-authored with President Peter McPherson, Vice President Howard Gobstein, and Research Director Christine Keller while I served as vice president for academic affairs at APLU (2006–2010). The conclusions reached are solely my own and not those of APLU. I express my gratitude to Christine Keller for deriving data from IPEDS.

1. "Areas of National Need" are determined by the Secretary of Education pursuant to the Higher Education Act. I refer here to the determination made by the Secretary for the purpose of awarding graduate fellowships in 2008.

2. The term *educational revenue* excludes revenues that flow from other activities, e.g., athletics, technology transfer, externally funded research.

3. The term *net tuition* is total tuition receipts minus tuition discount provided to students.

4. The HECA, or Higher Education Cost Adjustment, and its advantages over other price indexes are explained in Appendix III of Shulenburger and McPherson, pp. 86–87.

5. I find it useful to use the Carnegie classifications (2005) in examining groups of universities and do so in this chapter when such categorization data are available. In the figures and tables below, PU will be used to designate public institutions and PR, private. The Carnegie categories that accompany the public and private designations are: VH

= very high research, H = high research, D = doctoral, MA = masters, B = bachelors, and CC = community colleges. The categories are exclusive, so each higher education institution is assigned to one. For a full exposition on the Carnegie system of classifications see: http://classifications.carnegiefoundation.org/descriptions/.

6. "List" tuition is the published tuition rate. It contrasts with "net" tuition, the rate that students actually pay.

7. "Endowments Declined 18.7%," FY2009, NACUBO/Common Fund Study of Endowments, Washington, D.C.

8. Kane and Orszag, "Funding Restrictions at Public Universities"; "Financing Public Higher Education," 33–39; and Kane, Orszag, and Apostolov, "Higher Education Appropriations and Public Universities," 99–146.

9. 2007 figures computed from IPEDS for Very High Research Universities on 2/09/10 are Public Full Professor, $113,173, Associate Professor, $79,551, Assistant Professor, $68,703 and the Private counterparts, respectively are $144,363, $94,771, and $79,999.

10. For a glimpse at the continuation of this activity in 2008 see Anderson, "Applications to Colleges are Breaking Records." See also Finder, "Elite Colleges Reporting Record Lows in Admission."

11. For a description of the effort see Shulenburger, Keller, and Mehaffy, 48–54.

12. Note that I do not question whether graduating from college makes a difference in earnings, health, civic participation, etc. My argument focuses instead on whether adequate evidence exists to support contentions that graduating from one university with a bachelor's degree confers more benefits to the individual than graduating from another university. A thorough summary of the benefits associated with higher education is found in Baum and Ma; a beautifully crafted book summarizing the individual and societal monetary and non-monetary benefits of higher education is McMahon's *Higher Learning, Greater Good*.

13. The methodology used by PayScale to calculate ROI is unique. Di Meglio describes PayScale's methodology as follows: "The study, by PayScale, uses pay reports from 1.4 million graduates from U.S. colleges and universities supplied through online pay comparison tools in the past year. The study used pay reports from only full-time U.S. employees with bachelors' degrees and no advanced degrees, and pay reports averaged about 1,000 for each of the 554 schools in the study.

To calculate the 30-year net return on investment on a college degree from each school, PayScale first combined the median cash compensation (salary and bonus) for graduates for each of the past 30 years. It then calculated the cost of the degree (excluding financial aid awards) by combining tuition and fees, room and board, and books and supplies for the number of years it takes most students to graduate from each school. From the compensation figure, it subtracted the cost of the degree and the estimated median pay for a hypothetical graduate for the same period plus an additional 4 to 6 years representing the time he or she would have spent in school. The resulting figure, in 2010 dollars, incorporates the school's six-year graduation rate, so that a school where graduates have a net return of $2 million over 30 years and where the graduation rate is 50 percent will have an overall net return of $1 million. Annualized ROI includes annual wage inflation of 4.3 percent per year. Net return and annualized ROI for state schools were calculated twice, using college costs for in-state and out-of-state students, and are listed separately in the table. Data on school type, graduation rates, and total cost were supplied by the Integrated Postsecondary Education Data System."

14. Ibid. "Schools that performed poorly in the PayScale analysis took issue with the methodology. Among the complaints: PayScale based the study on a small, self-selecting sample of alumni from each school—on average, about 1,000—and failed to consider financial aid, which would have reduced total college costs and improved ROI for all schools. One school that argued in favor of incorporating financial aid in the calculations was Philadelphia University, which had a 30-year net return on investment of $218,000. Using the school's average financial aid award and more recent graduation rate, the 30-year net ROI would be $276,000" (2).

15. For an earlier discussion of "cost" and "price" see *Straight Talk About College Costs and Prices*, 8–10.

University-Based R&D and Economic Development

The Morrill Act and the Emergence of the American Research University

MICHAEL M. CROW AND WILLIAM B. DABARS

Our nation's research universities, both public and private, have served as the primary source of the discovery, creativity, and innovation that fosters economic and social development at all levels of analysis in the global knowledge economy. The research and development (R&D) enterprises of these institutions, conducted in coordination with undergraduate and graduate programs of advanced learning, have contributed incalculably to the standard of living and quality of life those of us in developed economies have come to take for granted.[1] The science-based technological innovation and industrial application that are the products of academic research are widely held to have been requisite to the trajectory of economic development that led the United States in the second half of the twentieth century to become what has been characterized as the "world's superpower." Economists contend that as much as 85 percent of measured growth in per capita income in the United States derives from technological change, according to research cited by the National Academies (Committee on Prospering in the Global Economy of the Twenty-First Century, *Rising Above the Gathering Storm*).

An open letter to members of Congress signed by the executives of sixteen leading technology corporations regarding proposed reductions in

119

federal support for academic research in 1995 alluded to thousands of technological breakthroughs that are the product of the partnership between research universities, the federal government, and industrial product development. "Imagine life without polio vaccines and heart pacemakers," the letter begins. "Or digital computers. Or municipal water purification systems. Or space-based weather forecasting. Or advanced cancer therapies. Or jet airliners. Or disease-resistant grains and vegetables. Or cardiopulmonary resuscitation" (Allen, Augustine, Clendenin et al.).

More recently, in the wake of the economic collapse of 2008, more than fifty public higher education leaders convened by the Carnegie Corporation of New York submitted an open letter to then president-elect Obama and his administration regarding a proposed Higher Education Investment Act. In the midst of crisis, the authors reaffirmed the partnership between the federal government and our research universities but even more eloquently underscored their critical societal role:

> America's colleges and universities, public and private, have always worked in the service of our nation, contributing to our social, economic, scientific, cultural, and technological preeminence by educating millions of citizens who contribute to every sector of society. Today, with millions of students, thousands of laboratories, and outreach that touches countless communities in rural and urban America, the great institutions of public higher education, along with our sister institutions in the private sector, have the capacity to produce the people, ideas, tools, solutions, and knowledge infrastructure our economy needs to regain its momentum and to set a new trajectory. ("Higher Education Investment Act")

Even more recently, Jonathan R. Cole, the longtime provost of Columbia University, has compiled a definitive compendium of some of the thousands of transformational "discoveries, inventions, devices, concepts, techniques, and tools" that originated at our nation's research universities. From lasers to magnetic resonance imaging to global positioning systems to the algorithm for Google searches, the breakthrough technologies of university-based innovation he enumerates have improved our quality of life immeasurably and contributed incalculably to economic growth.[2]

The intrinsic impetus to thus advance new knowledge, emphasizing in the context of economic development the focus of research institutions on scientific discovery and technological innovation, distinguishes the American research university from other institutional platforms in higher education. The economic contribution of research universities is closely tied to the basic and applied research conducted on their campuses, but of inestimable significance is their function in the production of human capital, which represents a critical national asset because of its impact on the creation of innovation capacity and thus the competitiveness of the American economy. In this context, a committee of the National Academies has posited that universities must perform "double duty: to educate and train not only those who will have careers in research, but also those who will become entrepreneurs, managers, consultants, investors, or policy makers." Their report on investment in science and technology calls for universities to become more proactive in preparing students for these roles, which are increasingly critical to national competitiveness (Committee on Prospering in the Global Economy of the Twenty-First Century, *Capitalizing on Investments in Science and Technology*, 56).

This chapter thus seeks to provide a brief overview of the interplay between integrated academic research, development, and education (RD&E) and its broad impact on local, regional, national, and global economic development, the majority of which derives most directly from the rise of scientific discovery and its interplay with technological innovation. While through preceding eras and well into the twentieth century most industries did not depend heavily on inputs from science, advances in knowledge fundamentally enabled by university science have increasingly driven the economy, leading to the development of entire new industries and the growth of national prosperity. Implicit in claims for the economic development function of the research university is the assumption that in this context it is a means to advance broad societal development. Our quality of life and standard of living depend on the accumulated success of academic research in ways that we normally fail to recognize, and without the emergence of the research university contemporary existence as we know it would be vastly impoverished.

As an intrinsic corollary dimension to this discussion, the chapter examines the fundamental impact of the land-grant institutions on the American research university, which assumed its defining structure and characteristics contemporaneously and in interrelationship with the formation of the land-grant colleges and universities during the final quarter of the nineteenth century. Among the institutions that were established as a consequence of the Morrill Act, and those already established which became its beneficiaries, a considerable number emerged in the decades following the Civil War as research universities. While nearly three dozen land-grant schools were founded within the decade following the enabling legislation, signed into law by President Lincoln in July 1862 in the midst of national crisis, seventeen had already been established as public colleges or universities prior to that year and would thereafter become designated land-grant institutions.[3] The contemporaneity of the emergence of the modern American research university and the land-grant system as well as their attendant reciprocal influence marks an important chapter in the history of American higher education. Indeed, in the estimation of former University of California president Richard C. Atkinson, the land-grant colleges were the "first quasi-research universities in the United States" (Atkinson and Blanpied 33).

The Land-Grant Institutions and the Emergence of the American Research University

There are approximately five thousand institutions of higher education in the United States, but of these only 108, both public and private, are categorized by the Carnegie Foundation for the Advancement of Teaching as major research universities.[4] While the definitive prototype for the American research university would come with the establishment of The Johns Hopkins University in Baltimore in 1876, fifteen institutions conclusively consolidated the structure and purposes of the American research university in the assessment of historian Roger L. Geiger. From a varied evolutionary pool and representative of the diversity of American higher education, these were five colonial colleges chartered before the American Revolution (Harvard, Yale, Pennsylvania, Princeton, and Columbia); five state universities (Michigan, Wisconsin, Minnesota, Illinois, and California); and five private institutions conceived from their inception as research universities (MIT, Cornell, Johns Hopkins, Stanford, and Chicago) (Geiger, *To Advance Knowledge* 2–3).

According to Geiger, these fifteen universities were unified by their collective identity as a unique and differentiated set of institutions and defined by their interrelationships, both competitive and cooperative; capacity to institutionalize and organize the proliferation of specialized knowledge into academic disciplines; success at leveraging burgeoning financial resources and academic infrastructure derived from growth; and commitment to research as a complement to the traditional function of teaching (Geiger, *To Advance Knowledge* 2–3).

Of the fifteen institutions singled out by Geiger as foundational to the American research university, six are land-grant institutions, both public and private: California, Cornell, Illinois, Minnesota, MIT, and Wisconsin. While in general usage the designation "land-grant" is often regarded as synonymous with state colleges and universities, a notable few are private, such as the Massachusetts Institute of Technology, or private with public colleges, such as Cornell University (Tobin 320). Of the seventy-six land-grant institutions that comprise the roster maintained by the Association of Public and Land-grant Universities, forty-two, including eight campuses of the University of California system, emerged as major research universities, with the majority in this category representing the definitive type of the flagship public research university. Twenty land-grant schools, including six University of California campuses, are member institutions of the Association of American Universities (AAU).[5]

The Morrill Act, with its provisions for the distribution of as many as ninety thousand acres of federal land to each state, would fund the establishment of collegiate institutions to provide instruction in agriculture and the "mechanical arts" to the sons and daughters of the working and middle classes.[6] The legacy of the utilitarian and egalitarian tenets specified in the Morrill Act, epitomized by curricula in the "useful arts"—identified by historian John Thelin as agriculture, mechanics, mining, and military instruction, thus leading to the designation "A&M" in the names of a number of such institutions (Thelin 76)—would play an important role in the ascendancy of the scientific and engineering disciplines in American research universities, thus shaping the research enterprises of the emerging set of American research universities (Rosenberg and Nelson 323–48). The legislation would produce a diverse and heterogeneous set of colleges and universities that have exerted a broad impact disproportionate to their actual number. By one estimate, land-grant institutions have educated one-fifth of all Americans with college degrees.[7] The act further set a precedent for federal support for higher education that would burgeon exponentially following World War II (Oleson and Voss xii). According to some assessments of American higher education, the global preeminence attained by American research universities in the postwar era is a direct consequence of federal patronage, beginning with the seed funding provided to many of the land-grant schools.[8] The federal precedent moreover encouraged state legislatures to provide annual appropriations for universities and colleges (Thelin 76; Oleson and Voss xii).

From the outset, the orientation and objectives of the land-grant schools thus informed and shaped the American research university as that institutional type evolved to become a dominant catalyst to regional, national, and global economic development. In order to appreciate the unique contribution of the land-grant institutions to this process, it will be necessary not only to consider the research enterprise of American universities but also briefly to survey the development of that enterprise over the course of the past 150 years as well as the trajectory of its interrelationships with business, industry, and governments. Our analysis necessarily conflates discussion of research universities, both public and private, with the subset of those that were established as or designated as land-grant institutions. Public research universities, including those established as a consequence of the land-grant legislation, are distinguished from their private research-grade peers less by their shared commitment to the public good than in their funding model and generally larger enrollments.

A Trajectory toward a Decentralized and Competitive "Academic Marketplace"

Although the organization and objectives of the contemporary American research university appear at first glance so self-evident as to have been inevitable from the outset, in reality the institution in its present form represents the culmination of a historical trajectory shaped by two centuries of what historians Hugh Davis Graham and Nancy Diamond have described as "haphazard evolution" rather than planning. The unique interplay of cultural, societal, and economic forces that led to the emergence of a set of heterogeneous institutions competitively engaged and capable of contributing to regional, national, and global economic development—a scenario aptly characterized as an "academic marketplace"—began in the earliest years of the American Republic (Graham and Diamond 9). This formative process, particularly in the late nineteenth and early twentieth centuries, was driven by regional competitive rivalries.

The emergence of a set of institutions of higher education competitively engaged and possessed of the capacity to contribute to national prosperity was by no means to be foreseen during the formative years of the Republic. During the Constitutional Convention in Philadelphia in 1787, James Madison called for the establishment of a national university and the legislative power to "offer premiums to encourage the advancement of useful knowledge and discoveries." The rejection of a proposal that may have led to the formation of a national ministry of higher education has been attributed to its conflict with the doctrine of states' rights.[9] The failure to enact the legislation would yield positive outcomes, setting the course for the decentralized configuration of American higher education, which would fortuitously unleash competition between institutions and contribute to this defining attribute of American higher education (Graham and Diamond 9).

"Decentralization" in this context thus refers to the absence in the United States of a centralized national ministry, or regional ministries, of higher education. Graham and Diamond consider the historical circumstances that contributed to the formation of this particular configuration: "Decentralization was accelerated by a colonial and revolutionary environment in America that combined community isolation, entrepreneurial incentives for upward mobility, fractious Protestant denominationalism . . . and revolutionary egalitarianism." Moreover, the authors attribute the aversion to centralized authority in this context in part to the U.S. Constitution, which, "shaped by classical liberalism's respect for contract and fear of centralized state power, created a federal system that limited and fragmented national authority and reserved education policy for state and local governments" (Graham and Diamond 9, 12–15).

Since the late nineteenth century, national systems of higher education in Europe have by contrast typically been subject to state control, characterized by centralized allocation of funding, planning, and policymaking, including determination of institutional specialization with an emphasis on advanced study, professional training, and research (Paradeise, Reale, Bleiklie, and Ferlie). But higher education in the United States would follow a different trajectory. In the estimation of Graham and Diamond, historical circumstance remarkably turned "fragmentation, incoherence, qualitative unevenness, and economic vulnerability" into assets. While the vicissitudes of the process would inform the emergence of the American research university in the nineteenth century, its remarkably productive apogee would come only in the decades following World War II, which produced a "decentralized, pluralistic, and intensely competitive academic marketplace fueled by federal research dollars" (Graham and Diamond 9, 12–15). While American research universities would assume their position of global dominance in the postwar years, as considered in the following discussion, the emergence of the academic research enterprise was robustly informed by the orientation of the land-grant institutions that took shape following the Civil War.

The entrepreneurial dimension of the American research university has been correlated with the Morrill Act by scholars who perceive in its utilitarian provisions the seed for teaching and research with the potential for contributions to economic development. Indeed, Nathan Rosenberg deems the trajectory of responsiveness of American universities to their economic environments the "most distinctive feature of American universities, at least as far back as the passage of the Morrill Act of 1862." Such institutions, he argues, comparatively autonomous and operating in a competitive environment devoid of centralized federal authority, have historically been "heavily beholden to the needs of local industries and to the priorities established by state legislatures." The attendant focus on "economic relevance" thus stems in his estimation from their need to be responsive to the shifting landscape of agriculture, business, and industry: "America's decentralized higher education system can be fairly described as 'market-driven,' rather than locked into a centralized system in which the reallocation of budgets and personnel is severely restricted by political and bureaucratic considerations, as well as by the constraints of past history" (Rosenberg 113–14, 116; Rosenberg and Nelson 326).

The Utilitarian Predication of the Land-Grant Institutions

The Morrill Act reflected the practical ethos intrinsic to our national culture from the earliest days of the American Republic. While the elite colleges of colonial New England perpetuated the classical curriculum deemed suitable for privileged young gentlemen, in the decades following the Civil War a groundswell of sentiment in favor of utilitarian instruction consistent with the mandate of the land-grant institutions would eclipse the model inherited from British and European institutions. As noted by historian Laurence Veysey, "During the ten years after 1865, almost every visible change in the pattern of American higher education lay in the direction of concessions to the utilitarian type of demand for reform." General societal approbation for instruction for "real life" fueled the demand for practical instruction (Veysey 61–66). By this time, the American public held a generalized conception of the knowledge disseminated at colleges and universities as "improvement" (Shils 28).

With its provisions for the distribution of federal lands to enable states to fund programs of instruction in agriculture and the "mechanical arts" for the sons and daughters of the middle classes, the Morrill Act responded to the normative ethos of what the political scientist Henry Steck has termed "practical people doing practical things, whether the practicalities of the earlier colleges of agriculture and mechanical arts or the advanced research of a Massachusetts Institute of Technology or Cornell" (Steck 73). Not only did the Morrill Act legitimize the utilitarian ideals that would shape the American university throughout the rest of the nineteenth century, but it also encouraged the perception that one of the primary purposes of an undergraduate education is preparation for professional life or direct entry into the workforce. To aid citizens of more modest social strata then entering universities in increasing numbers, instruction would stress application in everyday life. Unlike their British and European counterparts, Rosenberg and Nelson observe, American universities would be "perceived as a path to commercial as well as personal success" (325). The utilitarian conception of higher education not only encouraged ambivalence toward privilege but also, because of its association with the common good, was deemed to be more "democratic."[10]

Support from the general public for the concept of "practical utility" derived from higher education arose from the Morrill Act, according to Roger Geiger, and these inclinations would find expression in the utilitarian tenets formulated by Ezra Cornell, whose specifications for the establishment of the university that would bear his name include the oft-cited formulation, "I would found an institution where any person can find instruction in any study" (Rosenberg and Nelson 324–25). With its novel integration of the traditional humanities curriculum with science and "practical" fields, especially engineering and agriculture, Cornell University, established in 1865, represented a new vision for a "modern" university. According to Veysey, Cornell was the "first spectacular visible fruit of the Morrill Act" (82–86; Geiger, *To Advance Knowledge* 6). The utilitarian predilection of the land-grant universities was perhaps the primary force driving the dispersion of scientific and engineering skills in the decades following the Civil War and in important respects contributed to the role of science and engineering in the nascent American research university (Ross). The emergence of instruction in these fields, however, was by no means exclusively an outcome of the Morrill Act: Harvard had established the Lawrence Scientific School in 1846, followed by the Jefferson Physical Laboratory in the 1870s; the Yale Scientific School was established in 1847 (renamed the Sheffield Scientific School in 1861);

and Dartmouth had established the Chandler Scientific School in 1852 (Veysey; Atkinson and Blanpied 33). Nevertheless, in the estimation of some of the foremost experts in university-industry relations, public universities and "especially those established under the Morrill Act affected the direction of the academic research enterprise during this period to a greater extent than the private Ivy League institutions" (Mowery, Nelson, Sampat, and Ziedonis 2004, 9).

The utilitarian predication of the nascent American research university model would thus be especially conducive to the persistence of what Rosenberg and Nelson term "hands-on problem-solving" coupled with ambivalence toward the abstract and theoretical, an orientation expressed in the 1830s by Alexis de Tocqueville, whom the economists quote as follows: "In America the purely practical part of science is admirably understood and careful attention is paid to the theoretical portion, which is immediately requisite to application. . . . But hardly anyone in the United States devotes himself to the essentially theoretical and abstract portion of human knowledge." Tocqueville concludes that the motivation for scientific investigation is the pursuit of "every new method that leads by a shorter road to wealth, every machine that spares labor, every instrument that diminishes the cost of production, every discovery that facilitates pleasure" (Tocqueville 2: 48, 52–53).

Nevertheless, what we would term "applied science and engineering" did not generally appear in the curriculum of American universities until the 1840s because such an academic field was considered both "too practical and plebeian" (Metzger 129). While this orientation would persist into the 1920s, the practical inclinations of the republic perceived by Tocqueville would encourage the rise of engineering education in the United States, according to Rosenberg and Nelson, beginning in 1802 at West Point at the U.S. Military Academy, whose graduates lent expertise to the scientific exploration of the continent undertaken in association with the Lewis and Clark expedition. The trend toward practical applications intensified with the construction of vast national infrastructure projects such as the transcontinental railroad and the system of locks and dams erected on the Mississippi River. Demand for trained engineers would lead to the establishment of Rensselaer Polytechnic Institute in 1824, but not until the second half of the nineteenth century would sufficient demand from industry for engineers with more specialized training lead to the formation of additional schools and programs. Thus, the Massachusetts Institute of Technology was established in 1865, and courses of engineering were introduced at institutions such as Yale and Columbia during that same decade (Rosenberg and Nelson 327; National Research Council Committee on the Education and Utilization of the Engineer 25). While Veysey deemed Cornell the first institutional reification of the ideals of the Morrill Act, Henry Etzkowitz argues that the "key transition" for the transformation of the American research university into a "teaching, research, and economic development enterprise" took place at another land-grant institution, MIT. From MIT he traces the lineage to Stanford, where the "entrepreneurial academic model" was integrated into the academic culture of a liberal arts curriculum ("Research Groups as Quasi-firms" 110).

The Nearly Contemporaneous Emergence of the Land-Grants and the Prototype for the American Research University

The originating legislation for the land-grants came only fourteen years before the establishment of the institution that the consensus of scholarship widely holds to represent the definitive prototype for the American research university: The Johns Hopkins University, in Baltimore, Maryland, which famously conjoined the British model of residential undergraduate education, epitomized and already well established on these shores by such elite colonial colleges as Harvard, Yale, Princeton, and Dartmouth, with the advanced scientific research of the German academic model.[11] According to one scholar of American higher education, the establishment of Johns Hopkins in 1876 would prove to be "perhaps the single most decisive event in the history of learning in the Western hemisphere," a claim which Geiger deems "extravagant" but not unreasonable (Shils 28–29; Geiger, *To Advance Knowledge* 7). For our purposes, we underscore the near contemporaneity and inevitable interplay between this prototype for the American research university and the emerging land-grant institutions.

At Johns Hopkins, former University of California president Daniel Coit Gilman introduced into American higher education the pattern of specialized graduate study modeled on the practices of German scientific research institutes and thus an emphasis on complementary learning and research (Geiger, "Milking the Sacred Cow" 332). Until research achieved the status accorded it there and through this influence at other elite institutions, this sector that we regard as intrinsic to the purposes of higher education, writes Geiger, was "largely adventitious in the scheme of things" ("Milking the Sacred Cow" 333–34). Nannerl Keohane elaborates on the impact of the prototype: "Established universities such as Harvard and Yale, and new institutions such as Stanford or Chicago, adapted the Johns Hopkins/Germanic model by grafting it onto the traditional undergraduate liberal arts training by a collegiate structure within the larger university context" (5). The Germanic model would be "quickly Americanized," according to Graham and Diamond, as graduate schools were "superimposed" on existing colleges of arts and sciences (19). During the 1890s graduate schools modeled on Johns Hopkins were thus created with the establishment of the University of Chicago, for example, and with the transition of Harvard and Columbia from colleges into universities.

"Branches of learning as are related to agriculture and the mechanic arts"

As an expression of the social and cultural milieu of mid-nineteenth-century America, the Morrill Act engendered institutions in which teaching and research consistent with its purposes—as specified in its provisions, "without excluding other scientific and classical studies, and including military tactics, to teach such branches of learning as are related to agriculture and the mechanic arts" (National Association of State Universities and Land-grant Colleges 5)—would prove conducive to the emergence of scientific discovery and technological invention. Rosenberg and Nelson offer the following summary of fields of inquiry legitimated as suitable for academic inquiry as a consequence of the legislation: "agriculture and mining, commercial subjects such as accounting, finance, marketing, and management, and an ever-widening swath of engineering subjects, civil, mechanical, electrical, chemical, aeronautical, and so on" (325). All of these subjects were mechanisms for the development of human capital in cities and regions undergoing rapid industrial development.

Among the most significant contributions of the land-grant schools to economic development were training and research focused on agriculture. Rosenberg and Nelson underscore the extent to which these institutions exercised direct economic impact on their regions by "fostering the high productivity of the American farm through the teaching of food production skills." The Hatch Act of 1887 further expanded the role of the land-grant schools in this sector by funding affiliated agricultural experiment stations. Their cooperative arrangements with government regulatory agencies served to increase the legitimacy of the academy in the mind of the general public (Thelin 135–36; Rosenberg and Nelson 326).

The expansion of disciplinary fields during the final decade of the nineteenth century corresponded to the consolidation of academic practices that during prior decades had been regarded as reforms or innovations, Geiger explains. Among these measures were the elective system, programs in applied sciences, and graduate education (Geiger, *To Advance Knowledge* 10). While it was not until the early twentieth century that fields such as chemical engineering and electrical engineering were fully integrated into American research universities, the "institutionalization" of these and other applied engineering disciplines quickened the development of graduate programs, specialized journals, professional certification, and affiliation with professional organizations. The dynamics between academic research and technological development and the new status accorded these professions supported the formation of close ties between universities and industry (Rosenberg and Nelson 327). The emergence of these fields during the final decades of the nineteenth century brought engineers and scientists into industry, enabling the concurrent establishment of research laboratories by industrial enterprises (Mowery and Rosenberg 9).

Even before the advent of large-scale academic research, universities tended to enter into research important to local industries. Rosenberg and Nelson cite the example of the University of Akron, which supplied a skilled workforce for the local rubber industry and advanced research in the processing of rubber, which would be subsequently leveraged into expertise in the field of polymer chemistry. But in the first decades of the twentieth century, academic research began increasingly to differentiate itself from the specific requirements of industry. The emerging fields such as chemical engineering, electrical engineering, and, later, aeronautical engineering sought to replace industrial expertise with systematic and generalizable knowledge. The rise of academic science thus fostered the growth of science-based industry, which in turn increasingly correlated with economic development (Rosenberg and Nelson 327–31).

The American Research University as a Driver of Economic Development: World War II, Vannevar Bush, and Bayh-Dole

Seventy-five years of protracted debate regarding the role of the federal government in higher education would follow the initial deliberations of the Constitutional Convention, culminating in the Morrill Act, which set a precedent for federal support of higher education that would burgeon exponentially after 1945. The ascent of American research universities to global dominance has been a direct consequence of federal patronage, according to the consensus of assessments of American higher education, as we have observed (Atkinson and Blanpied 30–48).[12] While the relative lack of centralized federal regulation of higher education inherent in the American system from its inception stands in marked contrast to most other nations of the world, what has been described as the "compact" between the federal government and our universities nevertheless ensures an enduring and productive symbiotic relationship. Fierce competition among institutions in the competitive "academic marketplace" has focused on federal research dollars as well as support from industry and private investment, and has encouraged innovation and risk taking and led a number of ambitious universities to emerge as major research institutions (Graham and Diamond 9–25).

Federal support of academic research was hardly novel—Geiger traces federal patronage of agricultural research to the Hatch Act of 1887, for example, initiating what he terms a "tangled skein of relationships" that would prove incalculably beneficial to our collective well-being and the nation's research universities alike. But it was chiefly as a consequence of national defense interests that the patronage assumed its present contours. Thus was established the sometimes fraught relationship between American research universities and the "defense establishment" (Geiger, "Science, Universities, and National Defense" 26–27). The "military-industrial complex" to which President Eisenhower alluded in his famous 1961 farewell address to the nation is sometimes invoked to characterize that relationship (Eisenhower 1035–40). Even the establishment of what would become the chief federal funding sources for academic scientific research can be traced to national defense interests. As a consequence of wartime contracts associated with the Public Health Service, the federal government became the chief patron of biomedical research.[13]

While federal investment in university research has been a defining characteristic of the compact, the interrelationship, with implications for economic development, has been crucial in other respects. The Works Progress Administration (WPA), for example, created by the Franklin Delano Roosevelt administration and funded by Congress to address the economic downturn of that era, allowed for the construction of important academic infrastructure, much of it still in use today. The Servicemen's

Readjustment Act of 1944, known as the GI Bill, contributed to our national prosperity through its impact on millions of returning veterans of World War II. Federal support of financial aid programs, including the Pell grant, continues to exert broad impact.

Vannevar Bush and Science: The Endless Frontier

At the close of World War II, in July 1945, Vannevar Bush, the founding director of the Office of Scientific Research and Development (OSRD) under presidents Roosevelt and Truman, issued the science policy manifesto and social contract *Science—The Endless Frontier: A Report to the President on a Program for Postwar Scientific Research.* This document set the stage for peacetime federal investment in a national science enterprise envisioned as led by a handful of elite research universities and the nascent system of national laboratories in support of basic research in healthcare, national security, and economic prosperity for the American people (Bush). The unprecedented expansion of federal support for research was initiated in the charge to academic science implicit in the report, which propounded the vision of science as an "endless frontier" that would not only maintain American military preeminence but also drive economic growth and improve the quality of life through the production of science-based technologies for the benefit of all humankind.

Inasmuch as the Bush report codified the argument for continued government sponsorship of research and development, it led to the establishment of federal agencies such as the National Science Foundation (NSF) and National Aeronautics and Space Administration (NASA). For the National Institutes of Health (NIH), an agency that traces its lineage to the Marine Hospital Service established in 1798, the report justified massive expansion of federal investment in basic research in biomedical science and healthcare (National Institutes of Health). The system of national laboratories such as Los Alamos National Laboratory and Lawrence Livermore National Laboratory traces its inception to justifications for federal support for wartime research on nuclear fission articulated by Bush.[14] It is important to note that a significant amount of the research undertaken by university scientists and engineers is conducted within the system of national laboratories, which are funded by federal agencies such as the U.S. Department of Energy but administered by industrial contractors or universities (Atkinson and Blanpied 38).

Vannevar Bush proposed the idea for what would become the National Science Foundation as the principal agency for federal support for scientific research, and the agency was enacted into law in 1950. Although the status of elite American universities as the principal locus for research and development appears inevitable, funding for research could as well have been apportioned to industrial laboratories or independent research institutes. But the success of the Manhattan Project demonstrated the potential and the economic benefit of university-based research for the entire nation, and the Bush report consolidated the formal relationships between the federal government and research universities (Geiger, "Organized Research Units" 1). David H. Guston and Kenneth Keniston term the system of support for scientific research, centered in our nation's research universities, the "social contract for science." The authors formulate the following summary of the terms of this contract: "Government promises to fund the basic science that peer reviewers find most worthy of support, and scientists promise that the research will be performed well and honestly and will provide a steady stream of discoveries that can be translated into new products, medicines, or weapons" (1–2).

The Bayh-Dole Act (1980) Accelerates Academic Enterprise

To a remarkable extent the trajectory of economic competitiveness that marked the postwar era has been an outcome of scientific discovery and technological innovation. Such discovery and innovation are primarily the product of the teaching and research that takes place in our colleges and universities. With the passage by the U.S. Congress of the Bayh-Dole Act, enacted into law in 1980, allowing universities for the first time to patent the results of federally funded research, relations between academic institutions and business and industry were transformed. The Bayh-Dole Act provides the "legal framework for the transfer of university generated, federally funded inventions to the commercial market place." The legislation allows universities to exercise the option to license campus-based inventions, thus earning royalties, and to benefit from the ownership and commercialization of research undertaken with federal funding. According to the Council on Governmental Relations, "It was understood that stimulation of the U.S. economy would occur through the licensing of new inventions from universities to businesses that would, in turn, manufacture the resulting products in the United States."[15] While this would suggest that the legislation was enacted for the benefit of the economy, the immediate beneficiaries were research universities. Nonetheless, the attendant privatization and commercialization of knowledge exerted broad economic impact.[16]

The Commercialization of Academic Research and Economic Growth and Development

With economic growth increasingly tied to knowledge-intensive innovation, interactions between universities, industry, and government became critically important in the period after 1960. These interrelationships comprise what the economist Henry Etzkowitz terms the "Triple Helix" of university-industry-government innovation. Within this triad, while industry is the "key actor as the locus of production" and government serves as the "source of contractual relations that guarantee stable interactions and exchange," the role of the university is preeminent: "The university is the generative principle of knowledge-based societies just as government and industry were the primary institutions in industrial society." The concept embraces the nexus of relatively autonomous institutional sectors and hybrid organizations associated with innovation such as technology transfer offices and venture capital firms (*The Triple Helix* 1).

Through the development of products, processes, and applications across a range of fields and markets, academic research has the potential to generate significant economic returns to institutions themselves, a process that in turn further invigorates the broader economic contributions of universities, especially to their regions (Geiger, *Knowledge and Money* and "Milking the Sacred Cow" 332–48). Academic research attracts external funding from federal, state, and local government agencies and from business and industry. Research-related spending thus reflects the success of an institution in competing for funding from sponsors and is an important indicator of the overall contribution of an institution both to the knowledge base and the regional economy. As we have seen in the preceding discussion, the Bayh-Dole Act (1980) accelerated academic enterprise because it allowed universities to retain intellectual property rights to the ideas, products, and processes derived from federally funded research. The legislation was pivotal to the privatization and commercialization of knowledge (Slaughter and Rhoades 230).

Buoyed by the development of a knowledge-intensive economy, the growth of academic entrepreneurship, or the entrepreneurial university, has been described by Etzkowitz as the "working out of an inner logic of academic development" consistent with the inherent structure of academic research, which is often conducted by a "series of research groups that have firm-like qualities, especially under conditions in which research funding is awarded on a competitive basis." Etzkowitz observes that the "research university shares homologous qualities with a start-up firm even before it directly engages in entrepreneurial activities" (Etzkowitz, "Research Groups as Quasi-firms" 109).

A committee of the National Research Council charged in 2008 with evaluating technology transfer activities and intellectual property rights stemming from publicly and privately sponsored research within the context of the public interest produced a synopsis that suggests the scope and complexity of the commercialization, or "capitalization," of academic research:

> Discovery, learning, and societal engagement are mutually supportive core missions of the research university. Transfer of knowledge to those in society who can make use of it for the general good contributes to each of these missions. These transfers occur through publications, training and education of students, employment of graduates, conferences, consultations, and collaboration as well as by obtaining rights to inventions and discoveries that qualify for patent protection (intellectual property, or IP) and licensing them to private enterprises. All of these means of knowledge sharing have contributed to a long history of mutually beneficial relations among U.S. public and private universities, the private sector, and society at large. (National Research Council Committee on Management of University Intellectual Property 1)

The interdependencies and sequence of transactions between academic institutions and commercial firms in the commercialization process have been analyzed by Janet Bercovitz and Maryann Feldman. If the university-industry relationship that comprises technology transfer is to advance the interests and objectives of both partners, the formal and informal relationships in the "dyad" must mediate between the "rules, rewards, and incentive structures" of the university, an institution with a complex mission and commitment to scientists and researchers, and those of a firm with a "relatively simple profit motive" (Bercovitz and Feldman 175–76). Formal mechanisms in this sequence include sponsored research support, licensing of intellectual property, equity swaps, formation of spinoff firms, and hiring of students, which, the authors observe, is tantamount to a scientific apprenticeship.

While the majority of sponsored research is funded by agencies of the federal government, sponsored research may also represent a contract between the university and the firm wherein licensing agreements convey the legal rights to specific intellectual property, especially in terms of potential patents and trademarks and the division of royalties. A more complete schema of the relationships, Bercovitz and Feldman explain, requires an appreciation of "firm strategy, industry characteristics, university policies, the structure of technology transfer operations, and the parameters defined by government policy." Informal mechanisms cited include local networks, social interaction, personal communications, and "serendipity." Consulting arrangements between faculty members and firms represent another measure of economic impact. The complexity associated with negotiations involving intellectual property stems from the uncertainty of the technology transfer process. Bercovitz and Feldman offer the following assessment: "Knowledge is both difficult to value and difficult to appropriate . . . .The value of knowledge is uncertain, with uncertainty being highest for the most upstream, basic research . . . .Thus, negotiations are based on estimates of the subjective expected value of that portion of the knowledge that a firm will be able to appropriate." In this context, the authors quote Mowery and Rosenberg: "A new technology is a complex mix of codified data and poorly defined 'know-how.'" Finally, Bercovitz and Feldman underscore the significance of the policy environment for effective commercialization of academic research.[17]

Effective commercialization of academic research requires the judicious coordination of state and federal policies that encourage the diffusion of innovation. While the Bayh-Dole Act and related legislation facilitated patenting and licensing by academic institutions, continued government initiatives to spur innovation and competitiveness remain an imperative. If the United States is to leverage its dominant position in science and technology, academic and industrial endeavor will require support from programs and policies conducive to technology-based economic development.[18] Advocates of the laissez-faire approach that has dominated national policy in this context from the outset assume investment from the private sector is sufficient to foster innovation, but historic underinvestment from industry, with its limited incentive to value basic research without immediate commercial application, underscores the need for policies aimed at turning the nation's R&D capability to competitive advantage for the greatest possible public benefit. The much-contested policy environment for American science and technology requires continued evaluation and reconceptualization focused on consolidating its relevance to national economic objectives (Crow, "Science and Technology Policy in the United States" 202–12).

While academic research has increasingly served to advance industrial development and economic competitiveness since World War II, Bercovitz and Feldman attribute the acceleration of this collaboration in recent decades to four interrelated factors: "The development of new high-opportunity technology platforms such as computer science, molecular biology, and materials science; the more general growing scientific and technical content of all types of industrial production; the need for new sources of academic research funding created by budgetary stringency; and the prominence of government policies aimed at raising the economic returns of publicly funded research by stimulating university technology-transfer" (Bercovitz and Feldman 175).

While the formation of university spinoff companies with the potential to become high-growth firms is one of the more visible products of the commercialization process, the National Research Council committee found eight complementary mechanisms associated with the transfer of technology likely to contribute to economic development. These include the private or public sector employment of highly skilled graduates; publication of research; contact between researchers and private or public sector "users" of new knowledge; contract research projects; university-industry cooperative research facilities; consulting arrangements by researchers with firms; unrelated entrepreneurial ventures; and the licensing of intellectual property to established companies or new start-up firms (National Research Council Committee on Management of University Intellectual Property 2).

Research and development funding for academic institutions is potentially derived from five principal sources: the federal government; industry; academia; state and local governments; and the nonprofit sector, especially foundations. Estimated federal investment in R&D in 2011 is $111.4 billion with roughly 32 percent, or $36.1 billion, provided to universities.[19] In addition to funding the direct costs of a project such as salaries and laboratory equipment, federal investment provides universities with facilities and administrative (F&A) costs, sometimes referred to as "indirect" or "overhead" costs. These constitute significant reimbursements—in some cases as much as half of total award dollars—for the construction and maintenance of necessary research facilities, even when not directly associated with the given project. Recovered overhead costs can be directed to discretionary funding to support research in disciplines not associated with the initial project. Beyond covering the costs of sponsored projects administration and accounting, and operations and maintenance, overhead dollars provide funding for research facilities, start-up funds for faculty, support for graduate students, and the acquisition of library materials (Fossum).

The contributions of research and development to institutional advancement are thus critical to all aspects of academic operations. It is impossible to overstate the significance of sufficient endowment resources and increased revenue streams in building a great university because there is a direct correlation between fiscal robustness and the capacity of an institution to pursue excellence in teaching, research, and public service, as well as its potential to contribute to the standard of living and quality of life of communities and regions. An enhanced resource base allows institutions to invest in research infrastructure, for example, which attracts greater numbers of leading scholars and researchers, who in turn secure ever-larger levels of sponsored funding, a source of support critical to the success of a major research university. The financial resources of an institution exist to serve the community of students and scholars who are its spirit, and it is inconceivable to imagine a great institution without resources sufficient to express its higher aspirations.

While the commercialization of university research is one seemingly obvious avenue to move academic research at the "edge of newness" from the laboratory to the marketplace, our expansive usage of the concept of academic enterprise embraces all creative expression of intellectual capital and knowledge-centric change. Entrepreneurship is the process of innovation and spirit of creative risk taking through which the knowledge and ideas generated within universities are brought to scale to spur social development and economic competitiveness. Academic enterprise thus inspires discovery, creativity, and innovation—the intellectual capital that is the principal asset of every college and university.[20]

Innovation and Impact: Assessing the Economic Contribution of Academic Research

University-based research and development contribute to the creation and dissemination of new knowledge and through their utilization become catalysts spurring regional, national, and global economic development through practices and processes often insufficiently appreciated outside the academy. To the extent that our national prosperity and economic competitiveness are products of an educated citizenry, an increasing sector of which must be capable of advancing scientific discovery and technological invention in a knowledge-intensive global economy, the contributions of the American research university through the production of human capital are obvious to most observers. But the impact of these institutions on economic development is increasingly correlated with scientific discovery and technological invention. As formulated by the Committee on Prospering in the Global Economy of the Twenty-First Century, convened by the National Academies, "Knowledge acquired and applied by scientists and engineers provides the tools and systems that characterize modern culture and the raw materials for economic growth and well-being." In order to sustain economic growth in an economy characterized by increasing "knowledge density," the committee assesses, societies must "produce, select, adapt, and commercialize" knowledge.[21]

Estimates of the economic impact of technological innovation were first developed in the mid-twentieth century. Robert M. Solow initiated research on the determinants of economic growth, demonstrating that in addition to labor and capital, productivity depends on such "intangibles" as research and development and the acquisition and application of knowledge. According to the National Academies committee cited, even before the rise of ubiquitous information technology, Solow calculated that "as much as 85 percent of measured growth in U.S. income per capita during the 1890–1950 period could not be explained by increases in the capital stock or other measurable inputs" and could thus be attributed to technological change.[22] David C. Mowery and Nathan Rosenberg provide elaboration: "No more than 15 percent of the measured growth in U.S. output in the late nineteenth century and the first half of the twentieth century need be accounted for by the growth in measured inputs of capital and labor: The strikingly large 'residual' of 85 percent suggested that twentieth-century American economic growth was overwhelmingly a matter of extracting more output from each unit of input into economic activity." The "prime candidate" in this context was technological change (*Paths of Innovation* 4).

Economists who have studied economic growth have generally concluded that technological progress, broadly defined in economics, is key to continued growth in developed economies. For highly developed economies, research and development and higher education are key drivers of technological progress. Economic growth (alternatively termed productivity growth, which may be calculated as growth in gross domestic product per hour) is spurred by science-based technological innovation, which is largely a product of university-based research, development, and education. In research cited by Blakemore and Herrendorf, for example, Charles I. Jones determined that "70 percent of the improvement in productivity in the United States between 1950 and 1993 can be attributed to the direct and indirect effects of new knowledge" (220–39). Other research supports the hypothesis that higher education exercises its greatest impact on nations close to the "technological frontier" (Vandenbussche, Aghion, and Meghir 97–127). Peter J. Klenow and Andrès Rodríguez-Clare find that technological progress can account for more than one-half of economic growth as customarily measured in the United States since 1960 (73–103).[23] The economic impact of science-based technological innovation derived from commercialized academic research has been well documented in a number of more specialized sectors as well.[24]

Assessing the Economic Contributions of Knowledge

An assessment of the historical origins of the knowledge economy by the economist and historian Joel Mokyr provides useful perspective on the interrelationships between knowledge and economic development. The rise of the knowledge economy was precipitated not by political or economic factors, Mokyr argues, but rather primarily by the contemporaneous "knowledge revolution" produced by the Scientific Revolution of the seventeenth century and the Enlightenment of the eighteenth century. His focus begins with the broad economic impact of the growth of knowledge since the Industrial Revolution: "The central phenomenon of the modern age is that as an aggregate we know more." The stream of basic scientific knowledge about nature produced since the Enlightenment, Mokyr explains, has enabled the technological innovations and efficiency gains that brought about the unprecedented and sustained economic development of the West during the past two centuries (1–8).

The Industrial Revolution was produced by technological innovation, and "technology is knowledge," Mokyr explains. But scientific knowledge was required to make complex technological advances possible as well as adaptable to the vicissitudes of market demand: "The wider and deeper the epistemic base on which a technique rests, the more likely it is that a technique can be extended and find new applications, product and service quality improved, the production process streamlined, economized, and adapted to changing external circumstances, and the techniques combined with others to form new ones." Without the continued elaboration of scientific knowledge, the technologically driven economic development that has characterized the West since the Industrial Revolution—and increasingly the rest of the global economy—is certain to stagnate: "Without widening the epistemic base, the continuous development of techniques will eventually run into diminishing returns simply because the natural phenomena can be understood only partially and arguably only superficially" (Mokyr 1–8, 34–35).

Knowledge that leads to technological innovation and thus economic development is termed "useful knowledge" by Mokyr, following an earlier usage by the economist Simon Kuznets, who deemed such knowledge the source of economic growth in the modern era. Thus, "useful knowledge includes 'scientific' knowledge as a subset," but also what is variously termed "technological science" or "engineering science" or "applied science."[25] Moreover, the economic development of the modern era was determined not only by new knowledge but also by access to that knowledge through social networks and institutions such as universities and professional societies. Only with access does knowledge become "useful," Mokyr explains. As principal keepers and disseminators of the stock of knowledge, universities comprise the major access point to knowledge in the present and for subsequent generations. In his estimation, the global knowledge economy is thus in part a product of the universities and scientific institutes of the modern era and the social networks of disciplinary knowledge these have engendered. The contribution of research universities to economic development would seem obvious if not always readily apparent (Mokyr 1–8).

Assessing the Economic Contribution of Academic Research to Local Communities and Regions

An extensive literature on the broad economic contributions of academic research to national and global prosperity sometimes overlooks the more immediate impacts of research universities on their local communities and regions. External funding from federal, state, and local government agencies as well as from business and industry provides an economic return on investment to the communities that support universities in their regions. Research-related spending reflects the competitive success of an institution in this context and is an important indicator of its overall contribution both to the knowledge base and the regional economy. Academic research expenditures exert significant impact on private sector research activities, influencing both the level of industrial research and development and industrial patents.

The returns on investments made in any university are geographically localized. Local economic impact studies use various methodological approaches, beginning with calculations of the impacts of universities on employment, incomes, and the consumer spending of faculty, staff, and students. In many communities, for example, the university is one of the largest employers, and the institution itself is generally a major consumer of products and services produced by the local economy, including spending on construction projects. The multiplier effect of such spending within local economies generates upstream demands on other producers, which in turn produce additional tax revenues.[26] Calculations of such economic interdependencies are complex, and one analysis by a team of economists listed the following inputs:

> Direct employment and payroll, less federal taxes; expenditures for equipment, supplies, and services; construction costs; spending in the local community by faculty members, administrative staff, and students; public and private support of research grants and contracts; tuition and fees paid by students from outside the local area and by local students who would alternatively have attended college elsewhere; and expenditures by visitors, including alumni, who visit campus for academic and/or athletic events. Universities with medical centers include corresponding expenditures at their hospitals. Multipliers are applied to these sums to account for indirect and induced impacts. (Siegfried, Sanderson, and McHenry 2–3)

Apart from the more complex calculations associated with assessing the impacts of innovation, including technology transfer, considered in the following section, additional factors cited include "enhancements in the quality of the local work force, improvements in the quality of life, public service . . . and contributions to local culture" (Siegfried 3).

Earnings Premiums of Graduates and Higher Productivity

A complementary approach is to consider the earnings premium for college graduates. Using data from the U.S. Census Bureau, the government estimates that individuals who complete bachelor's degrees earn nearly $1 million more over the course of their lifetimes than those who have only completed high school.[27] Earnings for those with advanced and professional degrees increase markedly. Apart from the direct monetary benefits associated with a college degree, return on investment assumes many forms that benefit both the individual and society. The array of correlates of educational attainment begins with the intrinsic value of higher education to the individual, but the list of collateral returns undeniably redounds to broad societal benefits, including regional economic development. In addition to increased opportunities for more meaningful employment, for example, higher education influences lifestyle choices that correlate with better health and greater civic participation. Citizens able to make more informed choices benefit not only themselves and their families but also their communities and states. A more educated workforce generates greater tax revenues and influences quality-of-place decision making (Mortenson et al.). By one estimate, all wage earners benefit from an increase in the proportion of baccalaureate degree holders in a state's population. According to economist Enrico Moretti, the "social return to education may exceed the private return."[28]

Research Universities, Knowledge Workers, and Regional Innovation Clusters

While advances in communication and transportation that contributed to globalization might have led observers to expect geographic dispersion of industries, economists instead perceive the paradoxical persistence of local proximity and geographic "agglomeration" or "clustering" of economic activity based on new scientific and technological knowledge—for example, the start-ups and spinoffs of university research. The persistence of such regional innovation clusters may appear counterintuitive in this era of globalization, but knowledge still circulates through related firms, institutions, organizations, and professional and social networks bound by proximity. In an assessment of the role of clusters in building economic competitiveness, the business economist Michael E. Porter describes the diversity of actors in such agglomerations: manufacturers of complementary products, suppliers of specialized inputs, universities providing industry-specific R&D and education, vocational schools, and government agencies promoting specialized training, information, and infrastructure. While potential synergies may sometimes remain unrealized because of a lack of coordination and collaboration between public and private sectors, and between the federal government, regional enterprises, and academic institutions, the most effective clusters promote the right mix of cooperation and competition. In optimally structured clusters, Porter explains, companies can tap into large pools of information, suppliers, and skilled employees. Repeated interactions among cluster participants foster trust and long-term relationships leading to more collaboration and innovation than might have occurred in a more geographically diffuse industry. Furthermore, clusters are strengthened by lateral competition among companies occupying the same space in a supply chain (77–90).

Economic and social analysts Joel Kotkin and Ross DeVol underscore the correlation of intellectual capital with competitive advantage for metropolitan areas by focusing on the regional economic impacts of research universities. Consistent with other estimates, Kotkin and DeVol contend that 60 to 75 percent of economic growth during the 1990s was driven by technological advances, and that nearly all major technological advances during recent decades have been enabled by fundamental scientific discovery. They point out that while the economic benefit of university research, most notably derived from research and development associated with the sciences and science-based technologies, is generally calculated and reported as an aggregate contribution to national prosperity, it actually accrues disproportionately to regions that are home to major research universities (vi-3).

Contradicting the assumption that place has become increasingly irrelevant to economic development, "knowledge spillovers" from university research occur, not surprisingly, most frequently in communities adjacent to research universities. Such research and development, moreover, correlate directly with the presence of "knowledge workers." Because a postindustrial economy does not require industries and workforces to settle in strategic locations—near waterways or natural resources, for example—companies and knowledge workers increasingly locate "not where they must, but where they will," according to Kotkin and DeVol. As a consequence, "wherever intelligence clusters, be it small town [or] big city, wealth will accumulate." Based on extensive economic data, the authors argue that the presence of research universities is key both to quality-of-place considerations for knowledge workers and the potential for economic prosperity in a given region: "Cities that tap the knowledge assets in their midst, such as universities and research centers, will benefit from the talent that they attract to fuel local economic growth." The authors thus offer a compelling argument that suggests that in the global technology-based economy, "enduring competitive advantages still lie in location-specific competencies—knowledge, workforce skills . . . entrepreneurial infrastructure, and quality-of-place attributes" (vi-3). Their use of the term *knowledge worker* is consistent with the concept of the "creative class" put forth by regional economic development expert Richard Florida. He argues that economic development is promoted by the presence of a "creative class," which he defines as the social sector, representing more than 30 percent of the national workforce, comprising artists, musicians, writers, designers, architects, engineers, scientists, and others for whom creativity is an essential dimension of livelihood. Florida sees creativity as a driving force in the growth of the economy, and almost without exception, higher education is a key determinant to inclusion in the occupations that compose this sector.

Assessments of the economic impact of research universities evaluate the importance of the clustering or agglomeration of institutions, organizations, and firms within a particular sector. Knowledge spillovers from academic research correlate with innovation, which is "spatially distributed" or "geographically mediated." Thus, despite globalization, the flows of knowledge to some extent remain localized.[29] Regional clusters are spatially determined by proximity to innovation and to some extent may implicate what is termed the "tacit dimension" of scientific and technical knowledge. The tacit dimension ("tacitness") in this context implies practical understanding of a given technology based on direct experience inherent in individuals embedded in organizational processes.[30] In contradistinction to "explicit knowledge," that is, the codified principles of science and technology, "tacit knowledge" represents the practical understanding of "how things are done," which is to say, the "know-how" underpinning the development of a given technology. The significance of the tacit dimension varies by sector and over time, wherein advance proceeds in accord with respective technological paradigms. Each sector is thus defined by a technological paradigm, which "co-evolves" through its "core technologies," industrial infrastructure, and supporting institutions, namely, universities and industry associations organized to support the advancement of a given core technology (Nelson 297–306).

The role of academic institutions as hubs of regional innovation clusters is most famously epitomized in the relationship between Stanford University and Silicon Valley and between Harvard University, MIT, and Route 128 in Boston (Saxenian). Ecologies of innovation similarly radiate from the institutions in North Carolina defining the Research Triangle (Duke University, University of North Carolina, Chapel Hill, and North Carolina State University); from the University of California, San Diego; and from the University of Rochester and Rochester Institute of Technology. The structure of Silicon Valley as an "incubator region" conducive to innovation has been assessed by Martin Kenney and Urs von Burg, who describe the interrelationships between what may be perceived as two economies, the first comprising established institutions such as universities and corporate research labs and existing firms; the second the "institutional infrastructure" of new firm formation, comprising start-ups led by entrepreneurs and supported by venture capitalists (69–74).

Assessing the Economic Contribution of Academic Research to Industrial Innovation

While our colleges and universities perform the dominant majority of the basic research conducted in the United States, industry remains the principal source of the nation's applied research and development (National Science Board 6). But in addition to their critical role in discovery and innovation, universities mediate the relationship between fundamental research and industrial application, spawning entire industries and anchoring innovation clusters. According to some estimates, 80 percent of new industries may be derived from academic research (Atkinson and Pelfrey 39). Inasmuch as the majority of the scientists and engineers working in private industry in the United States were trained in American research universities, these institutions constitute what Jonathan Cole terms the "main pipeline to our nation's industrial research laboratories." Cole offers the following breakdown: "As of 2003, over 70 percent of all science and engineering graduates were working in private industry. Forty-four percent of all the science and engineering students who had earned PhDs were working in industry" (195).

The interrelationships between American research universities and private sector innovation in industrial laboratories and firms are multi-dimensional and complex, differing among industries and, according to economists, even now still poorly understood (Mowery and Shane v). Quantification of the impact of academic research on regional, national, and global economic development requires explication of empirical findings through various analytic frameworks and theoretical models, an adequate synopsis of which lies outside the scope of this discussion. Models of economic development that attempt to quantify the contribution of new knowledge to gross domestic product growth, to cite but one approach, may weigh the impact of inputs from human capital, the quality of which is determined by the interrelationships between universities, industries, and governments.[31]

While the impact of academic research on industrial innovation has long been taken for granted, efforts at rigorous quantification of the relationship first came as recently as 1990 when the economist Edwin Mansfield sought to estimate the time lag between investment in a particular research project and its subsequent industrial operationalization or commercialization, and the rate of return on that investment. Mansfield termed his objective the attempt to "estimate the social rate of return from academic research." Mansfield undertook a random sampling of major American firms in seven manufacturing sectors—information processing, electrical equipment, chemicals, instruments, drugs, metals, and oils—and estimated the overall rate of return for these industries at 23 percent. Moreover "fully one-tenth of the new products and processes commercialized between 1975–1985 could not have been developed (without substantial delay) without recent academic research" (1–12).

In an assessment of the impact of "public science"—academic research performed at universities and research institutes funded by the government—on industrial technology and economic development, researchers found a striking correlation between citations in scientific research papers and U.S. patents. More than 73 percent of papers cited in industry patents were found to derive from research conducted at publicly funded academic and research institutions. The authors conclude, "The great majority of the science base of U.S. industry comes from the public sector." Moreover, "Public science appears to be crucial to the advance of U.S. industrial technology" (Narin, Hamilton, and Olivastro 317, 328). While the exact figures vary, their estimate is confirmed by the National Science Board, which offers the following assessment: "Over 60 percent of the

U.S.-authored articles cited on U.S. patents have academic scientists and engineers as authors, indicating the link between academic research and valuable inventions" (National Science Board 12).

Networks and the National System of Innovation

The concept of "national innovation systems" refers to the network of institutions and policies supporting the processes of science-based technological innovation. As the central nodes of an integrative discovery and commercialization network, universities are key institutional actors in national systems of innovation, a concept that represents the most encompassing theoretical and analytical framework for the interrelationships between entities that determine the rate and direction of innovation. In the United States, in addition to universities, the term refers to the system of national laboratories and elements of business and industry. Broadly construed, the concept embraces the economic, political, and social institutions relevant to learning and discovery, including the patent system, the financial system, monetary policies, and even the structure and practices of firms (Tucker and Sampat 42). The concept is variously defined, including the following working definition: "A national system of innovation is the system of interacting private and public firms (either large or small), universities, and government agencies aiming at the production of science and technology within national borders. Interaction among these units may be technical, commercial, legal, social, and financial, inasmuch as the goal of the interaction is the development, protection, financing, or regulation of new science and technology."[32]

The concept of innovation is intrinsically interrelated with "entrepreneurship," especially as formulated by the economist Joseph Schumpeter, who as early as the 1930s described innovation as a process of "creative destruction" within which new products and processes supersede existing ones.[33] The related concept of "entrepreneurship policy" is associated with government support of entrepreneurial ventures intended to promote economic growth (Hart 5–6; Crow and Tucker 2–10). Indeed, innovation could be said to be "structurally determined" by both economic and political factors external to the firm. The concept of national systems of innovation, formulated in the 1980s in the work of Christopher Freeman and Bengt-Åke Lundvall, underscored the importance of social and political institutions for innovation. Indeed, Richard Nelson considers such systems to be dependent on government policy and regulation. While apart from universities most entities in national systems are firms and corporations, the state nevertheless often remains dominant because it finances or even executes some portion of research and development (Niosi et al. 208–12). Economic development is further advanced through "open" innovation systems, which encourage collaboration and coordination of effort through the formation of partnerships and consortiums (Chesbrough; Yusuf, 5).

The differentiation of knowledge enterprises further advances the integration of universities into coordinated and synergistic networks, thus expanding the potential of academia to offer multiple solutions and exert greater impact across broader swathes of knowledge. The imperative for transdisciplinary organization of teaching and research is obvious, but transinstitutional collaboration involving universities, industry, and government both aggregates knowledge and prevents unnecessary replication. Entrenchment in discipline-based departments corresponds to an academic culture that prizes individualism over teamwork and the discovery of specialized knowledge over problem-based collaboration. The amalgamation of transdisciplinary and transinstitutional frameworks has the potential to advance broader social and economic outcomes. Multiplying these types of university-industry-government partnerships throughout the leading institutions in America will drive the innovation that will be required to sustain our planet. As the United States engages competition from across the globe, the path forward will require both strategic collaboration and perpetual innovation (Kash 50–69; Crow, "Research University as Comprehensive Knowledge Enterprise").

Toward Perpetual Innovation and Academic Enterprise

While the institution famously characterized more than half a century ago by then University of California president Clark Kerr as a "multiversity"— "a whole series of communities and activities held together by a common name, a common governing board, and related purposes" (1)—has undergone incremental change, we contend that inherent design limitations in our colleges and universities diminish their potential for both innovation and optimal societal outcomes. The intrinsic impetus to advance innovation distinguishes the research university from other institutional types in higher education. Indeed, we seek to redefine the research university as a comprehensive knowledge enterprise committed to discovery, creativity, and innovation. Yet despite the critical niche that research universities occupy in the global knowledge economy, institutions thus committed primarily to innovation restrict the potential of their contribution unless they explicitly embrace a broader societal role (Crow, "The Research University as Comprehensive Knowledge Enterprise").

Innovation inevitably flourishes within a number of organizational settings, such as the R&D laboratories in our national innovation system, but with their uniquely multidimensional missions spanning teaching, research, and public service, research universities should arguably regard as an incumbent obligation the imperative to construe their purposes in a context of engagement. We mistakenly assume that the intellectual objectives of our institutions, especially in terms of scientific research and technological innovation, are automatically and inevitably aligned with our most important goals as a society. If research universities are to create knowledge that is as socially useful as it is scientifically meritorious, they must integrate their quest to advance discovery, creativity, and innovation with an explicit mandate to assume responsibility for the societies they serve.[34]

While American research universities retain global leadership in discovery and innovation, their capacity to mount adequate responses at scale and in real time to the grand challenges before us is diminished by entrenchment in bureaucratic constructs that serve primarily to perpetuate the academic infrastructure and practices of another century. Our institutions are internally adaptive when they should be more concerned with societal adaptation to the complexity and ambiguity that has become our default condition. In our accustomed effort to produce abstract knowledge, many research universities have lost sight of the need to give direction and purpose to scientific discovery and technological application. Our institutions might embrace ambitious and multifaceted public outreach and engagement programs dedicated to societal advancement and regional economic development. No less imperative is a commitment to the production in sufficient numbers of scientists and engineers and artists and philosophers and economists and doctors and lawyers—in short, the human capital from which we draw our future leaders in every sector.

More and more knowledge inputs are increasingly required to perform almost any job in the new and ever more complex global knowledge economy, and American research universities are the principal source of the advanced education that produces a skilled workforce. The economic success of individuals contributes to the success of a society—in fact, it is the main driver. Without it, the United States and the nations of Western Europe may face a reduction in our quality of life in the next generation, something unheard of in the past. As formulated by the Committee on Prospering in the Global Economy of the Twenty-First Century, convened by the National Academies:

> Without a renewed effort to bolster the foundations of our competitiveness, we can expect to lose our privileged position. For the first time in generations, the nation's children could face poorer prospects than their parents and grandparents did. We owe our current prosperity, security, and good health to the investments of past generations, and we are obliged to renew those commitments in education, research, and innovation policies to ensure that the American people continue to benefit from the remarkable opportunities provided by the rapid development of the global economy and its not inconsiderable underpinning in science and technology.[35]

Public sector investment in the infrastructure of higher education—and thus investment in human capital—during the twentieth century produced a level of educational attainment that served as a catalyst to innovation and thus American competitiveness in the global knowledge economy (Goldin and Katz 11–43). Yet with our success, public investment in higher education has progressively declined (Heller 11–37; Hossler et al. 160–90). American higher education cannot assume that its competitive position in the world is unassailable.[36] This erosion corresponds to a slackening in the pace of innovation and thus to a diminishment of our national competitiveness.[37]

The American economy is at a crossroads, and the prosperity we have known during the past seventy years is increasingly imperiled. For the first time since World War II, key benchmarks of national competitiveness suggest that American leadership in scientific discovery and technological innovation is threatened (National Academies Committee, *Rising Above the Gathering Storm*; National Science Board). Our global economic leadership is challenged by ambitious emerging nations that intend to compete by making massive investments in education and research. Around the world, national leaders understand that university research has been the chief catalyst for America's adaptability and economic dominance during the past century. While nations worldwide are investing strategically to educate broader segments of their populations for the new global knowledge economy, America has allowed its research universities, despite their historical preeminence, to lose their adaptive capacities. Unable to accommodate projected enrollment demand with existing infrastructure, our leading institutions define their excellence through admissions practices based on exclusion. And while our leading universities, both public and private, consistently dominate global rankings, our success in establishing excellence in a relative handful of elite institutions does little to ensure our continued national competitiveness. For the first time in our national history, we risk broad decline as a consequence of the insufficient adaptation of our institutions and the disinvestment that characterizes our policies toward higher education. If we are to prevail in this era of massively escalating complexity and competition, what will be required from our universities is perpetual innovation. Such innovation emerges not only through advances in knowledge but also imperatively requires evolution in the structure, practices, and interrelationships of our knowledge enterprises.

NOTES

1. Among other important discussions of this topic, see Cole, *The Great American University*; Duderstadt, *A University for the Twenty-First Century*; Rhodes, *The Creation of the Future*; Atkinson and Blanpied 30–38.

2. Cole, *Great American University* 4. The overview of academic research that comprises section 2 of the book, "Discoveries That Alter Our Lives" 191–342, suggests its scope and breadth, but as a supplement to the book intended to document the full range of discoveries from the past seventy-five years, Cole launched a Web site: http://university-discoveries.com.

3. Nevins, *The State Universities and Democracy* 26, n. 3, 27, cited in Tobin 320, n. 3. Nevins offers the following account of the establishment of the land-grant institutions: "Of the institutions benefited by the Morrill land grants, seventeen had been founded (often feebly) before 1862; eighteen more before the end of 1865; and sixteen others before the end of 1870." The Morrill Act is officially designated the Act of July 2, 1862, ch. 130, 12 Stat. 503, 7 U.S.C. 301 et seq.

4. For the purposes of this discussion, we follow the most recent classification scheme of the Carnegie Foundation for the Advancement of Teaching, which now designates institutions formerly termed "research-extensive" as either RU/VH ("research university/very high research activity") or RU/H ("high research activity"). One hundred and eight institutions are currently designated RU/VH and ninety-nine are classified RU/H. For a discussion of the methodology, involving both aggregate and per capita levels of research expenditures, see http://classifications.carnegiefoundation.org/methodology/basic.php.

5. Association of Public and Land-grant Universities (APLU), "Land-grant Heritage," http://www.aplu.org; for a list of member institutions in the Association of American Universities (AAU), comprising sixty-one leading research universities in the United States and Canada, see http://www.aau.edu/about/.

6. Thelin 75–77. Thelin explains that the distribution of federal land, widely misunderstood to be "literal gifts of land on which a state government would build a college," in reality represented a "complex partnership in which the federal government provided incentives for each state to sell distant Western lands" with the obligation to apply profits realized toward the establishment of collegiate institutions.

7. Moretti 190. Additional perspective comes with the estimate that the public research universities of our nation taken together have produced more than 70 percent of all baccalaureate degree recipients and conduct two-thirds of all funded research. See McPherson, Shulenberger, Gobstein, and Keller.

8. A concise discussion of federal support for American higher education is to be found in Atkinson and Blanpied 30–48. See also Graham and Diamond, and Geiger, *Research and Relevant Knowledge*.

9. Madsen 15–24. During his presidency, Madison urged the establishment of a national university during four annual addresses, according to Thelin. A bill to create such an institution brought before Congress in 1817 was defeated, however, by the House of Representatives. See Thelin 42.

10. By 1901 University of California president Benjamin Ide Wheeler could thus proclaim: "A university is a place that rightfully knows no aristocracy as between studies, no aristocracy as between scientific truths, and no aristocracy as between persons." Wheeler 2, cited in Veysey, *Emergence of the American University* 66.

11. Cole observes: "If the Germans provided us with a blueprint for advanced research, the British provided us with an outline for organizing undergraduate collegiate education" (18).

12. See also Geiger, *Research and Relevant Knowledge* 3–29; Graham and Diamond 9.

13. Federal support for biomedical research at universities in 2009 totaled $15.8 billion, 90 percent of which derived from the National Institutes of Health (NIH). NSF Survey of Federal Funds for Research and Development, cited in Blume-Kohout, Kumar, and Sood 1.

14. Westwick 27. Westwick provides a comprehensive overview and history of the origins and development of the system of federal laboratories. See also Crow and Bozeman.

15. Officially known as the Patent and Trademark Law Amendments Act (P.L. 96-517), enacted into law in 1980, together with amendments included in P.L. 98-620, enacted into law in 1984. Council on Governmental Relations 1.

16. Slaughter and Rhoades 230. For a close analysis of the extent of its impact as quantified by the growth of patenting and licensing by American universities, see Mowery, Nelson, Sampat, and Ziedonis 99–101.

17. Bercovitz and Feldman 176–81; Mowery and Rosenberg, *Technology and the Pursuit of Economic Growth* 7, cited in Bercovitz and Feldman 181. The significance of the policy context becomes apparent with their allusion to the analysis of the role of the political sphere and legal frameworks in the emergence of the Industrial Revolution in Rosenberg and Birdzell. See also Feldman 92–112.

18. Robert D. Atkinson provides a useful survey of legislation consistent with the objectives of the Bayh-Dole Act, including the Omnibus Trade and Competitiveness Act of 1988 and the National Technology Transfer and Advancement Act (NTTAA), signed into law in 1996; related programs and initiatives such as the Small Business Innovation Research program; and measures such as cooperative research and development agreements (CRDA), R&D tax credits, and adjustments to capital gains and corporate tax rates. See Atkinson 69–75.

19. Battelle Institute and *R&D Magazine*, "2011 Global R&D Funding Forecast" (December 2010): 6. Estimated 2011 gross domestic expenditures on R&D in the United States total $405.3 billion. A breakdown of R&D execution by sector includes the federal government,

industry, academia, federally funded research and development centers (FFRDCs), referring to national laboratories, and nonprofit organizations (research institutions).

20. Crow, "Research University as Comprehensive Knowledge Enterprise" 50–69. See also Colyvas, Crow, Gelijns, Mazzoleni et al. 61–72.

21. National Academies Committee, *Rising Above the Gathering Storm* 43–45. According to the OECD, "Underlying long-term growth rates in OECD economies depend on maintaining and expanding the knowledge base" (OECD, 1998 4), a point taken up by L. B. Holm-Nielsen (cited in National Academies Committee, *Rising Above the Gathering Storm* 43–45).

22. National Academies Committee, *Rising Above the Gathering Storm* 1, n. 1, 43–45; Solow 312–20. With the Solow growth model as the basis, economists have more recently modeled technological progress as total factor productivity (TFP), which Arthur Blakemore and Berthold Herrendorf define as the "efficiency by which capital and labor are employed to produce output." See Blakemore and Herrendorf 17. We are indebted to Arthur Blakemore for his contributions to this synopsis.

23. Blakemore and Herrendorf add, "Even more impressively, according to highly respected estimates, it accounts for 90 percent or so of cross-country differences in the *growth rate* of income per worker" (17).

24. While comprehensive discussions are to be found in Geiger, *Research and Relevant Knowledge,* and in Slaughter and Rhoades, more specialized studies abound. A recent report on the commercialization of academic research in the biotechnology sector, for example, reports a "flourishing global landscape of spin-offs, startups, and collaborations between biotechnology firms, financiers, and academia" (DeVol and Bedroussian 5). To cite but a few further representative examples, see Powell et al. 291–316; Mansfield and Lee 1047–58; and Etzkowitz and Leytesdorff.

25. Mokyr, *Gifts of Athena* 1–5. Mokyr paraphrases Kuznets: "Simply put, technology is knowledge, even if not all knowledge is technological." See Kuznets, cited by Mokyr 3, n. 1. Technology has similarly been defined as "applied knowledge embedded in tools, equipment, and facilities, in work methods, practices and processes, and in the design of products and services." Further, "It is 'know-how' in contrast to the 'know-why' that characterizes science. . . . In terms of traditional

stages of innovation, science is most closely related to pure, fundamental or basic research, while technology is most closely associated
with applied development and engineering" (Kassicieh and Radosevich 127). The historian Ronald Kline offers further conceptualization and modeling of the relationships between scientific advance and
technological innovation, parsing the generalized assumption that
"technology is simply applied science" (194–95). In this context Kline
cites Otto Mayr 663–72.

26. For an analysis of the local and regional impact of a major research
university, see, for example, Hill.

27. U.S. Census Bureau, "The Big Payoff: Educational Attainment and
Synthetic Estimates of Work-Life Earnings" 4. The estimates are
derived from calculations based on 1999 dollars over a hypothetical
working life of forty years (8).

28. Moretti 175. Moretti reports that a "one percentage point increase in
the supply of college graduates raises high school drop-outs' wages by
1.9 percent, high school graduates' wages by 1.6 percent, and college
graduates wages by 0.4 percent."

29. Assessments of clustering include Audretsch and Feldman 630–40;
Feldman, "The New Economics" 5–25.

30. The concept of tacit knowledge derives from the scientist and philosopher Michael Polanyi (1966). For the economic context of this
discussion, see especially Nelson and Winter. Feldman offers the following synopsis of the concept by Eric von Hippel: "Knowledge with
a low degree of tacitness may be easily standardized, codified, and
transmitted via journal articles, project reports, prototypes, and other
tangible mediums. In contrast, tacit knowledge has a higher degree
of uncertainty and the precise meaning is more interpretative . . . .As
a consequence, when knowledge is more tacit in nature, face to face
interaction and communication are important and geographic proximity may promote commercial activity" (von Hippel 429–39, cited in
Feldman, "New Economics" 17).

31. An invaluable overview of these interrelationships is to be found in
the collection of articles edited by Shahid Yusuf and Kaoru Nabeshima. Yusuf cites as particularly germane to this discussion the article
by Robert E. Lucas.

32. Niosi, Saviotti, Bellon, and Crow 207–08. The concept of "national
innovation systems" was coined by the Swedish economist Bengt-Åke

Lundvall and explored in "Innovation as an Interactive Process: From User-Producer Interaction to National Systems of Innovation," in Giovanni Dosi et al.

33. Schumpeter ascribed the innovation intrinsic to "creative destruction" to entrepreneurs: "The function of entrepreneurs is to reform or revolutionize the pattern of production by exploiting invention or, more generally, an untried technological possibility for producing new commodities or producing an old one in a new way" (8).

34. Crow, "Research University as Comprehensive Knowledge Enterprise" 212; relevant discussions regarding the imperative for universities to serve society include Bok; Duderstadt, *University for the Twenty-First Century*; and Kitcher.

35. National Academies Committee, *Rising Above the Gathering Storm* 13. See also the update to the 2007 report: *Rising Above the Gathering Storm Revisited: Rapidly Approaching Category 5*. The issue of decline in our national standard of living as a consequence of lack of investment in educational infrastructure is addressed in this and a number of other recent reports.

36. A sobering assessment of our competitive position is to be found in John Aubrey Douglass, "The Waning of America's Higher Education Advantage: International Competitors are No Longer Number Two and Have Big Plans in the Global Economy."

37. National Academies Committee, *Rising Above the Gathering Storm* (2007 and 2010). For an interesting perspective on the complex interrelationships between academia, business, industry, and government in spurring innovation, see Pisano and Shih 114–25. The authors argue that both outsourcing and lack of sufficient investment in research have sapped American competitiveness, especially in the high-tech sector. With reference to the "industrial commons," which they define as the "collective R&D, engineering, and manufacturing capabilities that sustain innovation," Pisano and Shih remark, "We cannot emphasize enough the importance of world-class universities in building the commons" (121).

From a Land-Grant to a World-Grant Ideal

Extending Public Higher Education Core Values to a Global Frame

JOHN HUDZIK AND LOU ANNA K. SIMON

Introduction

Talent development without borders is the twenty-first-century frame-work for knowledge access. In a rapidly expanding and "flattening" global environment, talent is found nearly everywhere. The best among students, scholars, professionals, and a skilled workforce are part of an increasingly mobile and global talent pool. In a twenty-first-century environment, student futures are strengthened and local competitiveness enhanced when graduates are globally informed and capable.[1]

In the twenty-first century we witness more and more the importance of global co-prosperity as the framework for advancing local prosperities. Research and education that are borderless widen access to cutting-edge knowledge and improve prospects for quality of life and a sustainable world. Development of intellectual structures, networks, and collective capacity to link local and global pathways of innovation becomes crucial. The talent we seek to access—and to build on—is resident not just within the academy but in public, private, and community entities here and abroad and in talent networks involving them all.

"The Morrill Act was the first of many federal policies to democratize access to higher education and to make public colleges and universities

159

instruments of advancement for the national and community well-being"
(WGI 3). Three core values—quality, inclusiveness, and connectivity—
have given direction to land-grant institutions since their inception and
over time increasingly to public higher education institutions in the United States more generally. These values guided land-grant institutions in
their contributions as the United States transitioned from an agricultural
to an industrial and service economy and, eventually, to a world power.
The objectives were the pursuit of quality in teaching and research relevant to societal needs, inclusiveness to diversify student access and widen
the content of subject matter for higher learning, and connection of higher education missions to community needs and aspirations.

The land-grant concept foretold a trend in U.S. public higher education to constantly "innovate" the university curriculum, research, and
engagement by imparting a practical emphasis to higher education and
extending its benefits beyond the elite social and economic classes. Connecting land-grant missions to global realities is not an end in itself but
a means—the next step of innovation—to advance core values in a new
environment.

This chapter begins by introducing the concept of the world-grant
ideal as an evolution of the land-grant concept. Subsequent sections expand on the basic concept and address: (1) the meanings, rationales, and
value locally, nationally, and globally of adopting the world-grant ideal;
(2) the transition from simple notions of international activity and internationalization as the frame of reference to a connection of those to
audacious goals for comprehensive internationalization as the engine to
drive the world-grant ideal; (3) tensions and barriers—some natural and
helpful and others dysfunctional—to achieving the ideal; and (4) the core
roles of scholarship, application, and the assist model of engagement for
co-creating co-prosperities.

As elaborated later, "co-creation" is a practice at the heart of both the
land-grant and world-grant ideals; the term labels a practice of partnership between institutions and communities and other external clientele to
solve problems and achieve advantage. "Co-prosperity" highlights a core
land-grant belief that institutional and community/clientele advantages
are drawn symbiotically from the advances of each.

This chapter is not about individual institutional reputations, stories
of what specific institutions have accomplished, or claims of preeminence.
In fact, this chapter and the world-grant ideal are about institutional relevance in a world needing sustainable prosperity and about constructing

a new framework propelled by the 150-year-old land-grant ideal that is relevant to a twenty-first-century global environment.

From a Land-Grant to a World-Grant Ideal:
Transitioning to a Twenty-First-Century Reality

World-grant is both a concept and a directional ideal for U.S. public institutions in the twenty-first century and beyond. Universities have not been "granted" the world in the sense that individual states were granted land by the Morrill Act as a funding mechanism to establish land-grant institutions (WGI 5). Rather, 150 years ago the Morrill Act also granted higher education the mission and responsibility to be connected to the fundamental issues unfolding in an institution's own backyard; the world-grant ideal recognizes the reality and importance of a worldwide backyard that stretches nearly seamlessly from the local to the global in mission and responsibility.

The challenges confronting the United States in the second decade of the twenty-first century parallel those challenges that led to the passage of the Morrill Act. Knowledge and information, particularly in science and technology, are growing at a faster rate than ever in recorded history. Keeping pace with and contributing to such growth is a staggering challenge, and so is the need for cross-cultural knowledge and values to drive these discoveries to humanistic purposes.

In a world as interrelated and complex as ours, it is increasingly difficult to imagine any significant challenge in the context of a single location; nothing occurs in a vacuum, and as global forces daily impact the local, so does the local shape the global. Examples are rife: banking and financial systems in the United States or in a few European countries or Asia impacting global credit and liquidity; food safety issues spanning continents as foods are imported and exported worldwide; virulent flu strains crossing species boundaries in a remote Southeast Asian locale and spreading globally; new forms of employment and unemployment from shifting global manufacturing patterns; impacts on world food supplies (and population) from the development in U.S. laboratories of high-yield disease-resistant or arid-climate crops; patterns of local and global energy consumption that impact world and local energy prices as well as environmental sustainability; with the advent of the World Wide Web, the utter inability of anyone or anything to control access to ideas that turn out to be good or dangerous and that expand knowledge and level advantage, at the same time compounding the difficulty of protecting intellectual property. The potential for globally connected public universities to drive societal growth and development for the greater good has never been higher, more appropriate, or more necessary. Consistent with the land-grant ideal, these universities are especially called upon now to do so by becoming a core part of the global intellectual highways of ideas, talent, and discovery, helping to fashion these highways as well as the traffic they carry.

Higher education itself is being reshaped into a global market, with inevitable comparisons and assessments being made about capacity, results, and opportunities for raising the bar of expectations across the world. U.S. higher education faces challenges in these terms. While other nations are adopting the U.S. approach to educational access and their entry and completion rates are rising steadily, educational attainment levels in the United States remain almost flat. The percentage of twenty-five to thirty-four-year-olds who have completed tertiary degrees in the United States has fallen from first place to well outside the top ten among Organization for Economic Co-operation and Development (OECD) countries (OECD, 2011). With the growth of higher education scholarship and research capacity elsewhere in the world, the dominance of U.S. higher education cannot be taken for granted. Global engagement will raise our own expectations.

Adoption of a world-grant ideal is not a paradigm shift, but rather preserves and strengthens historic core values and also builds on nearly seventy-five years of evolving U.S. land-grant and public institutional engagement abroad. However, the world-grant ideal is a call to innovation and change, which results in integrating a global perspective into instructional and research activity and mainstreaming access to it by students and other clientele (e.g., employers of graduates, community businesses large and small, government and social service agencies). It is not just another programmatic initiative for public institutions to take on, but a perspective that shapes all institutional missions and affects all institutional customers and clients.

Persistent Values and Missions in Societies Changing Utterly

Although the language used to describe land-grant values over the past 150-plus years reflects the character of particular times and challenges, the core values have remained remarkably consistent philosophical foundations and commitments of land-grant institutions.[2] From emphasizing agriculture and industrial development to the transition to a knowledge society, from focusing on local community, state, and nation to today's transitions to a global reality, the core values have remained steadfast.

The creation of land-grant institutions was indeed a bold step, yet we must remember that it was partly a reflection that the public believed that universities of the time were not working on behalf of society as needs for education and knowledge were being redefined. Emphases in basic and applied research and in understanding and meeting community needs broadly to advance opportunities for citizens were present at the inception of the land-grant ideal and today remain embedded in the core values—quality, inclusiveness, connectivity—that must now be called upon to drive the world-grant ideal.

Quality

This is a commitment to propel highly regarded research and education across the applied technical and liberal arts disciplines in a manner good enough for the best but also accessible to all including the poorest, contributing to a broadly educated and skilled citizenry. The primary challenge to higher education quality 150 years ago was not so much its quality per se, but rather its relevance to rapidly changing national and community realities and the need to expand fields of study and scope of legitimate inquiry in service to society (Simon, "Constructive and Complex Tensions" 2). The primary challenge to the quality of U.S. higher education in the twenty-first century remains access, but also crucial is the production of graduates ready for life and careers in the knowledge economy and a global environment where the half-life of cutting-edge knowledge seems constantly to shrink and where the "marketplace" of life and work is less and less local or national and increasingly borderless.

Inclusiveness

In the Morrill Act, inclusiveness meant widening access to the industrial classes, and it also meant widening the subject matter of higher education to include practical education along with liberal education. The liberal and the practical strengthened one another. It also meant providing access not only to students in the classroom but also to communities to promote economic preparedness and competitiveness. Over time, access has come to include a conviction that skills and knowledge derive from diversity (whether cultural, ethnic, racial, or gender); from cross-disciplinary concepts and methods; from global sources; and from maximizing considerations of alternative organizing paradigms and value propositions. These aspects of inclusiveness present the value proposition and necessity for twenty-first-century land-grant global engagement.

Connectivity

This is a commitment to work collaboratively with a wide range of partners, both within and beyond the academy, and to work across boundaries of communities, cultures, nations, fields of study, and institutions. The creation of knowledge—solving problems and realizing opportunities—requires direct engagement of communities and the building of paths of mutual engagement and co-creation where none existed before. The teams for co-creation must push well beyond local, state, and national boundaries to a world of no boundaries.

Twenty-first-century U.S. higher education, including land-grant institutions, must once again respond to challenges and critiques related to: (1) access and inclusiveness threatened by rising costs; (2) rapidly changing views of quality and relevance driven by dynamic knowledge-society needs; and (3) connectivity to a network of needs and opportunities that are not simply local, state, and national, but also global.

Global Engagement in an Evolving Context

It was not a global environment to which the Morrill Act initially responded. Almost since the nation's inception, a powerful inwardness drove U.S. social, political, and cultural frames of reference. Isolationist politics beginning with Washington's admonition to avoid "entangling alliances" were reinforced by broad oceans west and east and by the absence of threats north and south, particularly after promulgation of the Monroe Doctrine (Hudzik, "Comprehensive Internationalization" 14). Isolationism found an ally in a cultural championing of the yeoman farmer's fierce individualism and in restrictions placed on the powers of governments;

these formed a powerful ethos and preference for going it alone and for being left alone at both individual and national levels. Even in the late nineteenth and early twentieth centuries, the philosophy of American manifest destiny was a one-way street of engaging the world by projecting core U.S. values and practices outward, rather than importing any. Assimilation of diverse immigrant populations and cultures into the U.S. melting pot has been the goal for most, if not all, of the nation's history.

U.S. entry into World War II and widening U.S. roles and influence in the world afterward set the stage for a massive reorientation of the American frames of reference. Additionally, during the last part of the 1950s and early 1960s, disquiet arose about the United States' place in the world. The popular book of the late 1950s *The Ugly American* suggested that not all was necessarily right about U.S. objectives, methods, or worldview. The launch of Sputnik heavily shook the United States, with some Americans beginning to question the nation's preeminence (Hudzik, "Comprehensive Internationalization" 15).

These events not only began to reshape the country's global frames of reference but also the orientations and actions of U.S. higher education regarding engagement abroad. The availability of postwar reconstruction funds as well as broader growth of U.S. funding for international development was one reason. Among land-grant institutions in particular there was also a clear mission and value fit.

The National Defense Education Act (NDEA), passed in the aftermath of Sputnik, triggered unprecedented federal policy and support to build U.S. educational and research capacity and scope. Like the Morrill Act, NDEA was another groundbreaking, large-scale effort by the national government systematically to develop a portion of the nation's higher education capacity, this time particularly in science, technology, engineering, and mathematics, known as the STEM disciplines. As it turned out, the majority of NDEA graduate fellowships were awarded to persons who attained PhDs outside science and engineering (the plurality being in the humanities); so advantage was felt across a wide array of disciplines.[3] Title VI of the NDEA was groundbreaking in its potential scope and focus for building outward-looking, campus-based capacities in area/regional studies and in languages. The Fulbright-Hayes program enacted about a year later offered support for dissertation and faculty research abroad, adding a mobility dimension to the Title VI programs and to institutional engagement abroad.

However, the focus of Title VI was on developing expertise and not necessarily on developing mass education in international knowledge and learning (Biddle 67–69). Even so, Title VI unquestionably delivered the catalyst for higher education to bring the world more seriously into the classroom and onto the campus: it gave a boost to language study, including the less commonly taught languages, and it supported graduate work and faculty engagement abroad. Along with international development opportunities funded by entities such as the U.S. Agency for International Development (USAID), Title VI began to build a cadre of internationally experienced and engaged faculty on many campuses.

Many of the nation's land-grant and public institutions were prime locations for Title VI national resource area and languages centers, with 120 such centers in 53 institutions, many of which were members of what is now called the Association of Public and Land-grant Universities, the National Association of State Universities and Land-grant Colleges (Wiley 2001). With creation of the Peace Corps in 1961, an outlet was provided for the growing numbers of graduates interested in meaningful assistance and experience abroad. All but a few of the top twenty-five sending institutions for the Peace Corps have been land-grant or public institutions, and since 1961 the top five sending institutions, including three land-grant institutions, were publics.[4]

By the late twentieth century, many were acutely aware that the world was undergoing massive change with the breakdown of the bipolar cold war era, widening world development, and the emergence of a paradigm dubbed "globalization." Efforts to distinguish between globalization and internationalization created initial confusions, but eventually the latter came to mean relations between and among sovereign nations, while globalization was defined as the rise of factors and forces that transcend borders and sovereign states. "Even though global forces are mediated through the local context, they in turn shape local cultures and economies. Those local entities that remain largely unable to act effectively within these global currents are disadvantaged as never before" (Hudzik, "Comprehensive Internationalization" 15–16).

Benefits Locally and Nationally to Engaging Globally: Evolution of the Philosophy and Practice of Land-Grant Connectivity

Many U.S. land-grant and public institutions have passed through three stages on the local-global continuum of engagement, with evolving value-added implications for localities. The first stage had little if any cross-border engagement; the second stage adopted more pronounced and varied forms of international activity; and the third stage, under way and still evolving, reflects an integration of the local and global through more comprehensive internationalization and adoption of models for the co-creation of co-prosperities. In this third stage, the origins of transition are partly organic but increasingly can be shaped by institutional and higher education system directions.

Stage 1

Land-grant institutions began with a domestic focus on research and applications relating to food production, land use, sustainable agriculture, and rural development, including education, public health, nutrition, and community infrastructure. This was a strategic connection to people and communities and to national needs because agriculture was a dominant industry in the United States in the 1850s, with nearly 85 percent of Americans living in rural areas and 55 percent working in agriculture (Widder 3). Agricultural productivity made possible, and was followed by, growth in industrial manufacturing. Both trends quickened the shift of populations from rural to urban areas and toward a manufacturing economy. Land-grant higher education for agriculture and, subsequently, for industry focused on continuing economic and social development of the nation as well as of local communities.[5] While the land-grant mandate and much of public higher education were seen in local and state-based terms and, collaterally, as important to meeting national needs, the groundwork was laid for a systemic global engagement of land-grant institutions by the mid-twentieth century because the focal research and applications of land-grant institutions would ascend easily from a domestic to a global scale of priorities and needs.

Stage 2

The global engagement of many land-grant and public institutions expanded substantially after World War II along two tracks. One track focused on postwar reconstruction. The second track involved basic development assistance in other parts of the world, including in countries and regions being released from colonial rule and in countries grossly underdeveloped in terms of their economies, educational attainment, life expectancy, and health and nutrition. Land-grant engagement in these nations and regions was not reconstruction but rather establishment of basic foundations in sustainable agriculture, nutrition, and community infrastructure as essential antecedents to more advanced development.

International development work offered a natural fit with core land-grant values and also extended land-grant expertise and experience to the rest of the world. The global reputations of many land-grant and public institutions were built or enhanced through a commitment to local and global needs, dismissing a mutually exclusive choice between local and global. Value added nationally was mainly in the form of "soft diplomacy resulting from the engagement of Americans in development and problem-solving activity abroad."[6] As the number of faculty and staff who gained experience in various projects abroad expanded, capacity increased to internationalize portions of on-campus curricula and to connect the local community to peoples, places, and opportunities abroad.

With some exceptions, initial international engagement through development activity abroad was more assistance than partnership per se, and not manifestly a conceptualization of community engagement in the form of co-creation or co-production. Although it was moving away from isolationism as a dominant geopolitical philosophy, the United States retained a conviction of being best and took comfort in exporting inwardly derived values and practices via mechanisms such as the Marshall Plan and later through agencies such as USAID. The United States would teach but seemed less interested in learning. Thus, co-production, one of the hallmarks of a twenty-first-century land-grant institution's outreach (which had its origins in historical land-grant values and practices) spread only later to models for advancing sustainable development abroad.

Stage 3

The third stage of institutional engagement on the local-global continuum is under way and evolving. Engagement today is tied to a shaping of global co-prosperities, recognizing that a local versus global dichotomy is outdated. In this stage, higher education international engagement transitions from simple notions of assistance abroad to building local, national, and global networks with reciprocal and synergistic benefits locally and globally. Food, water, rural and urban land use, health, education, sustainable development, and environment remain focal issues but now are part of a global net of interconnected challenges and opportunities.

Benefits locally are reflected in the preparation of graduates and other clientele to become effective participants in a global marketplace of ideas and commerce as well as to become members of an increasingly mobile global workforce. Local and national benefits are tied to opportunities and problems that have global origins and solutions which encompass cross-border research paradigms and collaborations relating to the environment, health, energy, sustainable resources, food safety, and other issues. Soft diplomacy is advanced through educational exchange, joint education programming, collaborative research, and mutual problem solving.

Thus, in the third stage, local versus global is a false dichotomy and far removed from a zero-sum calculation. Global co-dependencies in the form of problems and their solutions, markets, and access to life-enhancing ideas and applications flow throughout a borderless environment. By involving the best faculty and staff globally, institutions themselves become more widely educated and experienced and can apply new knowledge and perspectives at home as well as globally.

Arising in part out of long-standing land-grant practices for community engagement and reinforced by early experiences and challenges in international development activity, the world-grant ideal fosters a unique kind of partnership in knowledge creation—the co-creation of knowledge through relationships not just among academic disciplines or even with other higher education institutions but also with local industries and businesses of a region and with public, private, and not-for-profit entities in a home state, in communities, or in any number of settings throughout the world.

In global financial and economic markets, we have come to understand the importance of co-prosperities or, at minimum, to have an appreciation for the negative ripples that economic problems in one region can have for others. Food sources, safety, and markets are borderless. As educational standards advance globally, pressure mounts to improve local educational outcomes to meet rising global competition. As knowledge-generation capacity flattens globally, the best ideas and applications that improve local life and solve local problems originate not just locally and nationally but globally. Communicable diseases—some new and exotic—cross national and continental borders as easily as they once spread from one village or town to the next. Local businesses increasingly must engage global markets for their own prosperity.

Rationales for Comprehensive Internationalization and Pursuing the World-Grant Ideal

The meaning of higher education internationalization and its fusion into core institutional missions and values have widened and solidified in the first decade of the twenty-first century. The notion of "comprehensive internationalization" began to gain traction (Knight and De Wit; Engberg and Green; NAFSA), and for many constituted a paradigm shift in higher education's conceptualization and actions relating to the outside world. For much of the post–World War II period, higher education internationalization was nearly synonymous with the term *international education,* and for many it was even more narrowly defined as student mobility across borders. It is coming to have a much deeper, wider, and institutionally infused meaning that anticipates and reinforces the world-grant ideal:

> Comprehensive internationalization is a commitment, confirmed through action, to infuse international and comparative perspective throughout the teaching, research, and service missions of higher education. It shapes institutional ethos and values and touches the entire higher education enterprise. It is essential that it be embraced by institutional leadership, governance, faculty, students, and all academic, service, and support units. It is an institutional imperative, not just a desirable possibility. . . . Comprehensive internationalization not only impacts all of campus life but the institution's external frames of reference, partnerships, and relations. The global reconfiguration of economies, systems and trade, research and communication, and the impact of global forces on local life dramatically expand the need for comprehensive internationalization and purposes driving it. (Hudzik, "Comprehensive Internationalization" 6, 10)

Comprehensive internationalization integrates three cross-border and world-content perspectives: (1) "international" for understanding and shaping bi- and multilateral relations; (2) "global" for understanding and mediating factors and forces that transcend political and geographic boundaries; and (3) "comparative" for a methodology that helps identify the saliency of similarities and differences across borders and cultures. While we use the term *comprehensive internationalization* to identify a totalized institutional commitment to teaching, scholarship, and engagement with respect to the international, the global, and the comparative, henceforth in this essay we will use the terms *international* and *comprehensive internationalization* in a second sense that comprises all three world-content perspectives.

The transition of international engagement from a desirable possibility to an institutional imperative is under way, pushed forward not only by globalization but also by growth in the size and quality of global higher education instructional and research capacity. This is not a paradigm shift in either land-grant missions or values or those of most public institutions but rather the latest manifestation of an evolving commitment to meet changing societal needs in practical terms. The need for such a transition was signaled and understood fifty years ago by John Hannah, then president of Michigan State University, who recognized the long-range implications of a changing world for U.S. higher education—even, or especially, for public institutions ensconced in the American heartland: "Time was when it was enough to prepare young people to be good citizens of their home communities, their states, and their country. But not today. No young man or woman can be considered educated who does not have some understanding of the world as a whole. . . . For the most part, [this is] the responsibility of the American college and university—and our responsibility cannot be avoided" (Hannah). The sustained sense of alignment of cutting-edge knowledge with a diverse socioeconomic profile of people "on the ground" in their practical circumstance requires agility on the part of public universities in responding to changing needs of peoples and in exhibiting leadership to adapt and recast themselves to meet new demands and opportunities for the nation and the world.

In his classic study *The Innovator's Dilemma,* Clayton Christensen outlines a pattern in which leading for-profit firms have ultimately failed because they focused too exclusively on past and current demand for existing products while overlooking the impact of "disruptive technology" on the longer range. In the world of twenty-first-century higher education, the analogy to disruptive technology illustrates a greatly expanding frame of reference coming from global challenges and opportunities (WGI 7) as well as the decreasing half-life of the value of cutting-edge information and discoveries in a knowledge society.

Higher education is being disrupted by a clientele that is global, a higher education supply system that is becoming global, and a competitive environment that requires reduced cycle time in learning and in discovery. A flattening of global higher education capacity and the multidirectional cross-border flows of students, scholars, and ideas are fundamentally game changers for U.S. higher education. It is conservatively projected that the number of higher education seats worldwide will grow from about 100 million in 2000 to 250 million or more by 2025 (Ruby). From 1995 to 2007, tertiary graduation rates doubled in OECD countries and entry rates increased 50 percent (OECD, 2011). Cross-border student mobility is projected to have similar growth from about three million to more than seven million by 2020 (Banks et al.; Haddad). Mobility numbers increased 70 percent from 2000 to 2008 alone (Hudzik and Stohl). Most of the aggregate seat growth will be in the non-Western world. The emergent systems will reshape the global higher education profile and affect established higher education systems, including the leading systems such as in the United States.

A recent National Science Board (NSB) study summarized a number of global trends with striking implications not only for global research capacity but also for emerging competition for the U.S. higher education research establishment. One NSB finding concerns the numbers and location of researchers, principally in the sciences and engineering. For example, between 1995 and 2007 the number of these researchers in the labor force grew annually between 7 and 11 percent in Asian countries and about 3 percent in North America and Europe. Cross-border joint publications, mainly intraregional, tripled from 1988 to 2007. Annual research and development expenditure growth from 1996 to 2007 averaged about 6 percent in North America and Europe; about 10 percent in India, Korea, and Taiwan; and between 15 and 20 percent in Thailand, Singapore, Malaysia, and China. The increased output of scholarly publications in the sciences and engineering between 1988 and 2008 was about 17 percent in the United States, about 60 percent in Europe, and in triple digits in Asia. Although much of the recent growth in the non-Western world is off a much smaller base and some of its quality is questionable, the trajectory is clear in policy and action to expand capacity terms (NSB).

Global higher education, into which the U.S. system is inextricably being drawn more tightly, will be characterized for some time by strong aggregate demand by students and short supply of faculty, leadership, and institutional capacity. There also is a rising inability globally—and clearly in the United States as well—for traditional public funding mechanisms to meet and sustain growing capacity needs. A philosophical switch to neoliberal notions that view higher education as less a public good and more a private investment directly challenges equitable access worldwide (Teixeira). Private for-profit and not-for-profit higher education is demand absorbing, and as a result it is becoming a growing proportion of capacity and enrollments in many countries—for example, about one-quarter in the United States, one-third in Mexico and Poland, 75 percent in Brazil, 77 percent in Japan, and 80 percent in Korea (PROPHE). Tuition costs continue to rise (OECD, 2011), and forces such as revenue diversification and surplus-producing activity, full-cost and market-demand accountability, and growth of a government-dependent private sector are reshaping public sector higher education globally as well (Teixeira).

Cross-border competition and collaboration are the consequences of such global higher education developments among widening types of higher education entities. For example, we already see trade and competition in the form of global circulation of talent, competition for a short supply of the best students, faculty, and administrators, and the emergence of global ranking schemes and quality competitions—and collaborations are forming via various networks and partnerships. While it is most unlikely that the United States will become unattractive to research scholars, and while we remain highly competitive in attracting the best, competition for the best is expanding globally. In the longer run, this has implications for the sources of the best talent in both students and faculty. Presently, it is estimated that about 22 percent of faculty members in U.S. higher education are foreign born; in some key areas, such as the STEM disciplines, this figure is estimated to be as high as 40 percent (Lin, Pearce, and Wang).

These pressures for collaboration reflect not only a flattening of global sources of cutting-edge knowledge but also the complexity of cutting-edge knowledge discovery. As Stephen Toope, president of the University of British Columbia, has noted, the cost and infrastructure of envelope-pushing research and discovery, particularly in the STEM disciplines, makes going it alone exceedingly difficult if not prohibitive; the expansion of research capacity globally in key disciplines pushes formation of cross-border collaborations out of competitive necessity. Toope suggests that the best cross-border collaborations are likely to grow organically out of the interests of research scholars rather than being pushed top-down by either governments or institutional leadership, the latter perhaps having a facilitative rather than creative role. Toope's views have implications for how land-grant and public institutions choose to orchestrate and shape or facilitate or constrain cross-border collaboration.

Increasingly, the clientele of U.S. public institutions is global, not just in terms of customers abroad but also of those at home. The rationale for global engagement and the conceptual shift from land-grant to world-grant becomes compelling and diverse.

Business Model Rationale

The business of higher education is ideas—the creation of ideas through research and the dissemination of ideas through education and application. Increasingly, the business of higher education is as much across as it is within borders—in the flow of ideas, students, and scholars, as well as the sources of societal problems and their solutions.

Client/Customer Rationale

An institution's customers are global. Most graduates will have to interact effectively with colleagues and organizations in many countries. As diverse immigrant populations join local communities, knowledge of their cultures is important. As businesses of all sizes engage global markets, they need access to country-specific and regional knowledge and expertise. So our customers "at home" are global customers, too.

Social Needs Rationale

Producing graduates and other clientele sensitive to the dynamics of democratic society enmeshed in a global environment requires building several understandings: of geopolitical relationships and influence; of factors shaping economic position in the global marketplace; of peace and justice; and of cultural differences. In ever-widening ways, the challenges we face at home have origins and solutions requiring cross-border collaboration in areas as diverse as public health, a sustainable environment, food safety, migration and emergence of a global workforce, and economic well-being, to name a few.

A Rationale of Innovation in Response to Challenge

U.S. higher education is challenged externally by the rapid development of global higher education capacity and internally by rising concerns about the value added of U.S. higher education—for example, falling completion rates, lengthening time to degree, and questions about the productivity and accountability of higher education and its responsiveness to emerging societal needs. World-grant comprehensive internationalization will play out within parameters and constraints that are likely to reshape significant features of the U.S. higher education landscape and to which the transition from land-grant to world-grant for public institutions will have to be responsive.

Redefining access from "international" expertise for the few to cost-effective mainstream access for the many becomes a core aspiration for the world-grant ideal. Comprehensive internationalization integrating such a perspective throughout institutional curricular and research fabrics, as opposed to being an added layer of new requirements, may be the most effective mechanism for doing so.

The pressure to innovate practice lies at the center of a world-grant ideal, particularly in how access to global connectivity needs to move beyond the few to the many. Innovation is not found merely in scaling up existing methods. Examples abound, but none more relevant than the innovations occurring in language instruction and learning or in active learning pedagogies. Budget constraints prioritize investments that produce synergies across institutional missions. Much as was the case with the original land-grant concept, the internationalization of learning, research, and outreach will benefit from their interconnection both on campus and in the strategic partnerships and engagements beyond our borders. Active learning through student participation in research and projects abroad is an example of such synergy.

The client pool for higher education is diversifying globally, particularly with respect to the nontraditional student becoming the norm. Responding to nontraditional students—part-time students, adult learners, lifelong learners, more socioeconomically diverse students, students with families and jobs—will challenge world-grant commitments to access for a far more diverse client pool. With rapid global expansion of higher education instructional and research demand and with short supplies of adequately prepared faculty and administrators, the global competition for the best faculty, administrators, and students will intensify.

From International Activities to a Comprehensive World-Grant Frame of Reference: Audacious Goals and Intentions

What distinguishes the world-grant ideal from earlier notions of higher education internationalization is the scale and scope of the intended internationalization of institutional ethos and missions, mainstreaming access, and cutting across all institutional missions. Such goals will appear audacious—or worse—to many.[7] Yet audacious goals are required if land-grant values are to be relevant in the twenty-first century and beyond and if the world-grant ideal is to have substance. Such goals would include the following:

- All undergraduate students should be given significant exposure to international perspective by its integration into their degree programs with learning outcomes established related to knowledge, attitudes, and skills. All students should have opportunities to enhance such learning, not only in the classroom but also in active learning education abroad, such as short- and long-term study abroad, internships, field research, and service learning.
- All faculty members should be encouraged and supported to enhance their international perspectives in their teaching and scholarship, and all graduate students should be provided opportunities to understand the practice of their professions and disciplines in other cultures.
- On-campus international students and scholars should be integrated into the campus living and learning environments.
- Community engagement should routinely include opportunities to connect local constituencies to global opportunities and learning.

Without a baseline of assets, network alignments, attitudes, and breadth of disciplinary engagement, such audacious goals will not be easily accomplished as part of achieving a world-grant ideal.

Assets

The core assets needed are several: (1) strong research, scholarly, and creative capacity; (2) distinguished faculty drawn competitively from throughout the world; (3) breadth of academic and professional disciplines and networks to support interdisciplinary approaches to problem definitions and solutions; and (4) borderless reach for ideas, resources, partners and partnerships.

Network Alignments

The alignments needed include: (1) permeable boundaries across academic disciplines and institutional support units; (2) collaborations accessing ideas and capacity across regions, nations, and cultures; (3) focus on new and evolving societal needs, many of which arise from a global environment; and (4) conscious consideration of local-global networks, recognizing that few if any absolute delineations remain between the domestic and international. The basic realignments signal the need for evolving partnerships with global reach among educational institutions, the private sector, and government and nongovernmental organizations as well as academic and professional disciplines.

Attitudes

A world-grant institution: (1) values advancing global understanding through its curricula both on and off campus, its programs of community engagement and outreach, and its liberal arts and professional curricula; (2) seeks mutual empowerment, engagement, and service locally and globally in meeting the needs of diverse cultures and peoples in diverse circumstances; and (3) accepts the need for nimble orientations, structures, and programs to address evolving social needs in cross-cultural and cross-border ways.

Breadth of Disciplinary Engagement

The world-grant ideal profits when every academic discipline reaches beyond its own discourse community, engaging its conceptual tools and knowledge to address issues that concern the world community at large as well as local and national communities. Just as the forces and demands of specialization that tend to yield the greatest rewards in the academy undermine the potential for engaging cross-disciplinary strengths, a focus on domestically defined issues and models of a discipline undermines its potential in a global environment.

Tensions and Barriers Moving Toward Comprehensive Internationalization and the World-Grant Ideal

Tensions are inherent in the land-grant model, and throughout its 150-year history they have forced land-grant and public institutions to realign priorities and practices in order to meet the changing needs of society. A movement toward comprehensive internationalization and a world-grant ideal likewise produces new tensions and intersections of challenge and opportunity mingling and aligning with core values.

Constructive Tensions

The Morrill Act created tensions between its offspring (including those that were established well before they were given land-grant designation) and the existing higher education establishment and, later, tensions within the land-grant institutions as they evolved to blend focal land-grant missions and programs with the full range of curricular and research thrusts of the best among the non-land-grant institutions. The ongoing tensions of the nineteenth and twentieth centuries were sources of innovation and change that strengthened the fledgling land-grants as they grew in stature and became increasingly important in supporting a rapidly diversifying economy and society. Determining how much a student's program should be devoted to liberal arts and how much to career and professional preparation was replaced with considering an integration of the objectives and delivery of both.

The tension between local and global—a contemporary parallel to urban and rural, or to liberal and professional education—is seen by many as a competition for knowledge and insufficient financial resources. There is considerable time wasted in thinking about how much institutional effort should be devoted to the local and how much to the global; more beneficial to the world-grant ideal as well as to traditional land-grant core values is thinking about how to blend and integrate local and global to common purposes. Research to detect toxins in food has application to food from domestic or global sources—both fill our grocery store shelves. Research on communicable diseases, conducted at home or abroad, has obvious implications for detection and control of their spread globally and locally. Knowledge of others' cultures, societies, and markets is essential to the development of marketing strategies for U.S. products abroad. The development of energy-saving technologies, policies, and practices abroad offers solutions at home. The general competition of global markets "ups" everyone's game—witness the impact of the Japanese and German automobile invasions on the American auto industry and subsequent improvements to quality. Years ago, Senator William Proxmire gained some notoriety for handing out the "golden fleece" award for seemingly wasteful government expenditures. In one case the award was given for a federal grant to study the mating habits of bees in South America; as it turned out the research involved the African killer bee and how its spread to North America could be controlled.

Constructive use of tensions—global/local, liberal/professional, rural/urban—bends and penetrates political, geographical, disciplinary, and cultural borders. Intentional boldness and risk taking are required; failures need to become learning points rather than reasons to blame or abort. A university in the world-grant ideal has a culture and capacity for the intentional, creative use of the tensions that are inherent in our global environment and sees tension as a constructive and complex tool to leverage change and advantage.

Counterproductive Tensions

Clearly, though, there are disruptive and counterproductive tensions that arise in several forms and affect achieving land-grant and world-grant ideals. These counterproductive tensions include the following:

DRAG OF SUCCESS

Past success and comfort in preserving what led to it create tension between comfortable frames of reference and the disruptive challenges of a changing environment that requires realignments. The world-grant ideal of engaging globally will challenge policies, practices, and orientations that have been developed within a largely local and domestic frame of reference. The allure of the status quo is reinforced among U.S. higher education institutions by decades of widely acknowledged top-tier status within the global higher education system and a sometimes blind eye to development and innovation taking place elsewhere.

RESEARCH CASTE SYSTEM

Historically, a large part of research engagement abroad has been characterized as project work, fieldwork, or applied research. Tensions arise from a research caste system distinguishing so-called pure or basic research and research applications, assigning greater value to the former. Project and applied field research are not only at the core of sustainable international development activity but also are at the core of institutional connectivity to community, whether at home or abroad. Yet basic research eventually is confirmed by applications, and good project work and fieldwork can achieve not only specific benefits but yield generalizable results—witness, for example, the Nobel Peace Prize given Norman Borlaung for development of high-yield, disease-resistant wheat.

DISCIPLINARY ARROGANCE

Culturally engrained disciplinary hierarchies, although real enough, also contribute to caste system tensions. Research on sustainable food production to limit death or ill health through poor nutrition should be valued no more or no less than research reducing death by controlling communicable disease. Ultimately, there is no difference between dying from starvation or tainted food and dying from AIDS or malaria. Yet "agriculture and applied research [part of the land-grant mandate] have traditionally been undervalued in academic-ranking schemes" (Gleason, 2010). For some, the source of research funding takes on its own caste importance, such as research funded by the National Institutes of Health versus research in food safety or production funded by the U.S. Department of Agriculture or USAID.

IT'S THEIR JOB, NOT MINE

A fundamentally unproductive tension is a supposed division of labor that sees some disciplines and professions as naturally inclined toward global engagement, thereby absolving the rest from needing to be involved. While humanities, languages, and social and behavioral science disciplines are traditional core elements in international education, professional disciplines take on importance not only because of the globalization of markets but also because of the globalization of problems and solutions in almost all areas. Indeed, all disciplines today seem more relevant in a twenty-first-century environment when informed by global perspectives and the practice of their professions in other cultures. Josef Mestenhauser, an early and highly respected leader and theorist in international education, saw "an advanced level of internationalization . . . involve[ing] not only internationalizing key courses but also identifying the international dimensions of every single discipline" (Mestenhauser). Beyond the mainstreaming of student access to international and global learning, the mainstreaming of academic unit contributions to this learning is at the core of the world-grant ideal.

ELITIST RANKING SCHEMES

The emergence of institutional ranking schemes—some domestically focused and some casting a global net—is antithetical to core land-grant values. In order to manage data collection and analysis, the schemes limit the variables chosen for measurement, on which subsequent rankings are based, and consequently the deliberate diversity inherent in land-grant missions and disciplinary foci is shoved aside. Ranking schemes that highly value aggregate SAT scores of admitted students ignore that high scores cluster around the more privileged school systems and communities, thus penalizing postsecondary institutions that provide access to students from less privileged schools and communities. Schemes that assign weight to the numbers of Nobel laureates or members of the National Academies at an institution ascribe value to research productivity in a limited set of basic disciplines and, by omission, denigrate or at least fail to recognize productivity in other areas, including many professional programs and disciplines. New and interdisciplinary areas of research and instruction tend to be ignored by ranking schemes until well established and familiar, if ever. Yet it is the constant addition of, and experimentation with, new research and curricular frames by land-grant and many other public institutions that have made them successful, whether domestically or globally. And some ranking-system criteria are directly counterproductive to land-grant and public higher education values. For example, the criterion of dollars spent per student—when more dollars spent is seen as a measure of quality—would militate toward limiting access through higher tuition costs, even though quality is not linearly related to expenditures.

Global Engagement as Either/Or

A focal tension arises from a belief that work done for domestic clientele and work done abroad is zero-sum. The belief arises partly from a mistaken if comfortable hope that somehow our well-being and prosperity can be separated from that elsewhere in the world. Resolution requires an understanding of the importance of global co-prosperities. A base zero-sum tension arises from viewing allocations of time, money, and other resources for international activity as pulling resources away from domestic and local activity. This view ignores that local has become global and vice versa, and it also ignores that this spurious dichotomy can be resolved by finding ways to integrate local and global efforts for mutual gain. Even though the tension persists in many quarters, there is evidence that the importance of international knowledge and global connectivity is well understood by the public.[8]

The world-grant ideal requires reconciling the disruptive and unproductive tensions between quality and access, research and outreach, the liberal arts and the professions, and home and abroad, and also requires rejection of the limitations imposed by caste systems and simplistic ranking schemes. Tensions are no less pronounced in the twenty-first century than they were in the nineteenth and twentieth centuries. But in the tensions are the messy intersections that fuel innovation and create new opportunities for locally relevant and globally respected institutions.

Reducing Internal Barriers

Serious challenges to achieving a world-grant ideal come from internal institutional barriers. A reinforcing set of strategies and tactics can help reduce self-imposed internal barriers to internationalization and achieve the world-grant ideal. Such strategies and tactics would include the following:

Building a World-Grant Institutional Culture

Successful world-grant comprehensive internationalization requires an institutional culture that provides overarching drive, purpose, and sustainability. Leadership communication and messaging by the president and provost provide highly visible advocacy for these purposes, but equally important for leading and building support are the roles of deans and faculty leaders, both within and outside the formal governance structure.

The driving culture for world-grant internationalization defines missions, values, and service in interconnected local, national, and global terms. It is not seen as an add-on responsibility but rather as a commitment to integrate global perspectives into the fabric of curricula and of institutional research and community engagement missions. It encourages the involvement of everyone. It is pervasive in institutional messaging and it is a broadly shared vision up and down and throughout the campus community about the necessity of effectively engaging and linking the local and the global.

This kind of culture and commitment is not synonymous with an action checklist that, once completed, allows the comfort of saying "mission accomplished." A sustaining culture drives an ongoing and evolving set of actions that flows from a continuous sensing of the global environment for opportunities and constraints and the interaction of those with the local environment and internal institutional dynamics. Much as the core values of land-grant engagement required an ongoing evolution of programs and priorities to meet changing environmental needs, so does the world-grant ideal in response to a much larger and more complex and dynamic global environment.

So success is dependent on a culture that combines persistence and adaptability. Because higher education institutions are dynamic entities with changing priorities and because the methods of globalization continually evolve, the world-grant ideal requires continuous evaluation and adjustment to changing circumstances.

DOCUMENTING VALUED OUTCOMES
A world-grant culture is not defined optimally by input or output measures such as dollars allocated to international activity, numbers of students studying abroad, numbers of international students and scholars on campus, numbers of internationally focused centers and institutes, or numbers and contract dollar values of research grants or projects abroad. Although these are indicators of capacity to engage globally, the real substance of the world-grant value added is defined by the intended impacts (Hudzik and Stohl).

Learning
Proportion of students achieving identifiable knowledge competency or learning objectives in the various "international" perspectives; evidence of

impact on students' knowledge, attitudes, beliefs, skills, careers, and capacity to learn and work effectively in other cultures; standardized levels of language competency; and evidence of enhanced community and clientele knowledge and skills to engage effectively in a global environment.

Research, Scholarship, and Engagement
Strategic, joint, or other ventures abroad that significantly contribute to core institutional mission objectives and values; incidence of faculty and staff refereed publications in international journals and invitational speaking engagements at international conferences; and cross-border collaborations that measurably strengthen institutional research, instructional capacity, and communities.

Inclusiveness and Connectivity Outcomes
Proportion and diversity of students exposed to the international perspectives on campus and through learning experiences abroad; proportion of majors incorporating such perspectives; proportion and diversity of faculty engaged in international teaching or research projects; and impact on the conditions of people and communities in areas such as economics, health, education, nutrition, safety/security, and access.

Faculty Engagement
Arguably, the most important ingredient in sustaining a drive toward the world-grant ideal is the faculty. Systemic barriers can arise that send conflicting signals for faculty engagement. For example, institutional messaging says "go global" but departmental cultures say "stay domestic," and hiring, tenure, and promotion practices may ignore or discount international interest and work. It is one thing to signal that it is permissible to include international activity in a tenure package, another to suggest that it carries weight, and quite another to say that it is an expected component or required.

Regardless of what is written on paper and in institutional tenure and promotion forms, the critical issue turns on what criteria are applied de facto by departmental promotion and tenure committees and administrators. What gets counted counts, and what does not get counted becomes a barrier. Perhaps the most important barrier to, or encouragement of, faculty engagement is whether international activity is seen as a core part of academic unit priorities. This is why integration of internationalization into core missions is so critical throughout an institution.

Designing Portals for Global Collaboration—Partnerships, Hubs, and Networks

A hallmark of the mission and values of land-grant institutions, and probably of all public institutions, is community engagement—working to identify community issues and to improve the condition of society and people where they live and work. Arising in part out of long-standing land-grant practices for community engagement and reinforced by earlier experiences in international development activity, "a key element of the world-grant ideal is a unique kind of partnership—a partnership designed to co-create knowledge in relationships not just among academic disciplines or even other higher education institutions, but also with local industries and businesses of a region and with government agencies in a home state, in communities, or in any number of settings through the world" (WGI 13).

In transitioning from notions of assistance to partnership, a university does not engage others "with the thought that it has all the right answers or knows assuredly which questions to ask. Instead, it brings a commitment to global engagement and a comparative research perspective that provides insight into how others are approaching similar challenges in other parts of the world—and then listens to its partners' ideas on how to address questions being considered, ultimately creating a solution or solutions through intellectually rigorous cooperative investigation of the problems being addressed" (WGI 13).

In a twenty-first-century knowledge society, access to global intellectual networks becomes a key element in being competitive and building co-prosperities. Borderless intellectual networks and hubs provide an important system of roads and portals to ideas, practices, and relationships that contribute fundamentally to such outcomes. The twenty-first-century relevance and value of land-grant institutions have become interdependent with building global partnerships and collaborations.

There is a persistence through time in the forming and waning of intellectual hubs—such as Athens 2,500 years ago, Renaissance Italy, and Confucian centers in China—that served as magnets for ideas and creativity reaching far across political boundaries. Some came to be associated with university settings, as in France and England in the sixteenth and seventeenth centuries and later in the German research universities. There are equivalents today in knowledge centers that typically have a constellation of research universities as part of their core. All such hubs attract scholars, intellectuals, and ideas from diverse places and cultures and typically affect multiple disciplines of thought and practice.

In a twenty-first-century environment of growing global capacity for research and education, these hubs are more numerous, and they exist as parts of idea networks and talent flows of people and ideas that run through multidimensional trade routes. Interconnections and patterns of flow frequently shift or reroute, depending on issues, interests, and needs, such as mangrove ecology in Vietnam and Louisiana; stem-cell research in the United States, Singapore, and Europe; and software development in the U.S. Silicon Valley and India. The issues and combinations are endless.

Twenty-first-century engagement abroad is far more complex than merely peering over the fence to gather intelligence about what others are doing or have learned or being "hub connected." And we are clearly beyond the one-way learning and assistance of older development models. The idea networks are proliferating and provide overlapping regional, national, disciplinary, and institutional cross-membership and access. Land-grant institutional access to multinational higher education networks and the institutions within them provides more diverse opportunities for collaboration than focusing on hubs. The flexible, varied, and shifting possibilities provided through networks fit better with the diversity of land-grant missions, values, and programming than does association via hubs alone.

Cross-border, interinstitutional partnerships or collaborations take many forms: bilateral memoranda of understanding defining collaborations between two institutions; the formation of cross-border associations or clubs of seemingly like-minded and similarly situated institutions; or the interconnection of learning hubs scattered globally and strategically linked through key elite institutions. However, meeting the particular and differing needs of local communities can easily get lost through intellectual hubs, just as they can via airline hubs.

None of these models or approaches alone is adequate to the challenge of land-grant and public institution global engagement in the twenty-first century because the flow of ideas is multidirectional and along shifting pathways of connections. And with a rapid flattening of intellectual advantage in a global knowledge society, being flexibly connected to networks may carry more value than being focused on an intellectual hub. With the rising complexity of problems, solutions, and global interconnections, the networks of value are multinational, multidisciplinary, and multi-institutional—and shifting.

For twenty-first-century land-grant institutions, a hybrid model of interinstitutional collaboration may offer the best means to engage a multidimensional global network of intellectual co-prosperity. One aspect of the hybrid can be the development of in-depth and bi- or multilateral partnerships with a few strategically selected institutions abroad in order to build collaborative synergies across instructional, research, and outreach missions as well as to provide a stable and sustainable core of cross-border relationships. Sustainable relationships to produce long-term mutual gain are the objective; they represent interinstitutional commitments not dependent on one or a few individuals.

Given the diversity of land-grant programming and missions, it is unlikely that a small number of deep interinstitutional partnerships will meet all needs for all time. Accessing flexible multi-institutional and multiregional networks can serve to widen opportunities and also provide for diverse borderless collaborations to arise organically.

Scholarship, Application, and an Assist Model of Engagement

By their very nature, land-grant institutions bring a blend of research, scholarship, and hands-on application to both local and global engagement. Throughout all three stages of engagement on the local-global continuum described earlier, success has required a hands-on presence in communities, countries, and regions.

The research settings and laboratories of tens of thousands of faculty from land-grant and other public institutions are not just on the campus but in local community projects, cooperative extension, and development project settings abroad. It is a community-based engagement informed by scholarship from diverse disciplines and geographic locations, including, among many other possible examples, creation and production of disease-resistant crops in the American Midwest and in Southeast Asia; advancement of arid agriculture in the U.S. Southwest, Egypt, and the Asian steppes; reestablishment of a safe and sustainable water supply tainted by industrial pollution in U.S. and Eastern European industrial regions and in areas worldwide tainted by agricultural runoff; community building and empowerment in Michigan cities and villages in Malawi, Uganda, and Kenya; control and eradication of diseases such as AIDS in the United States and South Africa; and revitalization of urban brown zones in the industrial rust belts of the United States, Eastern Europe, and the central Asian republics. The basis for action is first-rate scholarship applied where it is needed—much of it replicable in multiple local/global settings.

Sustainable benefits, though, are not the product of hands-on efforts that are merely hand-outs in forms such as food aid, food stamps, and free medical supplies or equipment. Rather, benefits occur by building sustainable, indigenous capacity through collaborative learning, whether in the home state or abroad. The "doing" must be done as much by the communities in need as it is by institutional intervention.

The land-grant model is inherently an "assist" model in which institutional presence provides the support for community-based action—an effective model whether in urban or rural extension in the United States or development activity in Africa or other world regions. The measurement of value-added outcomes is as much in the assist as it is in the doing.

Summary Thoughts: Directions and Guiding Actions

The Morrill Act funded an idea—the pursuit of an ideal to expand access to quality higher education and to purpose higher education with the responsibility to advance community and social prosperity in all of its meanings. It did not try to micromanage the method or model to achieve that ideal. It did not create a bureaucracy to organize how institutions and states were to respond. Rather, it was left to institutions, states, and localities to choose the portals and routes by which the core values would be pursued, priorities set, and strategies developed. Over 150 years, results have been strengthened through the diversity of priorities and methods employed among the nation's nearly 1,700 public institutions.

Pursuit of the world-grant ideal similarly is not about championing a particular method or model. Rather, it is a call to extend core land-grant values into the twenty-first century by connecting them to the ideal of talent development without borders and to a realization that community and institutional co-prosperities are shaped increasingly by borderless forces and possibilities. The intended directional truth of the world-grant ideal is housed under a very large tent in order to accommodate a diversity of approaches just as the land-grant tent did 150 years ago. However, while homogeneity in method and priorities is not the goal, there seem to be a number of core elements common to any attempt to achieve the world-grant ideal.

Core Guiding Elements

The question that framed this chapter is: How should a major public university in the United States align its distinctive strengths to meet the needs and demands of a global society and strengthen its commitment to the public good? The answer given is linking historic land-grant values to comprehensive internationalization of institutional missions and involving communities served through models that blend research and application efforts through institutional, local, and global interactions and collaborations. Part of what distinguishes the world-grant ideal from earlier notions of higher education internationalization are goals of mainstreaming access and connection, preparing graduates to be effective in a global marketplace, and expanding societal benefits by linking to the global net of ideas, innovation, and opportunities.

Successful world-grant comprehensive internationalization requires visualizing internationalization not as an add-on responsibility but rather as a commitment to integrate global perspective into the fabric of curricula, research, and community engagement missions. There is an expectation of commitment to action, and a deliberateness and intensity in doing so to link the global and the local.

Diversity, not Homogenization

There is no action checklist that every institution can follow to achieve the world-grant ideal. There certainly is no detailed legislation, policy, regulation, or bureaucracy that should or could productively impose the route for transition from land-grant to world-grant. At the same time, one cannot ignore the role that funding for innovation has had throughout the last 150 years—funding through grants of land to create new kinds of institutions, funding to support cooperative extension and experiment stations, funding through a variety of means to build international engagement and expertise, and funding to support research here and abroad. However, it has been the kind of funding oriented toward achieving ends and values rather than funding intended for implementing particular methods that has been most productive and would be again in advancing the world-grant ideal.

Ultimately, the land-grant and world-grant ideals run counter to a strong current that flows today through much of higher education—a current that draws institutions to emulate the models and practices of a relatively small circle of research-intensive universities that are considered elite, drawing such status in part from simplistic national and global ranking schemes. Such emulation risks the tyranny of homogeneity and the loss of innovation provided through different approaches and priorities. In pursuit of the world-grant ideal, research-intensive universities in the land-grant tradition would not regard the production of knowledge that changes ideas and practices in the discipline as antithetical to engaged outreach. The need is for both, with a standard of shared excellence and synergism.

Neither the land-grant nor the world-grant ideal can be pursued without valuing heterogeneity in programming and flexibility in priorities and responses to diverse and changing needs. The practical meaning of public benefit is strongly rooted in the particular needs, practices, and priorities of distinctive communities, clientele, and cultures. From such differences and through differences among higher education institutions arises innovation for diverse public goods. The value is not just diversity in the size, mission, or type of higher education institutions but in the diversity of priorities and programs even within institutional types such as research-intensive institutions.

Competition and Collaboration

Competition and collaboration across borders and among widening types of higher education entities are the consequences of global higher education developments. It is more productive, however, to recognize and act on the strong pressures and high incentives emerging for cross-border collaboration than to worry about competition. Pressures for collaboration arise not only from a flattening of global sources of cutting-edge knowledge and recognition of fundamental global co-dependencies, but also from the complexity and costs of cutting-edge knowledge discovery, particularly in the STEM disciplines. Going it alone is increasingly difficult and sub-optimizing. The emergence of cross-border collaborations arises out of necessity and is recognized by those astute enough to see its value.

Advancing Individually, Organically, and Via Network Assists

There are aspects of the transition from a land-grant to a world-grant ideal that will continue to emerge organically through the natural pressures and opportunities presented by twenty-first-century globalization and through institutional diversity. While the Morrill Act transformed U.S. higher education, it was through individual land-grant institutions funded by the Act (and, eventually, through other public institutions) that pivotal instructional and research outcomes led U.S. development—in agriculture, in industrialization, and then in the knowledge society of the late twentieth century. U.S. public institutions now have signal roles to play in a global environment guided by the same core land-grant values envisioned 150 years ago.

The responsibility for individual institutional commitment and action remains a powerful necessity, but so does updating notions of necessary institutional networks and partnerships. The idea of working together—institutions and communities collaborating across institutions and across disciplines—is at the heart of land-grant methodology. But it now needs updating to encompass borderless formation of networks and collaborations.

The Power of Diverse Networks

As noted earlier, in a twenty-first-century knowledge society, access to global intellectual networks becomes a key element in being competitive and in building co-prosperities. Through flexible access to varied networks, diverse individual strengths can be multiplied many times if harnessed through the lens of Morrill Act values and facilitated by local and global collaborations of like-purposed higher education institutions along with public, private, and not-for-profit entities. Flexibly accessing changing networks enhances capability. Diversity in the form of partnerships, partners, and relationships is required to pursue the land-grant mission effectively within a world-grant ideal.

Collaborative Knowledge Development and Sharing among Public Institutions

There would be payoffs from collaborative development and knowledge sharing among public institutions of approaches and methods that advance the world-grant ideal. Support for various means to explore and share ideas and practices among public institutions in pursuit of the world-grant ideal would enrich both ideas and practice. Among some of the issues that dialog could advance are the following:

- New metrics that would provide evidence of the value added by the continuing internationalization and global engagement of institutions. These metrics need to focus outward, measuring outcomes and impacts on various local, national, and global clientele. Some metrics, though, need to focus inward to measure outcomes and impact on the institutions. The development of metrics that document the "assist" contributions of higher education (as discussed earlier) in the development of co-prosperities is also needed.
- An evidence-based documentation of new institutional models of public university engagement in a borderless world. This would aid collective understandings of similarities and differences in how institutions are coming to engage globally. It would benefit all to build a storehouse of the options for engagement and underscore a diversity of approaches that could be matched to varying institutional interests and conditions.
- The regular sharing of knowledge about opportunities and approaches to engage globally and link locally, about barriers encountered and solutions adopted. The systematic and ongoing sharing of emergent practice would collectively yield more positive outcomes across the entire system—to enhance the power of learning from one another and the spread of innovative ideas and methods.
- Means for higher education institutions to build and work in networks, both formally and informally in virtual networks, to tap the collective capacities of institutions with common values in pursuit of the world-grant ideal.

Sustaining and Advancing Globally: Like-Minded Institutions and the Land-Grant Covenant

The need to advance the public good presses itself on universities throughout the world. The response needed is not simply for renewed higher education purpose through the action of individual colleges and universities but for building domestic and global partnerships and networks of institutions that share in the common values of the Morrill Act and the twenty-first-century orientation of the world-grant ideal.

It is the combination of research and engagement that holds the greatest potential to address local and world challenges. Mediating the tension between research and engagement is required, not forsaking one for the other. The tensions play out at times as seemingly insurmountable differences between quality and access, research and outreach, liberal arts and applied knowledge, and institutional rankings and engagement of community partners in the co-creation of knowledge.

Just as any public university that pursues a research-intensive mission feels attracted and obligated to succeed in terms that the academy itself defines, so must any such institution in the land-grant model pursuing the world-grant ideal engage to serve the public good through meeting the needs of diverse communities and clientele—now as often far from home as at home.

A key strength of the world-grant ideal is to make a positive difference for the "have-nots" as well as the "haves." The tide of prosperity rises with an increase in the proportion of the latter.

The challenge before diverse but like-minded institutions is twofold: (1) renew and update a commitment and approaches to core Morrill Act and land-grant values and (2) knit together networks within localities, across the country, and around the world to meld and grow the power of individual strengths. In so doing, higher education also offers a model of how to work more effectively as an agent of empowerment for individual learners, communities, states, and nations to address challenges interwoven with the global fabric of our time.

A commitment to a world-grant ideal and comprehensive internationalization does not play out in homogenous fashion across all institutions but is dependent on institutional missions, priorities, cultures, and capacities to engage. What is common across all institutions seeking to be true to the world-grant ideal is that each is committed to: (1) expanding the global reach of all students, faculty, and institutional clientele; (2) integrating a comprehensive approach to internationalization across all teaching, research, and engagement missions; (3) adopting collaborative strategies for mutual benefit not only at home but abroad; and (4) engaging flexibly in borderless and cross-sector networks.

The vision of the land-grant model is in its energies and commitment to communities, in recognizing the tension between similarities and differences across communities, and in how higher education must adapt to meet this diversity. The vision of the world-grant ideal is to expand knowledge creation, knowledge dissemination, and partnerships in a borderless world.

NOTES

1. This chapter significantly builds on and interconnects work done and previously published individually by the authors, most notably: Lou Anna K. Simon, "Embracing the World Grant Ideal" (hereafter cited parenthetically as WGI) and John Hudzik, "Comprehensive Internationalization."

2. According to the Title 7, Chapter 13, Subchapter I, § 304 of the U.S. Code on Agriculture (part of the original Morrill Act) titled "Investment of proceeds of sale of land or scrip," the original objective of the land-grant university was primarily to teach agricultural sciences, but also mechanical arts, military tactics and liberal arts: "Provided, That the moneys so invested or loaned shall constitute a perpetual fund . . . [for] the endowment, support, and maintenance of at least one college where the leading object shall be, without excluding other scientific and classical studies and including military tactics, to teach such branches of learning as are related to agriculture and the mechanic arts, in such manner as the legislatures of the States may respectively prescribe, in order to promote the liberal and practical education of the industrial classes in the several pursuits and professions in life." The fusion of the liberal and the practical, of the classical and agricultural, in the goals outlined by Congress demonstrates the intention that these colleges would have a unique purpose in educating Americans not just for a job, but for life. Mention of the "industrial classes"

is a clear allusion to spreading higher education access to a wider pool of citizens. Widening the subject matter of higher education equally expanded the meaning of access and inclusiveness respecting subject matter. Quality can be generally inferred as a core value, because to assume the opposite intent would seem impractical, but quality in practical education as well as liberal education seems to be the wider intent. Connectivity to community is clear in the reference to "the several pursuits and professions of life."

3. The language in the original NDEA act reads: "The Congress hereby finds and declares that the security of the Nation requires the fullest development of the mental resources and technical skills of its young men and women. . . . We must increase our efforts to identify and educate more of the talent of our Nation. This requires programs that will give assurance that no student of ability will be denied an opportunity for higher education because of financial need; will correct as rapidly as possible the existing imbalances in our educational programs which have led to an insufficient proportion of our population educated in science, mathematics, and modern foreign languages and trained in technology." However, upon consideration of the report of the National Research Council Commission on Human Resources to the U.S. Office of Higher Education we see that this act did not necessarily result in its intended outcome. The report notes that "Title IV was intended to alleviate the then existing and projected shortage of college teachers, and to achieve a wider geographic spread of strong graduate programs" (iv). Indeed, Title IV provided fellowships for over 45,000 individuals throughout its tenure. But in Table 2 of the Report, we see that while NDEA may have been enacted as a response to a shortage of mathematicians and scientists in the United States in the buildup to the cold war, it was actually more generous in its awards to students outside of these disciplines. The act thus expanded higher education across the board, as did the Morrill Act, which also had a similar intention of educating students in science, particularly the agricultural and mechanical arts, but benefited students more widely (see previous note).

4. In order, University of California, Berkley; University of Wisconsin-Madison; University of Washington; University of Michigan; Michigan State University (Peace Corps).

5. By 1880, nearly twenty years after passage of the Morrill Act, there were sixty chartered and functioning land-grant institutions

throughout the nation. Although each had significant commitments to the agricultural sciences, most also had educational and applied research programs in engineering, the sciences, and many of the liberal arts disciplines (Johnson 226).

6. John Hannah, twelfth president of Michigan State University, often described this idea as part of the mission of public universities: "One of the striking developments of recent decades has been the discovery by our government that American colleges and universities, and especially those drawing their support in part from public funds, represent vast reservoirs of human resources readily available for use in implementing our national policy in international affairs" (Hannah).

7. See also Hudzik, "Comprehensive Internationalization" 35.

8. Just before 9/11 (Institute for Public Policy and Social Research, SOSS-19), and then a year later (Institute for Public Policy and Social Research, SOSS-25), Michigan State University commissioned a random statewide public opinion poll regarding views about the importance of institutional international programming and international engagement. In virtually all areas in which the public was questioned about the reality of global impact on Michigan and the need to understand and connect with these realities, large majorities recognized the realities and the importance of engagement. Afterward, based in part on the Michigan survey, the American Council on Education (ACE) commissioned a national randomized survey on many of the same issues and found similar results (Green, Porcelli, and Siaya). The public is not the problem; rather, it may be us in higher education. See also ACE's 2003 report, "Mapping Internationalization on U.S. Campuses," which followed the ACE survey.

Statewide University Systems

Taking the Land-Grant Concept to Scale in the Twenty-First Century

NANCY L. ZIMPHER AND JESSICA FISHER NEIDL

The passage of the first Morrill Land-grant Act in 1862 marked a ground-breaking development in higher education in the United States. The legislation not only established a novel means of support for new institutions of higher learning but also defined an influential new educational mission, one riveted on expanding curricula and access in ways previously unseen in the United States.

The fundamental idea of the federal land-grant legislation, as Justin Morrill described it, was "to offer an opportunity in every state for a liberal and larger education to larger numbers, not merely to those destined for secondary professions, but to those much needing higher instruction for the world's business, for the industrial pursuits and professions of life" ("An address on behalf of the University of Vermont"). The land-grant institutions offered what Morrill called a "practical education of the industrial classes" (*Morrill Act of 1862*)—not study for the sake of erudition but education for the purpose of advancing knowledge in practical applications with the aim of helping both individual students and entire communities, rural and urban, improve their positions and quality of life.

The mission espoused by the Morrill Acts of 1862 and 1890 proved to be a watershed not only in American education, but also in the formation of the democratic American identity and the American Dream—the promise of opportunity and the possibility, with enough hard work,

197

gumption, and mettle, of individual success and prosperity. While land-grant colleges, universities, and university systems continue to make good on this mission, we propose that university systems, land-grant or not, are best positioned to make good on and expand the Morrill vision, extending educational opportunity and resources to the widest possible body of American students and thereby having the greatest positive impact on improving the quality of life in communities throughout the country and into the twenty-first century.

Cultivating *Systemness* to Take the Land-Grant Mission to Scale

Justin Morrill's vision emerges in the missions of many public university systems in the United States, even in those that are not land-grants, through systems' dedication to advancing the triad of teaching, research, and service while expanding access for students from all walks of life. The size, stature, and reach of public university systems position them to take the land-grant mission to unprecedented scale, not only preparing a growing population for the modern workforce but also playing a valuable role in strengthening or rebuilding local, regional, and state economies. To realize this potential to take the Morrill Act to new heights, university systems are well served to cultivate coherent, functioning "*systemness*"—that is, the effective coordination of multiple, complex components that when working together create a system that is more powerful than its individual parts and that is empowered to deliver on the progress-oriented goals of the land-grant mission.

The institutions established by the provisions of the Morrill Act have never operated together as a system or network in the ways that many public university systems operate today. The land-grant institutions, in their design and beginnings, *stem* and *benefit* from a common mission but do not constitute a comprehensive operating educational system in itself. Between and among the land grants, there is no universal or agreed-upon curriculum, no transfer pipeline or assurances of articulation, no umbrella for administrative oversight or shared administrative functions. These schools were not originally designed to function thus; they were designed as individual and separate institutions to serve local needs and to bolster local agrarian and industrial economies.

Today's public university systems differ from the land-grants in that they not only consist of multiple related institutions but also operate with a character-defining and mission-delivering *systemness* that occurs when many campuses come together. The term *systemness* cannot be found in any printed dictionary (not yet, anyway), and online searches yield only loose terminology lately used in the health care industry and a few scant references to information technology. But the as-yet-unofficial status of this key word does not diminish its power, especially when plugged into the vernacular of higher education administration, where we propose to use the term to describe the core strength of today's public university systems and how they are delivering far more than our educational forebears could have ever imagined, and in particular with regard to meeting the land-grant goals.

To be clear, the distinction between a public university and a public university *system* is that the latter consists of two or more public *institutions*, each with its own identity and a certain level of autonomy but operating under the administrative umbrella of a single legal entity such as a board of trustees, a board of governors, or a board of regents. Systems such as The State University of New York, the University of California system, The University of North Carolina, and the University System of Ohio are among the largest university systems in the United States that operate in this way. This structure is not to be confused with "free-standing" public universities that maintain several satellite or branch *campuses*, such as the University of Connecticut, Idaho State University, Kansas State University, the University of New Mexico, New Mexico State University, or The Ohio State University, to name a few examples. Each of the fifty states maintains at least one public university and/or university system; each state also has at least one land-grant university.

Creating university systemness, then, with an eye toward making good on the land-grant mission, is ultimately about achieving three things:

Effective Systemness Creates Strength

One of Aesop's fables, "The Bundle of Sticks," tells of a life lesson a man demonstrates for his sons by using a simple bundle of sticks. As the story goes, the father commands his children to snap the entire bundle in two, a challenge at which they fail because the bundle, as a whole, is too strong to be compromised. The father then instructs his sons to untie the bundle and break the individual sticks, a task easily achieved. In this example is the timeless lesson that there is strength in unity, an aphorism that university systems can embrace and live by. Systems are teams. They are groups and networks. They are natural solutions to complex problems, the product of a strength-in-numbers approach that is engrained in our humanity as a survival skill. The collective strength of an effective system, then, can prove greater than that of a single entity, and in the case of higher education, of a single institution.

On the reverse end of this is the premise that welcoming an already-existing institution into the fold of a system can strengthen the formerly independent school by making it part of a larger, established, well-known brand and a body that has more resources or support. Such mergers and absorptions became common in the three or four decades after World War II and represent important benchmarks in the development of today's university systems.

Effective Systemness Encourages Smart Growth

As Michael Bugeja, director of the Greenlee School of Journalism and Communication at Iowa State University, highlights in his September 2011 article "Twelve Ways to Survive 2011–2012," growth has been the primary guiding principle for higher education institutions for decades. The challenge before us now, however, is to reform institutions so that they live within their means and grow in responsible ways with an eye toward meeting the needs of students as well as of the communities in which institutions are located.

When it comes to public universities, there are cost advantages to obtaining system-wide contracts or undertaking shared-services measures, which can maximize revenue and thereby aid a system's ability to expand access as well as grow its campuses, departments, programs, initiatives, and services. In university systems, good systemness is the major determiner of smart growth. Driving sound systemness is a positive self-awareness of both institutional and community needs. With the right mechanisms in place, there can be a coordinated effort to ensure that institutions within a system work in concert with one another, limiting curricular glut, program duplication, and administrative redundancy, promoting the vibrancy of individual institutions, the system as a whole, and the communities served by those institutions.

Effective Systemness Allows Universities to Exceed Their Traditional Grasp and Re-envision Themselves as Powerful Community-Building Partners and Economic Engines in Service to Improve Quality of Life in Host Communities and Regions

Colleges, universities, and university systems are emerging as leading partners in how communities—and entire states—throughout the country are redefining and rebuilding themselves in today's challenging economy. Just as Justin Morrill understood education's role in building stronger communities, many individual colleges and universities are embracing their roles as "anchor institutions"—enterprises that are not likely to pick up and move away because of their large size and deep roots in the community. They are, in effect, anchored in place and serve as reliable and powerful forces for economic development, and from this position they help drive and determine the local quality of life.

Universities, as well as hospitals, museums, performing arts centers, sports complexes, and other large cultural institutions, all serve or have the potential to serve as anchor institutions. And each type of anchor bears a spin-off benefit—beyond its intrinsic purpose to educate, serve, or entertain the public and above providing direct employment—that fosters measurable, proliferative economic development and collateral quality-of-life enhancements.

There is widespread consensus among specialists in economic growth that universities function as anchors in singular ways. Higher education institutions pack a powerful triple punch because they (1) are in themselves sources of a wide range of jobs, from faculty to administrators to the necessary support staff without whom the university could not operate; (2) act as incubators for new ideas needed to create jobs in the twenty-first-century economy; and (3) are the key to developing a workforce prepared to fill those jobs.

The economic benefits that colleges and universities bring to a community are specific and sustained. Reliable, annual influxes of new students, many of whom commit to two or four or more years in the area, support host communities by seeking recreation and a wide variety of services. And the town-gown relationship is a symbiotic one: campuses vibrate with the energy of discourse and research, attracting community members to attend cultural and sporting events. Businesses catering to students, faculty, staff, and visitors are established, providing additional jobs and services. Furthermore, the populations of communities that host colleges and universities tend to be younger, better educated, and more diverse, profoundly shaping the sense of place.

If one college or university can have a profound impact on its local community, imagine then what a coordinated, fine-tuned university system can do on a larger scale for the economy and quality of life across a region or an entire state. As an example of the kind of economic impact generated by a university system, The State University of New York reported that in 2008–09 it had a statewide economic impact of a minimum of $19.8 billion, based on the spending of students, employees, and institutions—a better than five-to-one return on the state taxpayers' spending for SUNY (Nelson A. Rockefeller Institute of Government 4). The SUNY system's other measurable contributions to building New York's economy include not only educating a competitive workforce but also partnering with employers large and small to adopt new ideas and technologies and transfer university research findings into commercial use.

Identifying Challenges and Threats to Systemness

Through effective systemness, public university systems can work to eliminate obstacles that get in the way of taking the land-grant mission to scale and can position themselves to realize the mission writ large. However, developing systemness is in itself a challenge because of university systems' multifaceted compositional complexity and the need to orchestrate the governance of multiple institutions, each with its own set of departments, programs, faculty, students, staff, agendas, concerns, and cultures—all of which are subject to the push and pull between the rules and requirements of system administration and the needs and desires of the institutions that make up the system. Thus, there are certain inherent challenges that systems face that potentially limit their capacity to advance the land-grant mission.

The first challenge to creating systemness that can deliver large scale "land-grantness," as it were, might simply be identifying a system's components—which components are already in place, which components function and do not function, and which new components are needed to make the system function optimally. The California Master Plan for Higher Education of 1960 articulated for the first time in one place emerging challenges facing higher education in the United States and proved useful to other states orchestrating the organization of their public higher education systems. Clark Kerr, president of the University of California in 1960 and architect of the Master Plan, articulated at the outset of the report the challenge of cultivating university systemness when he stated that the "structure, function, and coordination of a university system are so closely interrelated that they must be dealt with as a single problem" (California State Department of Education xi). In this, Kerr identified the operational conundrum of any university system—creating a *structure* that effectively *coordinates* each part of the system so that it *functions* as a fluid, productive whole that serves to educate and prepare for the workforce a large and diverse student body.

Based on the Master Plan's findings and recommendations, California established a three-tier postsecondary education system designed to serve hundreds of thousands of students functioning along the spectrum of academic achievement and ambition and seeking to obtain degrees in a vast and growing array of fields and disciplines. The new system created a functional relationship between the already-existing University of California (UC), the California State College (CSC) system (now California State *University*), and the California Community Colleges (CCC) system. While other states have not adopted California's structure per se, the plan, with its comprehensive and thorough examination of higher education challenges in California, established an exemplary approach for how to identify system needs and coordinate already existing and perhaps discordant public postsecondary institutions into a system or body that efficiently and effectively serves the public's changing needs.

Approaching the twenty-first century, the National Association of State Universities and Land-grant Colleges (NASULGC, now the Association of Public and Land-grant Universities or APLU) saw the late 1990s as the optimal time to examine the state of public higher education in the United States. In 1996, NASULGC enlisted the W. K. Kellogg Foundation to support a national commission to explore and rethink the role of higher education. The resulting Kellogg Commission on the Future of State and Land-grant Universities, which met between January 1996 and March 2000, comprised the heads of twenty-five major public universities, land-grant and non-land-grant, who convened to address the challenges public higher education faced and to ascertain how public colleges, universities, and university systems could continue to fulfill and further the land-grant college mission and ensure that *public* universities function as the *public's* universities (Kellogg Commission, *Returning to*

Our Roots: Executive Summaries, preface). The commission acknowledged that "unless public universities become the architects of change, they will be its victims" and that, in order to meet cultural and economic changes, state universities and systems would need to rethink and renew their efforts to strengthen their legacy of world-class teaching, research, and public service (Kellogg Commission, *Returning to Our Roots: The Student Experience,* executive summary).

While the Kellogg Commission's findings, discussed in detail over the course of five topical publications released between 1997 and 2000, do not speak specifically to the challenges faced by university systems only, the warnings, lessons, and recommendations presented in the reports are as relevant to systems as they are to individual institutions and continue to drive conversations about the state of higher education. Pervasive challenges such as accommodating a growing population, meeting the educational needs of the knowledge-based workforce, and working with limited institutional flexibility were all identified as concerns—and each has an impact on defining an institution's systemness and its ability to realize the land-grant vision. In addition to these general concerns, specific challenges include finding systemness-promoting answers to surviving and thriving in spite of dwindling state support, reconciling competing needs between institutions within a system, answering calls for regulatory relief, and maintaining individual institutions' identities.

Dwindling State Support

The current economic climate in the United States has done much to direct the discourse among higher education professionals and experts toward addressing the specific challenges public higher education faces today and the solutions that may be possible with the shrinking pool of available resources and diminishing public support. For example, seven successive cuts to The State University of New York's budget over the past four years—amounting to $1.4 billion or one-third of the university's operating budget—have defined a new fiscal reality in the state.

A spate of articles authored by higher education experts speaking to this issue has emerged this year, each fraught with observations and solutions calling for protecting and strengthening systems, not dismantling them. Systems, though beset with many of the same problems individual institutions face, are often best equipped to meet such economic challenges—but only if and when they create effective systemness. This is especially so in light of the Kellogg Commission's assertion that simply because we as a nation face unprecedented challenges it does not follow that we ought to scale back our collective ambition (Kellogg Commission, *Returning to Our Roots: Executive Summaries* 1). Rather, we should scale *up* our ambitions to meet those challenges. Many public university systems, because of their size and systemness, are armed to put this call to confidence into action.

Competing Institutional Needs and Calls for Regulatory Relief

Institutions within a system have individual identities, often resulting in competing needs. In his June 2011 article "When Systems Evolve," Daniel J. Julius, vice president for academic affairs at the University of Alaska, underscores how university systems reflect multiple factors, including "geographic interests in states (rural vs. urban), philosophical differences (egalitarian vs. elitist), and political traditions (the relative value placed on public education and the willingness to use tax dollars for it)." Each of these factors plays a role in shaping an institution's identity and, further, determines how an institution fits into a system—whether an institution fully participates with a view that the system's sum is greater than its parts or whether the institution balks and, in extreme cases, attempts to untie itself from the system, arguing that it is better off operating independently, free from system regulations, and even free from system supports.

The problem of competing needs is especially evident in the tensions that arise between a system's flagship school and its smaller institutions. It is no secret that when the economy takes a turn for the worse, public universities, and particularly flagship and large research universities, call for regulatory relief and attempt to free themselves from system constraints with the argument that the bureaucratic mandates inherent in systems hurt rather than help institutions grow and thrive. Of course, in many cases the call for some sort of administrative reform is justified. Jane Wellman, executive director of the National Association of System Heads, and Charles B. Reed, chancellor of the California State University system, point out that the "myriad rules and regulations still operating in many states were developed in another time and place, before universities grew into multi-billion dollar enterprises with hundreds of thousands of students and tens of thousands of employees." Wellman and Reed further maintain that "relief from obsolete and ineffective state controls is appropriate for all of higher education, not just a few of the research universities, and not just because of funding reductions" (Wellman and Reed).

On one side of the argument there are the institutions within a system contending that the flagship's leaving the fold would inevitably cause harm, weakening or destabilizing the system overall. A perception of an unfairly lopsided allocation of resources or attention paid to a flagship breeds not only systemness-undermining tension but often resentment toward the flagship and also toward a system's administrative body, which may be perceived as playing favorites, leaving the smaller institutions in the system feeling slighted and short on the support or recognition they feel they need or are due.

On the other side of the debate are the flagships or research universities, which argue that, released from the strictures of the system, the institution on its own would be stronger and better able serve the population by mustering more flexibility on tuition setting, hiring, managing facilities, and purchasing (Lederman). The common complaint heard from flagship institutions is that other institutions in the system divert precious resources away from them. Arguments for regulatory relief are ongoing in many states, such as Wisconsin, Virginia, Oregon, Louisiana, and New York, to name a few, with requests for varying degrees of autonomy, ranging from outright separation from a system to a preferential flexibility or relaxation of regulations.

Maintaining Identity

A common goal for all institutions within a system is to maintain their unique identities. Specific departments and programs define campus cultures, and institutional pride and school spirit are powerful forces that generate a sense of community, belonging, and good will. None of these factors is to be underestimated in its power for promoting and supporting an institution. It follows, then, that as systemness increasingly informs operations, especially new initiatives that are implemented by an off-campus administrative body, campuses grow nervous that their identities will be subsumed by the overall brand and the interference of a remote system head. In this way, institutions in a system can become suspicious of and resistant to systemness-driven changes.

Identifying and Implementing Systemness
Components and Solutions

States strive to create university systems that best serve the unique needs of the population, and, as described above, this is particularly challenging in times of economic constraint. No matter what the economic conditions, however, there will always be some display of resistance toward aspects of systemness because going along with systemness means, to a point, relinquishing some control for the sake of the greater good of the system.

But healthy, operating systemness manifests the best not only of what universities have to offer but also of what the land-grant mission has to offer. As an example, The State University of New York's targeted initiatives teach broader lessons that can be used to illustrate comprehensive, functional systemness in a large university system.

SUNY was established in 1948 to answer the educational needs of a growing, diversifying population. But at its founding, SUNY was decidedly not meant to be any kind of educational powerhouse. Rather, if anything, it was explicitly intended to be something of a catchall, a supplement to work in cooperation with the state's "priceless private colleges and universities," as was explained by Governor Thomas E. Dewey in 1950 at a symposium on the "Functions of a Modern University" (State University of New York 30–31). Dewey argued that the relationship between SUNY and New York's private colleges should not be at all competitive, that they must "supplement each other with neither weakening the other."

Under its original establishing provisions, SUNY's reach was rather limited, as is described in *SUNY at 60: The Promise of the State University of New York*: "Opponents of SUNY's independence from the Regents prevented the creation of a permanent Board of Trustees until 1954. There were informal bans on teaching liberal arts or training secondary teachers in academic subjects (except at Albany), engineering except at Maritime Academy, and a prohibition on raising private funds. Significantly, doctoral programs and research were also out of bounds" (Clark, Leslie, and O'Brien xix).

But unfolding events proved influential in defining SUNY's role in higher education in New York. New federal policies, such as the introduction of the GI Bill in 1944 and the establishment of the National Science Foundation in 1950, had had their impacts, as did the wave of baby boomers preparing to enter college. More specific to the development of SUNY, however, was the 1958 election of Nelson A. Rockefeller as governor of New York State. Rockefeller's vision for SUNY was of a very different kind of university and most certainly invoked a stepped-up concept of systemness. Under a proposed new model, "Former state teachers colleges would become liberal arts colleges, community colleges would rapidly expand, and students would help support the expansion by paying tuition for the first time. Most dramatically, SUNY faculty would undertake significant scholarly research . . . at four university centers offering doctoral programs spread across the state at Stony Brook, Binghamton, Albany, and Buffalo. Finally, SUNY would be an independent force, freed from the restrictions of earlier compromises and from the [Board of] Regents' interference" (Clark, Leslie, and O'Brien xix).

Since that time, SUNY has grown into the largest comprehensive public university system in the country and the world. Following Rockefeller's vision, the system includes sixty-four schools, a mix of twenty-nine state-operated campuses, and five statutory colleges—including research universities, liberal arts colleges, specialized and technical colleges, health science centers, and land-grant colleges—and thirty community colleges. These institutions offer programs as varied as ceramics engineering, philosophy, fashion design, optometry, maritime studies, law, medical education, and everything in between. The system also operates three hospitals, a veterans' home, and numerous research institutes.

SUNY currently enrolls more than 467,000 students; employs 88,000 faculty and staff; and counts more than 3 million living alumni. As a system, SUNY is embedded in virtually every community in New York State: 93 percent of New Yorkers live within fifteen miles of a SUNY campus, and nearly 100 percent live within thirty miles. In many communities, SUNY is the region's largest employer.

Since its founding, the SUNY system and its essential systemness have evolved to meet the changing needs of New York's students, communities, and workforce. Several key components of SUNY's systemness, below, can be examined to better understand the concept in action.

Comprehensive Visioning

One of the most important factors contributing to systemness in universities is that an institution has at its core an identity and a vision. Further, a system's vision can be defined in a cohesive, comprehensive strategic plan that serves to guide over an extended period of time the growth and progress of the constituent units and of the system as a whole.

A vision, as embodied in a strategic plan, is best derived through the collaboration of many, reflecting the ideas, ambitions, and determination of a broad base of contributors from throughout the system and the state. For example, in 2010 SUNY launched a new strategic plan called *The Power of SUNY*, the origin of which is rooted in information gleaned from a one-hundred-day statewide tour of all sixty-four campuses. At each stop on the tour, SUNY held town-hall style meetings for students, faculty, and interested members of the community so that they could come and hear and speak about what they wanted from their university system or an individual institution within the system. It was from these events and from subsequent meetings and input of an assembled "Group of 200"—a broad mix of SUNY faculty, staff, students, and alumni as well as community members and other external stakeholders—that SUNY devised what would become the six "Big Ideas" of its strategic plan: SUNY and the Entrepreneurial Century, SUNY and the Seamless Education Pipeline, SUNY and a Healthier New York, SUNY and an Energy-Smart New York, SUNY and the Vibrant Community, and SUNY and the World. These ideas are the supporting, driving tenets of *The Power of SUNY*, the university's roadmap for the next decade.

In an overarching way, SUNY's goal with its strategic plan is to exceed its reach as an educator in the traditional sense and fulfill its role as an anchor institution, as discussed above, in the largest sense—bolstering economic vibrancy and improving the quality of life throughout the entire state, campus by campus, community by community, region by region. This same goal is treated in the Kellogg Commission's report "Returning to Our Roots: The Engaged Institution," and it is in our view an authentic, contemporary realization of land-grant school intentions. In this vein, SUNY's economy-driving power is demonstrated by the university's partnership role in Governor Andrew M. Cuomo's Regional Economic Development Councils, established in the summer of 2011. The governor's decision to consistently include the State University system at the table speaks to the powerful relationship higher education can foster between businesses and local communities as well as to its ability to move the dial on job creation and workforce development.

Implementation of a strategic plan of this scope involves extensive planning in itself and the invention and application of unique methodologies and collaborations both within the university system and with outside partners—another opportunity for the application of effective systemness. The implementation of *The Power of SUNY*, for example, is driven by two types of teams: *Innovation Teams*, one for each of the six "Big Ideas," and *Transformation Teams*, including groups focusing on academic excellence, strategic enrollment management, budget, leadership development, innovative instruction, information technology, and shared governance. These teams, the members of which come from throughout the system, meet on a regular basis to work toward their targeted goals to build stronger communities through improved university engagement.

In order to achieve goals of this significance and magnitude, it is also essential that university systems consistently and creatively perpetuate a sense of system cohesiveness. Leadership must drive the mission and vision through the interplay of words (spoken and written: town hall–style meetings, conferences, a system-wide Web site) and images—an appealing, system-unifying visual brand that is readily identifiable across a spectrum of mark-making opportunities, from signage and banners, to business cards and letterhead, to magnets, lapel pins, apparel, and a range of branded specialty items. A correlated operating network of colleges and universities also supports critical programs such as online learning, interlibrary loan, study abroad opportunities, and alumni and retiree networks, just to name a few.

Another aspect of effective systemness critical to realizing a university system's mission is transparency—putting out key information in an accessible and digestible way so that stakeholders and anyone interested in following the arc of an initiative can easily track its progress. This is where regular "report cards" can be very effective in checking the metrics developed to track an initiative's progress, its successes and shortfalls. It is important that universities hold themselves accountable, and that they are held accountable, for the goals they have set.

Student Mobility—Ensuring Access and Completion

The democratic notion of allowing an expanded body of students access to higher education was laid out by the Morrill Act, and modern public university systems picked up this concept and incorporated it into their systemness, implementing mechanisms that encourage access and degree completion. Clearly, among the primary purposes of a university system is to educate the widest possible pool of students. And in order to ensure that students graduate, and to promote efficient time to degree, fluid and easy mobility within the system is critical. All institutions within a university system should work together to ensure ease of transfer—that credits are transferable and that coursework and programs are as portable as possible between and among schools. Thoughtful articulation and transfer mechanisms shorten time to degree, save students money, and get them out into the workforce sooner.

There are several steps university systems can take to enhance student mobility throughout the system. Ease of transfer and efficient time to degree may be ensured by instituting policies whereby students transferring within a system are treated by their receiving institution, for all academic purposes, in the same way as native students of that institution. Credits for general education courses successfully earned at one institution in the system should be accepted at another, whether a student is transferring from one two-year institution to another or from one four-year institution to another or from a four-year institution to a two-year institution or from a two-year institution to a four-year institution. Students should not be required to repeat such courses after transferring. In the plainest of terms, this means that transfer students will be able to enter a four-year institution within the system with an array of completed coursework that will allow them to finish in the same time as students who have completed equal coursework and earned credits at the receiving campus. This same type of policy also encourages retention within a university system. Establishment and maintenance of system-wide electronic databases of approved general education courses and courses within majors would also help institutions within a system counsel students on degree and transfer options and help campuses efficiently process transfer evaluations.

The most common type of transfer agreement stems from negotiations between a system's institutions, primarily controlled by the faculty in each discipline in the receiving institutions. Historically, this was the practice, for example, at SUNY. In another approach, some states have mandated that all community college courses be accepted by the campuses to which a student transfers. In Florida, for example, common courses at all public colleges in the state carry the same titles and numbers, promoting ease of transferability.

The state of Ohio, as determined by its Board of Regents, took a different tack, requiring for all state-supported colleges that there be four courses in the major for each discipline that would be accepted statewide by all public institutions. The content for each course is determined by a faculty committee. Transfer of general education course credit is not course-by-course but by number of course credits in different types of academic disciplines (a certain number of credits of natural science, of social science, of humanities, etc.) (http://regents.ohio.gov/transfer/policy/index.php).

Over the last few decades SUNY has cultivated student mobility and articulation policies that contribute to its functional systemness and promote the core goal of promoting access. In particular, SUNY's governing body, the Board of Trustees, has gradually coordinated efforts between the system's thirty community colleges and its four-year schools, bringing the latter to accept an increasing number of courses from community colleges with regard to both general education requirements and courses in majors. The process at SUNY has evolved over time such that credit-transfer decisions—and therefore student mobility—are determined by "faculty" writ plural. That is, decisions are rendered by groups of faculty in each discipline from throughout the system, representing both two-year and four-year campuses, rather than by "faculty" writ singular or by individual faculty members on each campus deciding what constitutes suitable content for a particular course and whether to accept or reject a course a student has taken at another campus.

In the past several decades community colleges have played an increasingly important role in higher education and workforce training and, in particular, in promoting student mobility. Driven by developing technologies and the commensurate requirement for a highly specialized, knowledge-driven workforce, community colleges have evolved to meet new needs, all while maintaining their original mission to provide universal access to higher education by removing economic, social, and geographic barriers. They offer opportunities beyond the traditional liberal arts and business offerings, including degree and certificate programs in the widest possible range of practical disciplines.

So it is that more and more often the path to a four-year degree starts at a community college. Generally more affordable than four-year colleges, often situated more conveniently for commuting students, and with open admissions and flexible class schedules that accommodate employment, community colleges have seen consistent enrollment increases. In the 1960s alone, the number of community colleges in the United States doubled, from 412 to 909. By the beginning of the twenty-first century, they enrolled 44 percent of all college students in the United States

(Dubb and Howard 19). In addition, there has been a shift toward transfer degree paths (such as associate of arts and associate of science degrees) and away from career-oriented terminal associates degrees (such as associate of applied science and associate of occupational studies), indicating that students pursuing transfer degree paths at community colleges intend to continue their studies at four-year schools. To take advantage of this talent pool and enhance the chances that community college students intending to transfer will succeed in attaining a bachelor's degree, a system's mobility policies should encourage students to take the courses that will fulfill bachelor's degree requirements and ensure that they receive credit at their receiving schools for courses they complete successfully in community college.

There is another spoke in the accessibility wheel, an emerging one that turns on the concept of wider community engagement. More and more, universities are looking to primary and secondary schools to see what measures can be taken at earlier ages to best prepare all schoolchildren, from pre-kindergarten through twelfth grade, for college and beyond. This is but one of the many recommendations for improving access discussed in the Kellogg Commission report "Returning to Our Roots: Student Access"; it is also explored in SUNY's "Education Pipeline" part of its strategic plan.

Comprehensive Strategic Enrollment Management

Comprehensive strategic enrollment management goes hand in glove with student mobility—both work to ensure that students have access to the programs and courses they need to graduate prepared for twenty-first-century careers. There are several actions university systems can undertake to coordinate strategic enrollment management.

First of all, a university system's administrative body should work to have a cogent sense of system capacity, which means defining the system's *collective* capacity by exploring the capacities of *individual* campus programs and their relationships to the system as a whole. Examining transfer of students using enrollment and capacity data across all of a system's institutions is a critical part of this exercise. From there, the system can identify and work to remove obstacles to initial entry and/or transfer and can devise mechanisms for data-driven capacity evaluation by academic program. The system may require campuses to analyze system-wide capacity information on proposed new or revised programs and may encourage cooperative program development and delivery between campuses through the system's shared-services initiatives. It is also important to pay attention to and discourage program development where there is no measurable need and to monitor the impact of proposed discontinuation of programs system-wide.

In addition, systems can devise new funding models that take into account the types of degrees and programs campuses offer, providing more funding for the more expensive programs such as engineering, technology, natural sciences, and applied health sciences when those areas have been identified as "high need."

Comprehensive strategic enrollment management speaks to a large university system's understanding of itself as a potential mega-anchor institution that stands to serve not only students and communities but entire regions and states. SUNY, for example, plans to invest in helping campuses start or expand programs that have been identified as high-need areas for the state using the type of analysis that can be found in the 2011 report "How SUNY Matters: Economic Impacts of the State University of New York" (Nelson A. Rockefeller Institute).

Strategic enrollment management is a continual process, one that must be fine-tuned and consistently tracked as new data emerge and are collected. Doing so should be the duty of any and all university systems because having access to this vital information is essential to ensuring that programs and majors are applicable and relevant to the current job market.

Innovative Resource Allocation

Resources are not inexhaustible, and this goes for any system. Thoughtful, innovative allocation of resources is critical to effectively supporting a system and its many working parts.

New methodologies are developing with an eye toward improving efficiency and reducing costs by empowering a system's individual institutions to directly manage more of their academic and financial affairs. Campus input is a critical component in the development of a new model and is perhaps best served by involving campus academic and business officers as well as faculty. This new model can identify differences in resources required for various types of academic programs and provide incentives for campuses to grow enrollment and external research activity.

There is a trend toward greater simplicity and flexibility in allocation methodologies and, in many instances, a movement toward greater campus autonomy in the internal distribution of resources. As campuses exercise more authority in academic and fiscal matters, they also assume greater responsibility for the cost variations that result from local decisions. In New York, for example, difficult fiscal circumstances and the desire to reflect the priorities of the strategic plan prompted a review of the resource allocation model and methodologies. In this effort, SUNY tapped into its systemness by assembling a working group of campus presidents, provosts, vice presidents for administration and finance, and faculty governance to develop the technical details of a new model to be implemented for the 2012–13 fiscal year. For the same reasons—a challenging economic environment, which has led to diminishing state support, and a desire for increased autonomy for the university system from the legislature—New York State recently instituted a policy that gives SUNY control over its tuition setting over a five-year period. The plan includes what SUNY calls a fair, rational, and predictable policy and also includes a maintenance-of-effort provision, which means new tuition dollars are reinvested in the university system with the goal of protecting and enhancing academic programs, allowing for smaller class sizes and better preparing students for postgraduate opportunities.

When it comes to determining resource allocation across an entire system, it is important to consider specific adjustments to ensure no campus is unduly harmed—that is, that no campus experiences an unfair reduction in resources. The best allocation methodologies, however, reduce the reliance on special adjustments and continue farther down the path toward model simplicity. Shared-services plans are one significant way to achieve this because they reduce administrative costs on campuses, allow more resources to be spent on academics and student support services, and reduce the need for a potential administrative subsidy. As part of methodology review, it is helpful to examine and understand the resources provided to campuses in a national context. A study of peer institutions, like the methodology developed by the Maryland Higher Education Commission to fund the colleges in the University System of Maryland, can provide a sense of the appropriateness of funding for each campus (Maryland Higher Education Commission).

Another way to streamline and simplify resource allocation is to look at state-funded, campus-specific programs and initiatives, many of which have been in place for years with little review or adjustment and are potentially outmoded. Eliminating allocations for "single-campus" programs can allow a system to redistribute funding to high-priority areas such as diversity programs, student scholarship and grant programs, and initiatives to support a strategic plan. For example, funding for high-needs programs such as nursing, allied health services, engineering, or technology can be enhanced and a new method for distributing and reviewing the funding implemented.

Shared-Services Initiatives

The concept of sharing services within public university systems is not new. One of the benefits of systemness in large universities is that there is opportunity to share services and promote efficiency so that administrative costs on campuses are reduced and more resources can be channeled to academics and student support services. In just the last few years, several of the largest university systems in the country have implemented shared-services initiatives:

- In 2008, the University System of Georgia instituted a new "shared services" strategy to provide administrators throughout the system's thirty-five public colleges and universities with a new model to handle key business operations. The objectives were to unify and consolidate the system's separate and unconnected business practices; provide enhanced risk management of the state's assets and dollars; maximize efficiency and effectiveness in a large and complex organization with more than 38,000 employees and an annual budget of $6.1 billion; and consolidate payrolls across the institutions. The key advantages of a Shared Services Center include the achievement of economies of scale, the identification and elimination of redundant activities, and the ability to incorporate best practices quickly. Since its inception, the shared-services model has increased quality and enhanced services in the University System of Georgia.
- The University of Wisconsin system, comprising thirteen four-year universities, thirteen two-year colleges, and a statewide Extension Program has a single integrated financial system that provides institutions flexibility and is shared by all financial users in the UW-System. The payroll functions are centralized at the

payroll processing center in Madison. The Central Processing Center processes payroll, maintains systems, regulates and controls the database, establishes standard rules and schedules for all campuses, and remits all employees' payroll deductions for taxes, health insurance, life insurance, garnishments, etc.

• In 2006, the University of Texas system, comprising nine universities and six health science centers, implemented a shared-services plan to consolidate information technology and business services in areas with multiple institutions in close proximity. The initiative was organized around three basic types of shared services: information technology (data center), business systems (software applications), and business processes (supply chain). Today, the plan has not only achieved centralization of services, but it has also enhanced shared governance and permitted greater flexibility, resulting in cost savings through economies of scale, improved processes through standardization and common data definitions, and the application of best practices throughout the system. The initiative has already proven quite valuable by adding more than $250 million of value to the University of Texas system institutions.

• In 2004, Bemidji State University and Northwest Technical College in Bemidji, Minnesota, developed a unique relationship within the Minnesota State Colleges and Universities system. BSU and NTC began to merge many of their operations, including finance and business, some student services, information technology, human resources, and facilities. Significant cost savings have been realized through this process. Currently, the two institutions share the positions of president, vice president for finance and administration, chief human resources/affirmative action officer, and vice president for student development and enrollment. The academic missions of the two institutions continue to be separate and distinct for each; however, the opportunity exists to explore greater collaboration in the future.

SUNY's shared-services initiative was mentioned above in the context of comprehensive strategic enrollment management and innovative resource allocation. Adopted by the Board of Trustees in June 2011, this initiative, which SUNY calls its Campus Alliance Networks, authorized the chancellor to direct the state-operated campuses "to collaboratively develop and implement strategies to improve efficiency, generate cost savings, build capacity, and increase resources available to the core academic and student service missions of campuses" (SUNY Board of Trustees). The intent of the resolution—to redirect resources generated through such cost-saving measures toward the system's academic and strategic missions—tracks with the SUNY strategic planning process and with its core values of collaboration and student centeredness.

Devising shared-services plans requires that institutions within a system work cooperatively to examine their operations for potential savings and develop plans to implement those savings. These plans can include different approaches, including schools partnering on a regional or mission basis to identify and implement shared administrative or business functions now performed individually by each campus. It also can mean fine-tuning efforts to enhance procurement effectiveness and expansion of system-wide contracting opportunities. Reviewing academic programs and course offerings and realigning them where possible to improve academic quality and administrative efficiency are also part of this effort.

The types of specific action examples described above are possible and effective on a large scale only when there is coordinated systemness in place. Further, each initiative is a measure toward fulfilling the university system's goal to put students first—and in doing so, to fulfill its land-grant-driven mission to best serve the needs of the community as a whole.

ᘎ   ᘎ   ᘎ

Justin Morrill's vision indicated a remarkable prescience of national need, for the goals of the land-grant mission reach across the span of 150 years and inform the core goals of major public university systems in the United States today. From his mid-nineteenth-century vantage point, Morrill saw agriculture as the lynchpin of America's economic prosperity, the determiner of the country's future strength and success, with urban industry emerging to play an increasingly important role. Though agriculture continues to be an important part of the American economy, in the twenty-first century it is not the country's mainstay. As the United States evolved from an agrarian society to an industrial one to the increasingly technology-reliant, knowledge-driven one of today, so too have colleges, universities, and university systems evolved in order to meet changing needs.

As the population has grown and the workforce demands of the last several decades have become increasingly specialized and complex, it makes sense that university systems have developed as they have. The most advanced university systems answer the constant call for progress by *driving* it forward while simultaneously *rising to meet* the intellectual, scientific, and social demands that same progress creates. The great challenge for university systems is to make it so that they are not lumbering behemoths crushing under their weight the very institutions and initiatives that form and drive them. Rather, it is essential always to strive to create streamlined systems that operate efficiently so that, first and foremost, they serve students and, by extension, the community, just as the Morrill Act would have it. Doing so successfully will not eliminate all campus-system tensions, especially with research-intensive units that see themselves as flagships, but it will almost certainly work to minimize and mitigate those tensions. It is our view that the benefits of systemness in this regard, as in so many others, far outweigh the costs. Paying attention to lessons learned by other systems is one way to build and fine-tune a system, and knowing what is and is not applicable to a particular system is also an important distinction to be able to make. Because each state is so unique, it follows that each system should be as well.

The correlated missions of public university systems and their land-grant relatives aim to expand access to education while also broadening degree and training offerings that enhance quality of life. This amelioration applies both to the individual, through gaining personal achievement, and, by extension, to society as a whole—because in formulating a mission, and in devising a system to deliver that mission on a large scale, we cultivate a more educated, productive, and fulfilled populace, one that inevitably cultivates thriving, successful economies and communities.

Creating the Future

The Promise of Public Research Universities for America

JAMES J. DUDERSTADT

America's public research universities are the backbone of advanced education and research in the United States today. They conduct most of the nation's academic research (62 percent) while producing the majority of its scientists, engineers, doctors, teachers, and other learned professionals (70 percent). They are committed to public engagement in every area where knowledge and expertise can make a difference: basic and applied research, agricultural and industrial extension, economic development, health care, national security, and cultural enrichment (McPherson and Shulenburger).

Ironically, America's great pubic research universities were not created by the states themselves but instead by visionary federal initiatives. During the early days of the Civil War, Congress passed the Morrill Land-grant Act (1862), which provided revenues from the sale of federal lands to forge a partnership between the states and the federal government aimed at creating public universities capable of extending higher education opportunities to the working class while conducting applied research to enable American agriculture and industry to become world leaders.

Some eighty years later, in the closing days of World War II, a seminal report, drafted by wartime research director Vannevar Bush, persuaded the nation to invest heavily in campus-based research and graduate education through new federal agencies such as the National Science Foundation (Bush). Once again, the key theme was sustaining a close partnership

221

between the federal government, the states, universities, and industry for the conduct of research in the national interest. This shaped the evolution of the American research university as we know it today (Cole).

The public research universities created by these two federal initiatives have become key assets in providing the steady stream of well-educated people, scientific knowledge, and technological innovations central to our robust economy, our vibrant culture, our vital health enterprise, and our security in a complex, competitive, and challenging world. In fact, it was the public research university, through its land-grant tradition, its strong engagement with society, and its commitment to educational opportunity in the broadest sense, that was instrumental in creating the middle class, transforming American agriculture and industry into the economic engine of the world during the twentieth century, and defending democracy during two world wars. Today, public research universities must play a similarly critical role in enabling America to compete in an emerging global economy in which educated citizens, new knowledge, and innovation are key.

Yet today, despite their importance to their states, the nation, and the world, America's public research universities are at great risk. Many states are threatening both the quality and capacity of their public research universities through inadequate funding and intrusive regulation and governance. Rising competition from generously endowed private universities and rapidly evolving international universities threatens their capacity to attract and retain talented students and faculty. While the current budget difficulties faced by the states are painfully apparent, and while the highly competitive nature of American higher education is one of its strongest features, it is also important to recognize that public research universities are critical national assets, key to the nation's economic strength, public welfare, and security. It would be a national disaster if the crippling erosion in state support and predatory competition among institutions were to permanently damage the world-class quality of the nation's public research universities.

Today's Challenges Facing Public Research Universities

Challenge 1: Shifting Public Priorities

Today the nation's public research universities face urgent and at times contradictory marching orders. They are challenged by their states to expand participation in higher education significantly and to increase baccalaureate degree production in an effort to enhance workforce quality. At the same time, the nation depends upon them to produce both the world-class research and the college graduates at all levels necessary to sustain an innovation-driven and globally competitive national economy. Aging populations are increasingly dependent upon the clinical services of their medical centers. Local economies depend both on their talented graduates and their entrepreneurial spinoff of companies to market their research achievements. In an increasingly fragmented and hostile world, the nation continues to depend, for its security, on the science and technology developed on their campuses. Meeting these myriad challenges is increasingly difficult as state support of higher education erodes and political constraints on public institutions multiply.

There is ample evidence from the past three decades of declining support that the states are simply not able—or willing—to provide the resources to sustain growth in public higher education, at least at the rate experienced in the decades following World War II. Despite the growth in enrollments and the demand for university services such as health care and economic development, most states will be hard pressed to sustain even the present capacity and quality of their institutions. In the wake of the recent global financial crisis, many states have already enacted drastic cuts in state appropriations, ranging from 20 to 50 percent (SHEEO). In this budget-constrained climate, public support of higher education and research is no longer viewed as an investment in the future but rather as an expenditure competing with the other priorities of aging populations, such as health care, retirement security, safety from crime, and tax relief. Instead, state governments are urging their research universities to wean themselves from state appropriations by developing and implementing strategies to survive what could be a generation-long period of state support inadequate to maintain their capacity, quality, and reputation.

Challenge 2: The Changing Relationship between Universities and Government

Ironically, even as state support has declined, the effort to regulate universities and hold them accountable has increased. To some degree, this is evidence of governments attempting to retain control over the sector through regulation even as their financial control has waned. Most state governments and public university governing boards tend to view their primary roles as oversight to ensure public or political accountability rather than as stewardship to protect and enhance their institutions so that they are capable of serving both present and future generations. Furthermore, many public research universities today find themselves constrained by university systems, characterized both by bureaucracy and system-wide policies for setting tuition levels and faculty compensation that fail to recognize the intensely competitive environment faced by research universities.

Yet something more fundamental is occurring. While it was once the role of governments to provide for the purposes of universities, today it is now the role of universities to provide for the purposes of government. As costs have risen and priorities for tax revenues have shifted to accommodate aging populations, governments have asked more and more stridently, what are universities for? The imperatives of a knowledge-driven global economy have provided a highly utilitarian answer: to provide the educated workforce and innovation necessary for economic competitiveness. Governments, in other words, increasingly regard universities as delivery agencies for public policy goals in areas such as economic development and workforce skills that may be tangential to their primary responsibilities of education and scholarship (Newby).

While it is certainly true that cost containment and accountability are important issues, it is also the case that most public universities can rightly argue that the main problem for them today is that they are both seriously underfunded through state appropriations and seriously overregulated by state policies in areas such as employment, financial affairs, tuition control, and open meetings requirements. Little wonder that public university leaders are increasingly reluctant to cede control of their activities to state governments. Some institutions are even bargaining for more autonomy from state control as an alternative to restoration of adequate state support, arguing that if granted more control over their own destiny, they can better protect their capacity to serve the public.

Challenge 3: A Rapidly Changing Competitive Environment

The highly competitive nature of higher education in America, where universities compete aggressively for the best faculty members, the best students, resources from public and private sources, athletic supremacy, and reputation, has created an environment that demands achievement.

However, while competition within the higher education marketplace can drive quality, if not always efficiency, it has an important downside. When serious imbalances arise in available funding, policy restrictions, and political constraints, such competition can deteriorate into a damaging relationship that not only erodes institutional quality and capacity, but also more seriously threatens the national interest. It can create an intensely Darwinian winner-take-all ecosystem in which the strongest and wealthiest institutions become predators, raiding the best faculty and students of the less generously supported and more constrained public universities and manipulating federal research and financial policies to sustain a system in which the rich get richer and the poor get devoured (Duderstadt and Womack).

This ruthless and frequently predatory competition poses a particularly serious challenge to the nation's public research universities. These institutions now find themselves caught with declining state support and the predatory wealthy private universities competing for the best students, faculty, and support. Of course, most private universities have also struggled through the recent recession, though for some elite campuses this is the first time in decades they have experienced any bumps in their financial roads. Yet their endowments and private giving will recover rapidly with a recovering economy, and their predatory behavior upon public higher education for top faculty and students will resume once again.

What to Do? Institutional Strategies for the Near Term
Streamlining, Cost-Containment, Productivity Enhancement

Clearly, in the face of the impact of aging populations and the global financial crisis on state and federal budgets and hence on support for higher education, the nation's public research universities must intensify their efforts to increase efficiency and productivity in all of their activities. In particular, they should set bold goals for reducing the costs of their ongoing activities. Many companies have found that cost reductions and productivity enhancement of 25 percent or greater are possible with modern business practices such as lean production and total quality management. While universities have many differences from business corporations—for example, cost reductions do not drop to the bottom line of profits—there is likely a very considerable opportunity for process restructuring in both administrative and academic activities (ITS).

Of course, in the face of deep cuts in state appropriations, most public research universities have already been engaged in intense cost-cutting
efforts, particularly in nonacademic areas such as financial management,
procurement, energy conservation, competitive bidding of services, and
eliminating unnecessary regulation and duplication. They have cut hundreds of millions of dollars of recurring costs from their budgets. But it is
now time to consider bolder actions that require restructuring of academic
activities as well. Some obvious examples include:

- Moving to year-round operation to maximize use of campus
  facilities;
- Working with peer institutions to develop better metrics and
  accounting practices to achieve efficiency and productivity;
- Making more extensive use of information technology (e.g.,
  online learning, research collaboration among institutions, and
  sharing of expensive research facilities);
- Exploring model programs to reduce time to degree (e.g., three-
  year BA/BS and five-year PhD);
- Developing new models for junior faculty development and
  senior faculty retirement.

In fact, it might even be time to take on third-rail issues such as faculty tenure by reconsidering the appropriate balance between the role of
tenure in protecting academic freedom and providing the security of ca-
reer-long employment, particularly in professional schools such as medicine and engineering where professional practice is comparable to faculty
scholarship in determining both faculty contributions and compensation.

Clearly, current financial models for most American research universities are unsustainable and must be restructured (Zemsky; Zemsky,
Massey, and Wegner). Yet, while efficiency, streamlining, cost reductions,
and productivity enhancement are all necessary, eventually stakeholders of
American higher education must address the dramatic decline in research
university support through investments from all sources—federal government (particularly for graduate education), states, private sector, and
students (tuition). As any business executive knows all too well, relying
entirely on cost-cutting and productivity enhancement without attention
to top line revenue growth eventually leads to Chapter 11!

Privatizing the Public University

Declining state support is driving many public research universities to emulate their private counterparts in the development of an entrepreneurial faculty culture and in the manner in which priorities are set and assets are managed (Ehrenberg). In such universities, only a small fraction of operating or capital support comes from state appropriation. Like private universities, these institutions depend on tuition, federal grants and contracts, private gifts, and revenue from auxiliary services such as health care for most of their support.

In fact, many states are encouraging their public universities to reduce the burden of higher education on limited state tax revenues by diversifying their funding sources, for example, by becoming more dependent upon tuition (particularly that paid by out-of-state students), by intensifying efforts to attract gifts and research contracts, and by generating income from intellectual property transferred from campus laboratories into the marketplace. Some states are even encouraging experimentation in creating a more differentiated higher education structure that better aligns the balance between autonomy and accountability with the unique missions of research universities. Examples include Virginia's effort to provide more autonomy in return for accountability for achieving negotiated metrics, Colorado's voucher system, performance funding in South Carolina, and cohort tuition in Illinois (Breneman, "Peering Around the Bend").

Yet such efforts to "privatize" the support of public universities through higher tuition or increasing out-of-state enrollments can also encounter strong public and political opposition, even though there is ample evidence that to date tuition increases at most public institutions have not been sufficient to compensate for the loss in state appropriations (Desrochers and Wellman). Furthermore, since state support is key to the important public university mission of providing educational opportunities to students regardless of economic means, shifting to high tuition funding, even accompanied by increased financial aid, usually leads to a sharp decline in the socioeconomic diversity of students (Haycock; Haycock and Gerald).

The privatizing strategy is flawed for more fundamental reasons. The public character of state research universities runs far deeper than financing and governance and involves characteristics such as their large size, disciplinary breadth, and deep engagement with society through public service. These universities were created as, and today remain, public institutions with a strong public purpose and character. Hence, the issue is not whether the public research university can evolve from a "public" to a "private" institution, or even a "privately funded but publicly committed" university. Rather, the issue is a dramatic broadening of the "publics" that these institutions serve, are supported by, and become accountable to, as state support declines to minimal levels.

Extending the Land-Grant Paradigm to a New Century

The success of the land-grant university suggests that this model could serve as the platform for the further evolution of the public research university. For example, both the role of research universities in contributing to the innovation necessary to compete in a knowledge-driven global economy and the changing nature of the research necessary to stimulate breakthrough discoveries and transfer into the marketplace may require new research paradigms. In particular, with the disappearance of many of the nation's leading industrial research laboratories (e.g., Bell Labs), there is a need for new university-based paradigms to conduct translational research, capable of building the knowledge base necessary to link fundamental scientific discoveries with the technological innovation necessary for the development of new products, processes, and services.

To fill this gap, the federal government has recently launched a series of "innovation hubs" involving research universities, national laboratories, and industry designed to link fundamental scientific discoveries with technological innovations (Duderstadt, Muro, Rahman). In reality, however, this is simply the repurposing of the land-grant agricultural and industrial experiment stations established by the Hatch Act of 1887, a partnership involving higher education, business, and state and federal government that developed and deployed the technologies necessary to build a modern industrial nation for the twentieth century while stimulating local economic growth. The highly successful model of land-grant experiment stations and cooperative extension services can clearly be broadened beyond agriculture and industrial development as an expanded mission for land-grant and other public universities to address major national challenges such as building a sustainable energy infrastructure, providing affordable health care for aging populations, and developing new, globally competitive manufacturing industries. In fact, one might even imagine shifting the nineteenth and twentieth-century land-grant priorities from developing the vast natural resources of a young nation to instead focusing on the key resources of the twenty-first-century knowledge economy: the skills, knowledge, innovation, and entrepreneurial spirit of our people. The field stations and cooperative extension programs—perhaps now as much in cyberspace as in a physical location—could be directed to regional learning and innovation needs.

The land-grant model of linking federal and state investment and interest with higher education and business to serve national and regional needs, while initially intended for agriculture and industry, remains a very powerful paradigm for the conduct of both basic and applied research aimed at a very broad range of contemporary needs and priorities.

What to Do? The State Role

Balancing Governance, Autonomy, and Accountability

Many of the most powerful forces driving change in higher education come from the marketplace, driven by new societal needs, the limited availability of resources, rapidly evolving technologies, and the emergence of new competitors such as for-profit ventures. Clearly, in such a rapidly changing environment, agility and adaptability become important attributes of successful institutions.

Unfortunately, the governance of public universities, whether at the level of state government or institutional governing boards, is more inclined to protect the past than prepare for the future. Furthermore, all of higher education faces a certain dilemma related to its being far easier for a university to take on new missions and activities in response to societal demand than to shed missions as they become inappropriate, distracting, or too costly. This is a particularly difficult matter for public universities because of intense public and political pressures that require these institutions to continue to accumulate missions, each with an associated risk, without a corresponding capacity to refine and focus activities to avoid risk. Examples here would include pressures to launch expensive new academic programs in areas such as medicine or engineering without adequate resources or to embark on high-risk economic development activities through university-business partnerships that may be incompatible with the academic culture. Furthermore, there are many demands from state and federal government, governing boards, and public opinion for increasing accessibility, decreasing costs, and accountability for learning outcomes. All of these forces have long constrained the agility of public universities (Miller).

Little wonder that one finds an increase in the efforts of public research universities to free themselves from the constraints of politically determined governing boards, the tyranny of university systems, and the intrusive regulation of state government in the hope of achieving the autonomy and agility to adapt to a future with limited state support. Steps should be taken to ensure that during a time of great financial stress on flagship public universities, they are provided with the autonomy and agility to restructure their operations to enable them to survive with their quality intact what is likely to be a generation-long period of inadequate state support. After all, should the states intentionally allow their public research universities to decline significantly in quality and capacity, it would be a major blow to the nation's prosperity and security, since public universities are the primary source of advanced degrees and basic research for the United States. Put another way, states should be warned not to add insult to injury by strangling their research universities with unnecessary regulation or intrusion on sensitive political issues such as climate change or gay rights, even as they starve them with inadequate support.

Mission Differentiation and Profiling

It is apparent that the great diversity of higher education needs, both on the part of diverse constituencies (young students, professionals, adult learners) and of society more broadly (teaching, research, economic development, cultural richness), demands a diverse higher education ecosystem of institutional types. Key is the importance of mission differentiation since the availability of limited resources will allow only a small fraction of institutions to become globally competitive as comprehensive research institutions (Duderstadt, "Aligning American Higher Education").

Although most states have flagship state research universities, they also have many other public colleges and universities that aspire to the full array of missions characterizing the comprehensive public research university. Community colleges seek to become four-year institutions; undergraduate colleges seek to add graduate degree programs; and comprehensive universities seek to become research universities. Since all colleges and universities generally have regional political representation, if not statewide influence, they can frequently build strong political support for their ambitions to expand missions. Even in those states characterized by "master plans" such as California, there is evidence of politically driven mission creep, leading to unnecessary growth of institutions and wasteful overlap of programs.

A differentiated system of higher education helps to accomplish the twin goals of enhancing educational opportunity and conducting research of world-class quality. But it assigns different roles in such efforts to various institutions. Clearly, limited resources will allow only a small fraction of institutions to become globally competitive as comprehensive research institutions.

So how many world-class research universities can a state—or the nation, for that matter—really afford? This is a highly charged question that usually engenders strong political rhetoric. But perhaps here we can rely upon (or blame) a calculation once made by David Ward, former president of the American Council of Education and chancellor of the University of Wisconsin-Madison. He estimated that supporting a public world-class research university with an annual budget in excess of $1 billion or more requires the tax base of a population of five million or greater. Ward's calculation would suggest that nationwide we could probably afford sixty of these comprehensive flagships. But here it is also very important to add the caveat that many a university that possesses neither the resources nor the scale to become a comprehensive research university has demonstrated the capacity to mount world-class research and graduate programs in more narrowly defined areas. By focusing resources, many regional universities and independent colleges have managed to create peaks of excellence that make significant contributions in particular areas of scholarship.

What to Do? The Federal Role

The Importance of a National Strategy

Nations around the world have recognized the importance of world-class research universities and are rapidly strengthening their institutions to compete for international students and faculty, resources, reputation, and the impact of university-driven research and advanced education on economic prosperity (Weber and Duderstadt, *Globalization* and *University Research for Innovation*). Yet currently the United States stands apart with no comprehensive policy for enhancing and sustaining its research universities in the face of growing international competition from abroad. In fact, many current federal policies and practices actually harm the competitiveness of American universities, for example, the failure to cover the full costs of federally funded research projects (indirect cost recovery, cost sharing requirements), a research appropriations process that favors political influence rather than national priorities, and regulatory constraints that discourage the recruiting of international students and faculty. There is an urgent need to develop a framework of national policies and funding goals capable of sustaining the nation's research universities at world-class levels, embedded in a broader federal R&D policy that addresses national priorities (National Academies Committee, *Rising Above the Gathering Storm*).

Within the broader framework of United States innovation and R&D policies, it is essential that the nation develop specific goals for sustaining the strong academic research, doctoral education, and research universities key to the nation's capacity to compete, prosper, and achieve national goals for health, energy, the environment, and security in the global community of the twenty-first century. These goals should include a framework of supportive federal funding and public policies adequate to maintain university research and graduate education at world-class levels (Berdahl; McPherson).

Fixing the Flaws

While the federal government continues to be the key sponsor of campus-based research, there is an urgent need for the federal government to end damaging fluctuations in research appropriations and research policy and instead provide steady, sustainable, predictable support for university research over the longer term. This would enable universities to plan their own investments in research facilities and staffing, and it would enable federal research expenditures to become more effective and efficient.

During the past two decades, an era during which external support of campus-based research by federal and industrial sponsors remained at relatively constant levels (at $32 billion per year and $2.5 billion per year, respectively), there has been a very significant growth in research supported from internal university funds, which now amounts to more than $10 billion per year (Berdahl). While some of this university-sponsored research has supported scholarship in important areas such as the humanities and social sciences where external sponsorship is limited, much of the growth in university research expenditures has also been driven by the serious underfunding, cost-sharing requirements, and regulatory burden of the research grants and contracts commissioned from universities by government, industry, and foundations. In fact, the present financial burden associated with research grants from federal agencies is estimated by some universities to be as much as 25 percent of the grant amount. Since the only way for most institutions to subsidize such unsupported costs of federal and industrial research grants is through the reallocation of student tuition revenue or clinical income from patients, universities have been forced into a very awkward and politically volatile position by current federal research policies.

There is an urgent need for the federal government to move over the next several years to cover the full cost of the research projects it funds at academic institutions, and it should do so across all federal agencies and universities in a consistent and transparent manner. Private foundations and industrial sponsors should also be advised not to pressure universities to waive or reduce administrative cost rates below actual expenses. In fact, research universities should actively discourage research grants and contracts characterized by inadequate funding or excessive cost sharing that would require unreasonable subsidies from other university revenue sources such as tuition, clinical income, or donor-specified gifts.

Earlier it was noted that a serious competitive imbalance has arisen in the marketplace for the best faculty, students, and resources, with private research universities now spending almost three times as much to educate each student and 20 percent more for faculty salaries (McPherson, Shulenburger, Gobstein, and Keller). This is due, in part, to the degree to which current federal and state policies in areas such as tax benefits, student financial aid, research funding, and regulation tend to preferentially benefit and subsidize the high-cost nature of private institutions. Since one of the great strengths of American higher education is the presence of a balanced system of world-class public and private research universities, it is important that federal and state policies treat both public and private universities in an equitable manner to achieve quality, diversity, and balance in America's higher education system rather than drive damaging predatory behavior.

Restructuring the Support and Conduct of Graduate Education

The erosion of state support of graduate education and research, particularly in areas of science and technology critical to national interests, suggests that the federal government must play a more significant role in graduate student support. In particular, the federal government should become the primary patron of advanced education in areas key to national priorities such as economic prosperity, public health, and national security, just as it accepted this responsibility for the support of campus-based research in the decades following World War II. Federal support of graduate education should be allocated to universities based on a combination of merit and impact. For example, competitive graduate traineeship programs might be used in some disciplines, while grants for other fields might be based on graduation rates or the size of graduate faculties or student enrollments (much like the capitation grants used in the health sciences). Other grants could be designed to stimulate and support newly emerging disciplines in areas of national priority such as nanotechnology or sustainable energy. A key objective would be a better balance in support among student fellowships, traineeships, and research assistantships.

For their part, research universities should commit to correcting the current flaws in doctoral education and postdoctoral training. Numerous studies confirm a strong consensus that by conducting graduate education in the same institutions where a large portion of the nation's basic research is done, our research universities have created a research and training system that is one of the nation's greatest strengths—and the envy of the rest of the world. Yet it is not surprising that during these times of challenge and change in higher education, the nature and quality of graduate education have also come under scrutiny. The current highly specialized form of graduate education no longer responds to the needs of many students nor of society, as evidenced by the difficulty many recent PhDs have in finding employment. Attrition in many graduate programs has risen to intolerable levels, with more than 50 percent of those who enroll in PhD programs failing to graduate (compared to attrition rates in law and medicine of less than 5 percent), while time to degree has lengthened beyond five years, only to be followed by required postdoctoral service for many disciplines. These factors have eroded the attractiveness of further graduate study for many talented undergraduates who now prefer to enroll in professional programs such as law, medicine, and business characterized by more predictable duration, completion, and compensation. It is time to launch a serious reform of graduate education in American universities comparable to those occurring in other areas of graduate and professional education (e.g., the Flexner Report in medicine).

Jump-Starting the Rebuilding of the Nation's Research Faculty During a Time of Financial Stress

There are compelling needs to replenish the faculties of the nation's research universities with new perspectives and capabilities. Yet it is also the case that many institutions are limited in their ability to add young faculty members by serious financial constraints, particularly in public universities now experiencing serious reductions in state appropriations. Furthermore, the recent recession has shaken the confidence of senior faculty enrolled in defined contribution retirement programs, delaying their decision to retire and resulting in a rapidly aging and heavily tenured faculty cadre without the turnover necessary to open up positions for new junior faculty hires. To address this current challenge, likely to last for the next decade, the National Academies has recently proposed a federal program of matching grants to establish endowments for the support of faculty positions, modeled after highly successful programs at the University of California Berkeley and in Canada (Birgeneau and Yery; Canada Research Chairs).

For the Longer Term: Broadening the Concept of the Public Research University

The American university has changed quite considerably over the past two centuries and continues to evolve today. Colonial colleges have become private research universities; religious colleges formed during the early nineteenth century gradually became independent colleges; junior colleges have evolved into community colleges and then into regional universities. Today public research universities continue to evolve to adapt to changes in students (from state to national to global), support (from state to national, public to private), missions (from regional to national to global), and perception (from education as a public good to a private benefit). They are rapidly expanding their public purpose far beyond the borders of their states, since the more mobile the society and global the economy, the broader the "publics" served by the university.

This broadening of the public purpose of the public research university is not only mandated by national and global needs for its services, but is also a consequence of the changing motivation of the states to invest in world-class institutions. At a time when the strength, prosperity, and welfare of nations demand a highly educated citizenry and institutions with the ability to discover new knowledge, develop innovative applications of discoveries, and transfer them into the marketplace through entrepreneurial activities, such vital national needs are no longer top state priorities (Courant, Duderstadt, and Goldenberg). The model of state-based support of graduate education and research made sense when university expertise was closely tied to local natural resource bases such as agriculture, manufacturing, and mining. But today's university expertise has implications far beyond state borders. Highly trained and skilled labor has become more mobile and innovation more globally distributed. Most of the benefits from the graduate training and research conducted at state research universities are public goods that provide only limited returns to the states in which they are located.

Hence, it should be no surprise that today many states, caught between the financial pressures of weakened economies and the political pressure of Tea Party activists, have concluded that they cannot, will not, and probably should not invest to sustain world-class quality in graduate education and research, particularly at the expense of other priorities such as broadening access to baccalaureate education or addressing the needs of aging populations. Unfortunately, today not only is state support woefully inadequate to achieve state goals, but state goals no longer accumulate to meet national needs.

While the declining priority that states have given to public higher education may be politically acceptable in the near term, though certainly not for their long-term prosperity, such a strategy could have disastrous consequences for the nation. The scientists and engineers, physicians and teachers, humanists and artists, and designers, innovators, and entrepreneurs produced by public research universities are absolutely vital to national prosperity, security, health, and quality of life in the global, knowledge-driven economy. It is clear that the production of these critical assets can no longer be left dependent on shifting state priorities and declining state support. It is essential to realign responsibilities for support of America's public research universities such that advanced graduate and research programs of major importance to the nation are both supported by and held accountable to the needs of key stakeholders beyond state borders. Here it should be noted that both the unusually broad intellectual needs of the nation and the increasing interdependence of the academic disciplines provide compelling reasons why such federal support should encompass all areas of scholarship including the natural sciences, the social sciences, the humanities, the arts, and professional disciplines such as engineering, education, law, and medicine.

More specifically, one might consider a hybrid structure for the public research university that is better distributed for both support and governance among the states, students, the federal government, industry, and private donors:

- The states, consistent with their current priorities for enhancing workforce quality, would focus their limited resources on providing access to quality education at the associate and baccalaureate levels, augmented by student tuition and private philanthropy.
- Students (and parents) would continue to provide support through tuition and fees, although perhaps increasingly augmented by need-dependent financial aid grants and income-contingent student loans.
- The federal government, in addition to being the leader in supporting university research, would become the primary patron of advanced education at the graduate level (i.e., master's and doctoral degree programs) across all academic disciplines (natural and social sciences, humanities, and the arts) through a coordinated system of fellowships, traineeships, and graduate student assistantships.
- Professional schools enabling high-income careers such as law, business administration, and medicine would become predominantly privately supported through high tuition (enabled by strong financial aid/loan programs) and private giving, similar to private universities.
- Foundations and individual donors would continue to play a major role in the support of both education and scholarship in selected areas while enabling the broader roles of the university such as the preservation of knowledge and culture and serving as an informed critic of society. Yet it should also be acknowledged

that while such private support will become increasingly important, for most public institutions it will provide only the margin of excellence on a funding base primarily dependent upon state support and student tuition.

Of course, such an approach would require a new social contract to reflect not only the interests of the states but those of the expanding array of stakeholders providing support for such hybrid institutions. Clearly, not only the governance but the statutory responsibility and authority of these emerging institutions would need to be renegotiated. In view of the likely inability of the states to sustain the essential contributions of their research universities at a world-class level, such an evolutionary path seems not only possible but perhaps inevitable.

The Future of the Public Research University in America

An important theme throughout the history of American higher education has been the evolution of the public university. The nation's vision and commitment to create public universities competitive in quality with the best universities in the world were a reflection of the democratic spirit of a young America. With an expanding population, a prosperous economy, and imperatives such as national security and industrial competitiveness, the public was willing to make massive investments in higher education. While elite private universities were important in setting the standards and character of higher education in America, it was the public university that provided the capacity and diversity to meet our nation's vast needs for postsecondary education and research.

Today, however, in the face of limited resources and the pressing social priorities of aging populations, this expansion of public support of higher education has slowed. While the needs of our society for advanced education and research will only intensify as we continue to evolve into a knowledge-driven global society, it is not evident that these needs will be met by further expansion of our existing system of state universities. The terms of the social contract that led to these institutions are changing rapidly. The principle of general tax support for public higher education as a public good and the partnership between the states, the federal government, and the universities for the conduct of basic research and education, established in 1862 by the Morrill Act and reaffirmed a century later by post–World War II research policies, are both at risk.

These forces are already driving major change in the nature of the nation's public research universities. One obvious consequence of declining state support has been the degree to which many leading public universities may increasingly resemble private universities in the way they are financed, managed, and governed, even as they strive to retain their public character. Public universities forced to undergo this privatization transition—or, in more politically acceptable language, "self-sufficiency"—in financing must appeal to a broader array of constituencies at the national—indeed, international—level, while continuing to exhibit a strong mission focused on state needs. In the same way as private universities, they must earn the majority of their support in the competitive marketplace, that is, via tuition, research grants, and private giving, and this will require actions that come into conflict from time to time with state priorities. Hence, the autonomy of the public university will become one of its most critical assets, perhaps even more critical than state support for many institutions.

In view of this natural broadening of the institutional mission, coupled with the increasing inability (or unwillingness) of states to support their public research universities at world-class levels, it is even possible to conclude that the world-class "state" research university may have become an obsolete concept. Instead, many of America's leading public research universities may evolve rapidly into "regional," "national," or even "global" universities with a public purpose to serve far broader constituencies than simply the citizens of a particular state who no longer are able or willing to provide sufficient support to sustain their programs at world-class levels. In fact, one might well argue that states today would be better off if they encouraged their flagship public research universities to evolve into institutions with far broader missions (and support), capable of accessing global economic and human capital markets to attract the talent and wealth of the world to their regions.

How might institutions embark on this path to serve far broader public constituencies without alienating the people of their states—or risking their present (albeit low) level of state support? One constructive approach would be to attempt to persuade the public—and particularly the media—that public research universities are vital to states in a far more multidimensional way than simply education alone—through health care, economic development, pride (intercollegiate athletics), the production of professionals (doctors, lawyers, engineers, and teachers), and so forth. The challenge is to shift the public perception of public research universities from that of a consumer to that of a producer of state resources. One might argue that for a relatively modest contribution toward their educational costs, the people of their states receive access to the vast resources, and benefit from the profound impact, of some of the world's great universities. It seems clear that we need a new dialogue concerning the future of public higher education in America, one that balances its democratic purpose with economic and social imperatives.

Today we face the challenges of a hypercompetitive global, knowledge-driven society in which other nations have recognized the positive impact that building world-class public universities can have. America already has them. They are one of our nation's greatest assets. Preserving their quality and capacity will require not only sustained investments but also significant paradigm shifts in university structure, management, and governance. It also will likely demand that public research universities broaden their public purpose and stakeholders far beyond state boundaries. Preserving the quality and capacity of the extraordinary resource represented by our public research universities must remain a national priority, even if the support required to sustain these institutions at world-class levels is no longer viewed as a priority by our states.

Challenges to Equilibrium

The Place of the Arts and Humanities in Public Research Universities

DANIEL MARK FOGEL

A discussion of the importance and value of the arts and humanities seems to me to be essential to the architecture of a volume that otherwise would not only have omitted an intrinsic element of Justin Morrill's vision and legacy but also would have missed a chance to correct a disturbing imbalance in the reigning cases for support of public higher education. Those cases appeal heavily to the vocational aims of higher education and to the undeniable importance of university-based research for economic development, innovation, and national competitiveness—always emphasizing research in science, technology, engineering, and mathematics (the STEM disciplines). When the case for higher education touches at all on the arts and humanities (or, for that matter, on such traditional social sciences as political theory and anthropology), it is almost always to attribute to them some marketable utility. Typically, communication skills and a capacity for critical thinking are valued as prerequisites for business success, or modern language and area studies as handmaidens of global commerce. With a little more flair, the arts may be invoked as drivers of "the creative economy," or, alternatively, liberal education may get a perfunctory nod as important to citizenship in a democracy. Probably the most influential case statement for research and education of the last ten years—the National Academies' superb 2005 report *Rising Above the Gathering Storm: Energizing and Employing America for a Brighter Economic Future*—was very effectively focused on the STEM disciplines and their importance for economic vitality and competitiveness and for national power, with hardly so much as an implied reference to any other disciplines.[1]

Even for those who do not in their hearts place the STEM disciplines above all others, the temptation to promote public higher education to policymakers as offering high returns on investment is irresistible. In asserting a university claim on declining public resources, proponents of higher education are eager to promise big bang for the public buck in terms to which legislators, business executives, and opinion leaders are presumed most likely to assent. I have made that pitch many times myself in the Vermont statehouse to Education and Appropriations committees as well as to chambers of commerce and to Rotary Clubs. In an opinion piece I wrote for the *Washington Post* in October 2005, I recalled the lecture my fourth grade teacher delivered with fearsome vividness in 1957, right after the launch of Sputnik (the message was that "we would all have to buckle down, focus, and apply ourselves assiduously to the study of math and science"). I went on to describe the intensity I had recently observed in the students at China's leading technological university, Tsinghua. And I asked, "Do our students understand that they must work at least as long, as hard and as smart as their Chinese peers if we are to maintain a viable place in the economy of a Chinese century?" We do what we have to do—if the argument of this essay is taken as a critique of all who have resorted to making utilitarian and economic cases for support of public higher education, then I myself plead guilty. I would argue that we have virtually no choice, given our fiduciary responsibilities to our institutions, except to make the only case that seems to have any currency. But we do so at a real cost, and it is incumbent on us to take stock of that cost and to be as constructive as we can in offsetting it by instituting corrective and recuperative measures.

First, however, I want to come back to the proposition that a treatment of the land-grant movement that leaves out liberal education would not be true to Justin Morrill's legacy, a vision of democratic opportunity in education across all disciplines, concisely captured in Ezra Cornell's motto for his land-grant university, "I would found an institution where any person can find instruction in any study" (Cornell). In sponsoring the Land-grant Act, Morrill was motivated by his urgent sense that the United States must not fall behind Europe in the advancement of agricultural science and technology. The historic legislation was headed thus: "AN

ACT Donating Public Lands to the several States and Territories which may provide Colleges for the Benefit of Agriculture and Mechanic Arts." But the text of the act that followed was careful to stipulate that colleges that derived support from its provisions were not to exclude "other scientific and classical studies," for the overriding purpose of the legislation was to enable the states to "promote the *liberal and practical education* of the industrial classes in the several pursuits and professions of life" (emphasis added). Not only were "classical studies" and "liberal education" specified as essential to the purposes of the Act from the outset, but years later, when Morrill spoke of the Act, he placed considerable emphasis on the inclusion in the founding idea of the importance of the liberal arts. In late June 1887 at ceremonies observing the twenty-fifth anniversary of the Land-grant Act, he spoke at the Massachusetts Agricultural College (now the University of Massachusetts-Amherst). It is worth quoting an entire paragraph from his address:

> The Land-grant Colleges were founded on the idea that a higher and broader education should be placed in every state within the reach of those whose destiny assigns them to, or who may have the courage to choose industrial vocations where the wealth of nations is produced; where advanced civilization unfolds its comforts, and where a much larger number of the people need wider educational advantages, and impatiently await their possession. The design was to open the door to a liberal education for this large class at a cheaper cost from being close at hand, and to tempt them by offering not only sound literary instruction, but something more applicable to the productive employments of life. It would be a mistake to suppose it was intended that every student should become either a farmer or mechanic when the design comprehended not only instruction for those who may hold the plow or follow a trade, but such instruction as any person might need—with "the world all before them where to choose"—and without the exclusion of those who might prefer to adhere to the classics.

The allusion to the closing lines of *Paradise Lost* ("The world was all before them, where to choose/Their place of rest") was nicely calculated to set up the conclusion of the paragraph, which Morrill ended thus:

Milton in his famous discourse on education, gives a definition of
what an education ought to be, which would seem to very completely cover all that was proposed by the Land Grant Colleges;
and Milton lacked nothing of ancient learning, nor did he suffer his culture to hide his stalwart republicanism. He says: "I call,
therefore, a complete and generous education, that which fits a
man to perform justly, skillfully and magnanimously all the offices, both private and public, of peace and war."

Here is strong testimony that liberal education was, by legislative intent,
integral to the design of the land-grant college system from the very start.[2]

One hundred and fifty years later, some may be inclined to dismiss
Justin Morrill's insistence on liberal education as a foundation of the land-
grant college idea as an obligatory nod to nineteenth-century pieties. If so,
it was a long nod, since Morrill was saying as much from 1862 to 1887. Far
from being a truism, moreover, Morrill's affirmation of the value of liberal
education contrasted sharply with the views of many contemporaries. As
Frank Donoghue shows in the first chapter of *The Last Professors: The Corporate University and the Fate of the Humanities,* the hostility between the
world of business and industry and the academy—with the humanities
dead center in the crosshairs—has been building for more than a century.
Four years after Morrill spoke at the Massachusetts Agricultural College,
Andrew Carnegie told the graduating class of 1891 at the Pierce College
of Business and Shorthand in Philadelphia that he rejoiced "that your time
has not been wasted upon dead languages, but has been fully occupied in
obtaining a knowledge of typing and shorthand" and avowed that "the
only worthwhile education is that which has 'bearing on a man's career
if he is to make his way to fortune'" (Donoghue 3–4). Donoghue notes
that such assaults on the content and conduct of higher education intensified in the early years of the last century. He mentions Clarence Birdseye
(inventor of modern methods of food preservation by freezing), who authored *Individual Training in Our Colleges* (1907), promoting alignment
of higher education with "business principles" (Donoghue 4). He cites
a series of attacks on higher education (1909 to 1911) by manufacturer
Richard Teller Crane, whose outright assault on liberal education disdains
"impractical, special knowledge of literature, art, languages or history." No
man, said Crane, who has "a taste for literature has the right to be happy,"
for "the only men entitled to happiness in this world are those who are
useful" (Donoghue 6). An article titled "Shall the University Become a

Business Corporation" by Henry S. Pritchett, president of MIT, inspired Andrew Carnegie to found the Carnegie Foundation for the Advancement of Teaching and to recruit Pritchett as its founding president.[3] In 1910, the foundation brought out as its first report *Academic and Industrial Efficiency*, by the prominent engineer Morris Llewellyn Cooke, a disciple of the father of scientific management theory, Frederick Winslow Taylor. Governing boards (already largely dominated by business executives) and senior campus administrators reconfigured university operations and programs, including curricula, to align them with corporate metrics and analytics designed to promote efficiency and productivity. Defenders of the academy sought to circle the wagons, with defenses ranging from Thorstein Veblen's moderate and conciliatory *The Higher Learning in America* (1916) to the aggressive counterattack launched by Upton Sinclair in *The Goose Step: A Study in American Education* (1923).[4]

World War II marked an epoch in American civilization and in higher education, with short, mid-term, and long-term consequences for almost all academic domains, not least of all the arts and humanities. In 1940, only 4.6 percent of the American population had completed four or more years of college; by 2005, the percentage among adults twenty-five and older had grown to 28 percent. In the years leading up to the war, the percentage of high school leavers continuing to college had increased threefold—from 2.5 percent in 1900 to 7.5 percent by the time the United States entered the war. But since the Allied victory of 1945, the percentage has multiplied nearly tenfold, rising steeply and rapidly to 45 percent by 1960 and then, settling into a more gradual upward trajectory, to 70 percent by 2009. That huge growth was spurred by many factors, including increased access for women and minorities. The initial postwar boost in institutional capacity to accommodate rapidly swelling enrollments was tied to the only single piece of legislation that rivals the Morrill Land-grant Act in its importance in the history of American human capital production, the GI Bill. Because public higher education experienced far greater growth than private higher education, making public colleges and universities the principal receivers of matriculating war veterans, that historic opening of access to a college degree may in some sense be considered a secondary echo of the Land-grant Act. And the same can be said of the consequent rise of the American middle class and of national prosperity in the second half of the twentieth century.

The war effort had drawn heavily, moreover, on academic expertise, for example on the university-based scientists who streamed from Berkeley,

Chicago, Columbia, Cornell, Harvard, MIT, Princeton, and other universities to the Manhattan Project as well as on social scientists, and, yes, humanists. Economists and mathematicians were enlisted to manage the wartime economy and to bring their analytic tools to the calculation of logistical and tactical effectiveness and efficiency (for example, to the development of algorithms to optimize the selection of bombing targets). Rapid advances in radar, sonar, and communications were the work not only of physicists, chemists, engineers, but also of literary scholars such as M. H. Abrams, who worked throughout the war at the Psycho-Acoustic Laboratory at Harvard. Rapid postwar expansion of university research capacity in science and engineering, inspired by the experience of wartime research and development (R&D), was fueled by the rise of federal funding for academic research, a development that was novel and of such a great scale as to be genuinely revolutionary. The new order of federally sponsored academic R&D was championed most notably by Vannevar Bush, who had been vice president and Dean of Engineering at MIT for half a dozen years before his election as president of the Carnegie Institution in 1938. As director of the wartime Office of Scientific Research and Development, he oversaw not only the Manhattan Project but also the development of radar, sonar, the Norden bomb sight, and many other technologies, all arguably keys to Allied victory. As a great entrepreneur of strategic big science, as a close advisor to presidents Roosevelt and Truman, and as a public intellectual, Bush promoted the rationale for government funding of scientific research and the rise of government agencies to allocate and administer the funds—a rationale that drew an unbroken current of energy from the experience of World War II and the perceived imperatives of the cold war, exemplified by the shock of the Soviet Sputnik launch (October 1957) and the passage of the National Defense Education Act less than a year later (September 1958).

Public investment in university-based research was channeled through government agencies such as the National Science Foundation, the National Institutes of Health, the Department of Defense, the Department of Energy, and many others. The universities themselves saw the creation of institutional research offices (to ensure that the metrics required for government reporting and compliance were continuously compiled and updated), offices of sponsored research administration (pre- and post-award), and beefed-up compliance, internal audit, and reporting functions. The transformation of the modern research university into a complex and increasingly bureaucratic corporation run on modern business principles, which accelerated in the early years of the twentieth century, was supercharged in the postwar boom. The academy thus participated in the corporatization of American life to which millions had become habituated through wartime mass mobilization in vast impersonal organizations such as the United States Army, and became aligned not only with corporate values and operating tenets but also very intensively and intentionally with the military-industrial complex. This development, moreover, pertained much more to research universities than to liberal arts colleges, and the two types of institution thus grew farther apart than ever before, differing not only in scale and degree but also increasingly, and radically, in kind.

Liberal arts colleges remained havens for the arts and humanities, but they were almost exclusively private. The vast majority of undergraduate students were enrolled in public institutions, which also housed the majority of the American professoriate. And while the arts and humanities departments in the public research universities grew with their mushrooming institutions to accommodate the new societal presumption that college was no longer a privileged bastion of the elite but a prerequisite for success in life for almost anyone with aspirations to attain or sustain middle-class status—and with doctoral programs in fields such as English booming through the 1960s and into the early 1970s—nevertheless professors in fields such as the modern languages and literatures, history, classics, art history, philosophy, music, theatre, the studio arts, dance, and creative writing have felt increasingly marginalized and embattled over the course of the last forty years.

The distress of faculty in the arts and humanities goes well beyond hand wringing over the changing demographics and economics of their disciplines, though there has been plenty of well-documented fulmination over the decades about a crisis in this or that discipline or set of disciplines or in the humanities generally. Some of the angst has specific, measurable objective correlatives. Prominent among these are the recurrent employment crises for new PhDs in fields such as English and history. In January 2011, for instance, *Perspectives on History* (a publication of the American Historical Association) reported that the number of jobs posted with the AHA fell 29.4 percent in 2009–10, to the lowest point in twenty-five years. Similarly, in a mid-year report on the 2009–10 Modern Language Association Job Information List, MLA reports one-year drops of 27.5 percent (for jobs in English) and of 26.7 percent (for jobs in the foreign languages), with the two-year drop of 45.2 percent (English) and 46.4

percent (foreign languages) "the steepest downtown in the thirty-five-year history of our counts" (1).

Behind these numbers lies real heartbreak. In 2009–10, nearly one thousand (989) new PhDs in history entered a job market with only 569 openings. The MLA report suggests that the higher education system is able to absorb annually only about four hundred of the roughly one thousand new PhDs in English produced each year, and only about 280 of about six hundred new PhDs produced annually in foreign languages. As a gauge of the human cost underlying the data, consider that in fields such as English and history only about one-half of students have completed their degrees ten years after first enrolling, and between one-fifth (history) and one-quarter (English) of the non-completers are still enrolled after ten years—long rows to hoe when the odds of employment, even as non–tenure track faculty, are so low. Faculty are further disheartened that the tenure track jobs they have rightly understood to be bulwarks of academic freedom, of the autonomy of the individual faculty member, and of shared governance are declining as a proportion of all faculty appointments, with part-time and full-time non–tenure eligible faculty now representing about 70 percent of all postsecondary faculty appointments nationwide. While the shift to such "contingent faculty" is most pronounced in the community college sector, it is increasingly the case in public research universities that all or nearly all the teaching in lower-division general education courses—including those in humanities fields such as English with typically heavy "service" teaching loads—is delivered by graduate teaching assistants and contingent faculty.

To cap the statistical gloom, the number of students studying in many arts and humanities fields has declined over the past half century. The visual and performing arts are in part an exception to the general trend, particularly at the bachelor's level, with graduates growing in absolute numbers and as a percentage of all degrees, from 30,395 in 1970–71 (3.6 percent) to 89,140 in 2008–09 (5.5 percent); the arts also saw an increase over the same span of time in master's production, from 6,675 to 14,918 (though at this degree level the percentage of all master's fell, from 2.9 percent to 2.3 percent). But in English, by contrast, bachelor's degree production peaked in 1971 at a little over 64,000, representing 7.6 percent of all bachelor's degrees awarded, whereas in 2009, the nearly 55,000 bachelor's awarded in English came to just under 3.5 percent of all bachelor's degrees. Similarly, English doctoral production peaked in 1973 at a little more than 1,900, representing just under 5.6 percent of all doctorates awarded that year, whereas in 2009 the 1,264 doctorates in the field represented just 2 percent of all doctoral production. The story in history is similar—a fall from nearly 45,000 bachelor's in 1971 (5.31 percent of all bachelor's degrees) to 34,704 in 2009 (just 2.2 percent), and from 1,140 doctorates in 1973 (3.28 percent of all doctoral degrees) to 926 in 2009 (just 1.51 percent). The same trend is manifested in languages and literatures other than English.

The distress among academic humanists and artists about these challenging realities is genuine and, for many, acute. Underlying these concerns, moreover, are deeper wellsprings of disquiet, some arising from political challenges inside and outside the academy, some from the persistence of a strong strain in American culture that marries utilitarianism to outright anti-intellectualism, and some from philosophical and even metaphysical interrogations of the value of academic work in the arts and humanities.

There are many aspects of the political marginalization of the arts and humanities inside the academy. Because the prestige of research universities is tied to external funding for research concentrated in science and technology disciplines, the arts and humanities are often marginalized in the rhetoric of institutional leaders, in their strategic and tactical agendas, and finally in resource allocation. Indeed, both intentionally and sometimes it seems almost without thinking (or acknowledging or even knowing that this is the case) administrators regularly export tuition dollars generated in low-cost areas like English to high-cost areas such as the physical and life sciences and engineering. Given the ascendancy of science and technology disciplines in the academic pecking order, it is hardly surprising that faculty in the arts and the humanities find themselves chafing under paradigms for measuring and rewarding the productivity and outcomes of faculty work that suit most research scientists reasonably well but that seem to most artists and humanists to do violence to any just appreciation of the nature of their teaching, creative activity, and scholarship. Here is a representative cry of protest from an English professor writing in a recent issue of *The Chronicle of Higher Education*: "For what I teach and what I seek to do—and for the . . . humanities in general—the assessment, accountability, and quantifiable outcomes movement is nothing less than a benighted Enlightenment fantasy of mastering the unmasterable, of quantifying what cannot be measured" (Cary Nelson).

Outside the academy, intensified concerns about the return on tuition investments that represent an increasingly high percentage of stagnant household incomes have raised the stock of vocationally oriented fields of study and have devalued areas of studies that are less certain of immediate payoff—English, philosophy, or history, anyone? Painting or dance? The politics of austerity have obvious harmonic resonance with the ongoing reverberations of culture wars over the last quarter of a century, which have largely featured disparaging attacks on academic humanists, as typified, for example, by Allan Bloom's *The Closing of the American Mind* (1987), Dinesh D'Souza's *Illiberal Education: The Politics of Race and Sex on Campus* (1998), and, more recently, by David Horowitz's *Reforming Our Universities: The Campaign for an Academic Bill of Rights* (2010) and Naomi Schaefer Riley's *The Faculty Lounges: And Other Reasons Why You Won't Get the College Education You Paid For* (2011).

For demoralized academic practitioners of the arts and humanities the standard defenses of their work offer little comfort. That a degree in English or history is good preparation for professional schools, that communication skills and critical thinking skills cultivated in general education humanities courses prepare one for success in the workplace, and similar propositions, however true, speak only to the use-value of limited aspects of teaching in the arts and humanities, merely as means to ends that can be monetized. The utilitarian rationales patently do not speak to the intrinsic value in and of itself of academic work in the arts and humanities, but unless that can be done persuasively anyone alert to the pressures of the present time knows the writing is on the wall that more and more of the teaching in these fields will be done by low-paid contingent faculty with little or no institutional or public expectation of or support for their engaging in scholarship or in the practice of their arts. The rationale for humanities scholarship that Stanley Fish rests on in a recent *New York Times* blog ("Crisis of the Humanities II," December 10, 2010)—that "the real benefit" of work in the humanities "is experienced by scholars who work in the field . . . and by scholars in neighboring or even distant fields" who see "a model or a vocabulary that will help them negotiate an impasse in their work," that "the real benefit, in short, is internal to the enterprise"—may be intellectually appealing to some. But it is a rationale so hermetically sealed within the academic domain that it offers little comfort to embattled humanists and artists and little real hope that presidents and chancellors could sell that rationale when asking state legislatures for money, though Fish suggests "it might even work"—and wouldn't it be, as he himself might say, nice to think so? But in a climate conditioned by the dogmatic insistence that we can no longer afford to support critical social services for the needy or investments in vital public infrastructure, what are the real odds of making a winning case for investment in scholarship and artistic activity essentially for their own sake?

More intellectually compelling than Fish's account of the benefit derived from the academic study of the humanities—and politically and morally far more comprehensive and challenging—is Martha Nussbaum's *Not for Profit: Why Democracy Needs the Humanities* (2010). Drawing heavily on the philosophies of John Dewey and of Rabindranath Tagore, Nussbaum deplores the cutting away of the arts and humanities "in both primary/secondary and college/university education, in virtually every nation in the world." Everywhere, she says, the arts and humanities are deemed to be "useless frills, at a time when nations must cut away all useless things in order to stay competitive in the global marketplace." "If this trend continues," she suggests, "nations all over the world will soon be producing generations of useful machines, rather than complete citizens who can think for themselves." Nussbaum sees the trend as sweeping up other broad disciplinary domains as well: "What we might call the humanistic aspects of science and social science—the imaginative, creative aspect, and the aspect of rigorous critical thought—are also losing ground as nations prefer to pursue short-term profit by the cultivation of the useful and highly applied skills suited to profit-making" (Nussbaum 2–3). The cost, she argues, is a loss in the capacity for "rich human relationships, rather than relationships of mere use and manipulation," and with that the forfeiture of any chance for the continuing success of democracy "because democracy is built upon respect and concern, and these in turn are built upon the ability to see other people as human beings, not simply as objects" and "to imagine sympathetically the predicament of another person" (Nussbaum 6–7). Nussbaum's powerful argument, however, boils down to saying that education in the arts and humanities is essential to the formation of the thoughtful, compassionate citizens she believes a humane democracy requires, in essence a subset of the general argument for education as foundational for citizenship. That position, however eloquently and frequently presented, has not stanched—and surely cannot by itself be expected to stanch—the hemorrhagic decline of tax-financed funding for public higher education.

If Nussbaum is right, however, then it is essential not only to faculty in the arts and humanities but also to the well-being of the nation that the public institutions educating the vast majority of our tertiary degree holders maintain strong programs in the arts and humanities. And yet, as was recognized by participants in a conference hosted by the University of Michigan's ArtsEngine on "The Role of Art-Making and the Arts in the Research University" in May 2011, "the case has not been made in a sufficiently sophisticated way" and faces significant challenges, including "disciplinary trends, cultural assumptions about the arts, the paucity of relevant research on student learning, the current fiscal state in higher ed, and ongoing debate about the purposes and value of a college education." As a contribution to meeting such challenges, I want to conclude by offering some further rationales for support of the arts and humanities in our land-grant and public research universities, as well as a modest prescription for presidents, chancellors, and other advocates of public higher education.

There is a nexus perhaps too poorly understood outside of the academy between the institution of tenure, so closely tied to academic freedom and the autonomy of the individual scholar, and the value of university-based research. If you are a social scientist—for example, an economist or agricultural economist—you can come out against price supports for the dairy industry, if that is the position to which your research leads you, even if you are employed by a public university in a dairy state, but only provided that you have tenure: if you do not, there is a good chance that commodity agriculture will have the political muscle to take you out. Only through a high degree of tolerance for work that has no present use-value or foreseeable application, moreover, are we able to foster, on a broad scale, the advance of pure knowledge and of basic understandings of the world in which we live. Since attacks on tenure are endemic among business leaders, it was refreshing and in fact inspiring to hear in March 2011 former vice chairman of the Ford Motor Company Allan D. Gilmour, now president of Wayne State University, tell a group of United States senators that universities are more important today than ever before as sites of basic research because of the abandonment by industry of such fabled research operations as AT&T's Bell Laboratories. Major innovations by business and industry, Gilmour told the senators, are often built upon research for which no immediate application is contemplated or foreseen. Again, tenure is germane here: faculty members who have now become the principal stewards of the nation's basic research capacity are only able to pursue their research free of political interference and the expectation of immediate utility because they enjoy the academic freedom and autonomy that tenure alone can confer. If you are a chemist employed by industry, then you work on what you are told to work on, almost always with product-related, profit-driven outcomes in mind. But if you are a tenured chemist at the most outcomes-oriented land-grant institution we can imagine, you are still free to follow your own inclinations in selecting your research topics and you can report, and teach, your findings as you see them. The arts and humanities are the canary in the mine for all academic disciplines—if our institutions of higher learning lose their commitment to apparently "useless" scholarship and creative activity in the arts and humanities, then that commitment may well be imperiled over time for every disciplinary domain, with potentially grave long-term consequences for all of the human and societal benefits that can and do flow from work that was once seen as useless.

Some may rejoin that between basic research in the physical and life sciences that may someday contribute to unforeseen applications and humanities scholarship and artistic activity that only by a stretch can be supposed to provide any discernible societal benefit there is a vast difference. In an essay published in 1972, M. H. Abrams observes, "Rather than to exaggerate the commonalty of method in science and criticism, it would be more profitable to say that while criticism involves the use of logic and scientific method, it must go far beyond their capacities if it is to do its proper job . . . initiating its chief functions in an area where these simplified calculi stop, for the models of logic and of scientific method achieve their extraordinary efficiency and their diverse modes of certainty by the device of systematically excluding just those features of experience that, humanly speaking, matter most." For Abrams, critical discourse operates in a region "where the rules are uncodified and elusive and there is room for the play of irreducible temperamental differences, yet decisions and judgments are not arbitrary, but are subject to broad criteria such as coherent-incoherent, adequate-omissive, penetrating-silly, just-distorting, revealing-obfuscatory, disinterested-partisan, better-worse," and where knowledge, though not judged by the "alien criterion" of scientific certainty "must satisfy an equivalent criterion in its own realm of discourse, for which, in lieu of a specialized term, we use a word like valid, or sound." Then, invoking Wittgenstein on "language-games" and J. L. Austin on the recognition that "language is not an ideal form, but is designed for use 'in the human predicament,'" Abrams concludes thus:

> One way to describe criticism and related modes of inquiry is to say that they are a language-game—or a family of language games—designed to cope in a rational way with those aspects of

the human predicament in which valid knowledge and understanding are essential, but certainty is impossible. This is of course
an extremely difficult undertaking, but as Wittgenstein remarks,
what cannot be gainsaid is, "This language game is played"; and
what its great exponents have achieved shows how well and how
profitably the game can in fact be played. The name of this game
is the humanities. (Abrams 52–54)

The arts, like the humanities that "theorize about the arts," are also
in their own diverse ways modes of inquiry into, and expressions of, the
human predicament—and in some respects I would say that the arts and
humanities are not simply the canary in the mine but the mine itself, or
at least one of the richest lodes of ore within it. And how, without them,
might we expect those burdened with the power for good and for ill of
scientific and technological knowledge to make wise decisions in those
domains where, as Abrams says, "knowledge and understanding are essential, but certainty is impossible," the domains of policy and ethics, of competing choices and conflicting goods, and of human costs and benefits?

No one of course knows the limitations of science better than our
best scientists. In his Nobel Prize biography, chemist Roald Hoffmann
writes that "[p]erhaps we scientists do [have knowledge that is barred
to humanists], but in such carefully circumscribed places of the universe," whereas, he continues, "[p]oetry soars, all around the tangible, in
deep dark, through a world we reveal and make" (Hoffmann). Similarly,
physicist Freeman Dyson observes in a highly favorable review of Daniel
Kahneman's *Thinking Fast and Slow* that Kahneman's method as a psy-
chologist is "necessarily limited" because Kahneman studies only "mental
processes that can be observed under rigorously controlled experimental conditions," so that the method can only handle "everyday decisions,
artificial parlor games, and gambling for small stakes." In contrast, the
"violent and passionate manifestations of human nature, concerned with
matters of life and death and love and hate and pain and sex, cannot be
experimentally controlled and are beyond Kahneman's reach." For this
reason, Dyson believes that Kahneman's experimental psychology should
embrace its complement in the more literary psychology of figures such
as Freud, who "can penetrate deeper than Kahneman because literature
digs deeper than science into human nature and human destiny" (43).

This brings me to an anecdote by which I hope to illustrate the last
rationale I will offer here for the importance of the arts and humanities in

our great public research universities. Some years ago, when I was graduate dean at Louisiana's land-grant university, LSU, I attended a lecture by
a brilliant colleague, a veterinary parasitologist. As he spoke, he ran slides
on two screens illustrating his work on host immune response to nema-
tode infection. The ugly and impressive color shots of worms spilling from
the guts of dead horses bore importantly on work aimed at protecting
human beings from crippling and blinding diseases caused by the same
parasites; twenty years later I see from my former colleague's Web site
that he is working under an NIH funded program to develop recombi-
nant protein vaccines against parasitic nematodes in humans. As I walked
out of the lecture in the company of a senior professor in mathematics, I
remarked disconsolately, "Here's Tom doing work that may contribute to
the eradication of the scourge of loathsome diseases on three continents,
and here am I continuing to write about how Virginia Woolf and James
Joyce struggled with their anxieties about the influence of Henry James,
and what good is that to anyone?" To which, instantly, the mathematician
replied, "And why should we want to feed the hungry or cure people suffering from disease unless it is to make it possible for them to listen to
Mozart and Bach and to read Henry James and James Joyce?"

I might have said that the alleviation of suffering and the restoration
of health are worthy ends in themselves, but that would perhaps have
been an ungracious response to the luminous generosity of spirit with
which my colleague had spoken. Still, I continue to find his point not
only consolatory but also very powerful. I would never be so feckless, not
to say callous, as to argue that public funds should go to the academic
study of the arts and humanities at the expense of programs to help those
who are ill or hungry or verging in old age on destitution. But I am with
Martha Nussbaum in declaring that an education that reduces everything
to use-value, that sees students only as production units, and that values
only work that can be commoditized and only relationships that can be
monetized, is profoundly dehumanizing. Were we to cease to uphold the
value of the academic study of the arts and humanities in our great public
universities, it is not only those institutions that would lose their souls—
the nation itself, with the vast majority of its educated citizens coming out
of those same schools, would find its own soul greatly diminished and in
some sense sold.

The scope of this essay has not allowed me to discuss all of the good
arguments that can be made for the importance of the arts and humanities in public research universities. In her keynote address to the recent

Michigan conference on the role of the arts in research universities, Princeton's president Shirley Tilghman, a distinguished molecular biologist, touches on one of the arguments with which I strongly agree but that I have largely left out here, that much value is derived for students and their teachers when "the arts themselves are intertwined with social, economic, and political forces, as well as scientific and technological ones," a formulation that I infer assumes that when you have strong programs in the discrete disciplines you can then realize in well-grounded and legitimate ways the richness of interdisciplinary approaches to knowledge and understanding. I hope that without having offered every argument that might be made I have even so said enough to suggest how wise Justin Morrill was in including literature, the classics, and liberal education in his vision of the future of public higher education. And in the end my modest prescription for presidents, chancellors, and other advocates of higher education is that they not shirk from making any of the arguments that can be made for support of public universities, neither neglecting the utilitarian rationales that Nussbaum and others deplore nor the loftier aspirations of the enterprise that go beyond the physiological needs at the base of the Maslow hierarchy—food, shelter, warmth, sleep—to the highest levels of human self-actualization represented by the arts and humanities. In seeking to keep our public universities accessible, affordable, and productive, we know that what is at stake is not only the future of our institutions, but also the future well-being and soul of the nation. In making the case we must therefore use every tool at our disposal while seeking to protect the academy as a preserve for the disinterested pursuit and transmission of knowledge and creative expression in all of the disciplines with respect to "all the offices, both private and public, of peace and war," for from the preservation of disinterested and "useless" teaching, scholarship, and creative activity across the broad disciplinary domains—from the arts and humanities and the social sciences to the physical and life sciences, technology, and the professions—ever-greater virtuous effects in students and enhanced applications of knowledge for the benefit of society will continue to flow.

NOTES

1. *Rising Above the Gathering Storm* is widely cited as having come out in three different years: circulated in draft in 2005 and formally released

by the National Academies on October 12 of that year, it was the subject of extensive public discussion throughout 2006, and was published in book form by the National Academies Press in 2007.

2. Morrill, "Address." Morrill's use of Milton beautifully illustrates the high level of literary culture that he, like other self-educated Americans of his time (such as the president who signed the Land-grant Act), attained despite not having had the benefit of the postsecondary education he made possible for millions.

3. Pritchett 289–99. Pritchett's article is more nuanced and sensitive to academic values than one might presume. Consider, for example, the first two sentences of his concluding paragraph: "For after all, we can never too often remind ourselves that the first purpose of the university is not to further industrial development or to increase the wealth of a state, but that it is the development of the intellectual and spiritual life. This development can take place only in the air of freedom, however evident are the dangers which freedom brings with it." Pritchett espouses scientific and businesslike university administration in a shared governance arrangement among trustees, administrators, and faculty, evidently a less autocratic regime than what was then prevalent in American universities.

4. Material throughout this paragraph is drawn from the first chapter of Donoghue's *The Last Professors*, "Rhetoric, History, and the Problems of the Humanities" 1–23.

References

2011 Academic Ranking of World Universities. http://www.shanghai-ranking.com/ARWU2011.html.

2011 Global R&D Funding Forecast." Battelle Institute and *R&D Magazine*, December 2010. http://www.battelle.org/aboutus/rd/2011.pdf.

Abrams, M. H. "What's the Use of Theorizing about the Arts." In *In Search of Literary Theory*, ed. Morton W. Bloomfield. Ithaca: Cornell University Press, 1972.

Adams, James D. "Is the U.S. Losing Its Preeminence in Higher Education?" NBER Working Paper no. 15233. Cambridge, MA: National Bureau of Economic Research, August 2009.

Alexander, F. King. "The Silent Crisis: The Relative Fiscal Capacity of Public Universities to Compete for Faculty." *The Review of Higher Education* 24, no. 2 (Winter 2001): 113–29.

Allen, W. Wayne, Norman R. Augustine, John L. Clendenin, et al., "A Moment of Truth for America." *Washington Post*, 2 May 1995.

Anderson, Karen. "Public College Tuition Increases Prompt Concern, Anguish, and Legislation." *New York Times*, 30 August 2003.

———. "Applications to Colleges Are Breaking Records." *New York Times*, 17 January 2008.

ArtsEngine Working Group Reports. http://artsengine.umich.edu/topics.php.

Arum, Richard, and Josipa Roksa. *Academically Adrift: Limited Learning on College Campuses*. Chicago: University of Chicago Press, 2011.

Atkinson, Richard C., and William A. Blanpied. "Research Universities: Core of the U.S. Science and Technology System." *Technology in Society* 30 (2008): 30–38.

Atkinson, Richard C., and Patricia A. Pelfrey. "Science and the Entrepreneurial University." *Issues in Science and Technology* 26, no. 4 (Summer 2010): 39–48.

Atkinson, Robert D. "Deep Competitiveness." *Issues in Science and Technology* 23, no. 2 (2007): 69–75.

Audretsch, David B., and Maryann P. Feldman. "R&D Spillovers and the Geography of Innovation and Production." *American Economic Review* 86, no. 3 (June 1996): 630–40.

Banks, Melissa, Alan Olsen, and David Pearce. *Global Student Mobility: An Australian Perspective Five Years On*. Canberra, Australia: IDP Education, 2007.

Baum, Sandy, and Jennifer Ma. *Education Pays: The Benefits of Higher Education for Individuals and Society*. College Board, 2007.

Bercovitz, Janet, and Maryann Feldman. "Entrepreneurial Universities and Technology Transfer: A Conceptual Framework for Understanding Knowledge-Based Economic Development." *Journal of Technology Transfer* 31 (2006): 175–88.

Berdahl, Robert. "Maintaining America's Competitive Edge: Revitalizing the Nation's Research University." Testimony to the National Academies Committee on Research Universities. Washington, DC: Association of American Universities, 2010.

Berrett, Dan. "Why They Move." *Inside Higher Education*, 31 May 2011. http://www.insidehighered.com/news/2011/05/31/.

Biddle, Sheila. *Internationalization: Rhetoric or Reality*. ACLS Occasional Paper 56. American Council of Learned Societies (2002): 67–69.

Birgeneau, Robert J., and Frank D. Yery. "Rescuing Our Public Universities." *Washington Post*, 27 September 2009, A23.

Blakemore, Arthur, and Berthold Herrendorf. "Economic Growth: The Importance of Education and Technological Development." Tempe: W. P. Carey School of Business, Arizona State University, January 2009.

Bloom, Allan. *The Closing of the American Mind*. New York: Simon and Schuster, 1987.

Blume-Kohout, Margaret E., Krishna Kumar, and Neeraj Sood. *Federal Funding and University Research and Development*. Santa Monica: RAND Corporation, December 2010.

Bok, Derek. *Beyond the Ivory Tower: Social Responsibilities of the Modern University*. Cambridge: Harvard University Press, 1982.

Bonnen, James T. "The Land Grant Idea and the Evolving Outreach

Community." In *University-Community Collaborations for the Twenty-First Century: Outreach to Scholarship for Youth and Families*, ed. Richard M. Lerner and Lou Anna K. Simon. New York: Garland, 1998.

"Booker Taliaferro Washington." *The African American Almanac*, 7th Ed. Farmington Hills, MI: Gale Cengage, 1996. http://www.gale.cengage.com/free_resources/bhm/bio/washington_b.htm.

Bowen, William G., Matthew M. Chingos, and Michael S. McPherson. *Crossing the Finish Line: Completing College at America's Public Universities.* Princeton: Princeton University Press, 2009.

Breneman, David. *Are the States and Public Higher Education Striking a New Bargain? Public Policy Paper Series.* Washington, DC: Association of Governing Boards and Colleges, 2005.

———. "Peering Around the Bend: The Leadership Challenges of Privatization, Accountability, and Market-Based State Policy." Association of Governing Boards, Washington, DC, 2005.

Brooks, C. "Report to the Council of 1890 Presidents/Chancellors." Dallas, TX. 13 November 2010.

Bugeja, Michael. "Twelve Ways to Survive 2011–12." *Inside Higher Ed*, 6 September 2011. http://www.insidehighered.com/views/2011/09/06/12-ways-survive-2011–12.

Burke, Joseph C. *Funding Public Colleges and Universities for Performance: Popularity, Problems, and Prospects.* Albany: Rockefeller Institute Press, 2002.

Bush, Vannevar. *Science, the Endless Frontier: Report to the President on a Program for Postwar Scientific Research* (1945). Washington, DC: National Science Foundation, 1990.

California State Department of Education. "A Master Plan for Higher Education in California." 1960.

Canada Research Chairs. www.chairs-chaires.gc.ca. Last updated 24 November 2011.

Chesbrough, Henry. *Open Innovation: The New Imperative for Creating and Profiting from Technology.* Boston: Harvard Business Review Press, 2003.

Chesterton, G.K. "The Ethics of Elfland." *Orthodoxy.* New York: J. Lane, 1914, c1908. http://www.pagebypagebooks.com/Gilbert_K_Chesterton/Orthodoxy/The_Ethics_of_Elfland_p1.html.

Christensen, Clayton. *The Innovator's Dilemma.* Cambridge: Harvard Business School, 1997.

Christy, Ralph D., and Lionel Williamson. *A Century of Service:*

Land-Grant Colleges and Universities, 1890–1990. New Brunswick and London: Transaction Publishers, 1992.

Clark, John B., W. Bruce Leslie, and Kenneth P. O'Brien, eds. *SUNY at 60: The Promise of the State University of New York.* Albany: State University of New York Press, 2010.

COGR. *The Bayh-Dole Act: A Guide to the Law and Implementing Regulations.* Washington, DC: Council on Governmental Relations, October 1999.

COGR, AAU, and APLU. "Regulatory and Financial Reform of Federal Research Policy." Recommendations to the National Research Council Committee on Research Universities. Council on Governmental Relations, Association of American Universities, and Association of Public and Land-Grant Universities. 21 January 2011.

Cole, Jonathan R. *The Great American University: Its Rise to Preeminence, Its Indispensable National Role, and Why It Must Be Protected.* New York: Public Affairs, 2009.

College Board Advocacy and Policy Center. "Tuition Discounting Report Finds that Discounting Continues to Increase at Private Colleges but Levels off at Public Colleges." 2010. http://advocacy.collegeboard. org/college-affordability-financial-aid/trends-higher-education/ news/tuition-discounting-report.

Colyvas, Jeannette, Michael M. Crow, Annetine Gelijns, Roberto Mazzoleni, et al. "How Do University Inventions Get Into Practice?" *Management Science* 48, no. 1 (2002): 61–72.

Comer, Marcus M., Thasya Campbell, Kelvin Edwards, and John Hillison. "Cooperative Extension and the 1890 Land-Grant Institution: The Real Story." *Journal of Extension* 44, no. 3 (June 2006): 3FEA4. http://www.joe.org/joe/2006june/a4.php.

Commission on the Future of Higher Education. *A Test of Leadership: Charting the Future of U.S. Higher Education.* U. S. Department of Education, 2006.

Cornell, Ezra. Letter to Andrew Dickson White. 23 February 1868.

Courant, Paul N, James J. Duderstadt, Edie N. Goldenberg. "Needed: a National Strategy to Preserve Public Research Universities." *Chronicle of Higher Education,* 3 January 2010, A36.

Cross, Coy F., II. *Go West, Young Man! Horace Greeley's Vision for America.* Albuquerque: University of New Mexico Press, 1995.

———. *Justin Smith Morrill: Father of the Land-Grant Colleges.* East Lansing: Michigan State University Press, 1999.

Crow, Michael M. "Science and Technology Policy in the United States: Trading in the 1950 Model." *Science and Public Policy* 21, no. 4 (August 1994): 202–12.

———. "The Research University as Comprehensive Knowledge Enterprise: A Prototype for a New American University." In *University Research for Innovation,* ed. Luc E. Weber and James J. Duderstadt. Geneva: Economica, 2010.

———, and Barry Bozeman. *Limited By Design: R&D Laboratories in the U.S. National Innovation System.* New York: Columbia University Press, 1998.

———, and Christopher Tucker. "The American Research University System as America's *de facto* Technology Policy." *Science and Public Policy* 28, no. 1 (2001): 2–10.

Dale, Stacy Berg, and Alan B. Krueger. "Estimating the Payoff to Attending a More Selective College: an Application of Selection on Observables and Unobservables." *Quarterly Journal of Economics* 117, no. 4 (November 2002): 1491–528.

———. "Estimating the Return to College Selectivity over the Career Using Administrative Earning Data." Working Paper #563. Princeton University, Industrial Relations Section, 2011.

Desrochers, Donna, Colleen M. Lenihan, and Jane Wellman. *Trends in College Spending 1998–2008.* Washington, DC: Delta Cost Project, 2010. http://www.deltacostproject.org/resources/pdf/Trends-in-College-Spending-98-08.pdf.

Desrochers, Donna, and Jane Wellman. *Trends in College Spending 1999–2009.* Washington, DC: Delta Cost Project, 2011. http://www.deltacostproject.org/resources/pdf/Trends2011_Final_090711.pdf.

DeVol, Ross, and Armen Bedroussian. *Mind to Market: A Global Analysis of University Biotechnology Transfer and Commercialization.* Santa Monica: Milken Institute, 2006.

Di Meglio, Francesca. "College, Big Investment, Paltry Return." *Business Week,* 28 June 2010. http://www.businessweek.com/bschools/content/jun2010/bs20100618_385280.htm.

Donoghue, Frank. *The Last Professors: The Twilight of the Humanities in the Corporate University.* New York: Fordham University Press, 2008.

Douglass, John Aubrey. "The Waning of America's Higher Education Advantage: International Competitors Are No Longer Number Two and Have Big Plans in the Global Economy." Berkeley, CA: Center for Studies in Higher Education, University of California, 2006.

———. *The Conditions for Admission: Access, Equality, and the Social Contract of Public Universities*. Stanford, CA: Stanford University Press, 2007.

Dow Jones Industrial Average (DJIA). *Historical Time Line*. http://www.djaverages.com/.

D'Souza, Dinesh. *Illiberal Education: The Politics of Race and Sex on Campus*. New York: MacMillan, 1998.

Dubb, Steve, and Ted Howard. *Linking Colleges to Communities: Engaging the University for Community Development*. The Democracy Collaborative at the University of Maryland, August 2007.

Duderstadt, James J. *A University for the Twenty-First Century*. Ann Arbor: University of Michigan Press, 2000.

———. "Aligning American Higher Education with a Twenty-first-century Public Agenda." *Higher Education in Europe* 34, no. 3–4 (2009): 347–366.

———, Mark Muro, and Sarah Rahman. "Hubs of Transformation: Leveraging the Great Lakes Research Complex for Energy Innovation." Brookings Institution Policy Brief 173. Washington, DC: Brookings Institution, 2010.

———, and Farris W. Womack. *Beyond the Crossroads: The Future of the Public University in America*. Baltimore: Johns Hopkins University Press, 2005.

Dyson, Freeman. "How to Dispel Your Illusions." *New York Review of Books* 58, no. 20 (22 December 2011): 40–43.

Ehrenberg, Ronald G. "The Perfect Storm and the Privatization of Public Higher Education." *Change* 38, no. 1 (January/February 2006): 46–53.

Eisenhower, Dwight D. "Farewell Address to the Nation, January 17, 1961." Public Papers of the Presidents (1960): 1035–40.

Engberg, David, and Madeline F. Green, eds. *Promising Practices: Spotlighting Excellence in Comprehensive Internationalization*. Washington, DC: American Council on Education, 2002.

Etzkowitz, Henry. "Research Groups as Quasi-firms: the Invention of the Entrepreneurial University." *Research Policy* 32 (2003): 109–21.

———. *The Triple Helix: University-Industry-Government Innovation in Action*. New York: Routledge, 2008.

———, and L. Leytesdorff. *Universities in the Global Economy: A Triple Helix of Academic-Industry-Government Relations*. London: Croom Helm, 1997.

Evans, Teri. "Penn State Tops Recruiter Rankings." *Wall Street Journal,* 13 September 2010. http://online.wsj.com/article/SB100014240527487 043589045754776433696663352.html.

Ewell, Peter, and Marianne Boeke. *Critical Connections: Linking States' Unit Record Systems to Track Student Progress.* Lumina Foundation, January 2007.

"Faculty Salaries Vary by Institute Type, Discipline." *Chronicle of Higher Education,* 11 April 2011. http://chronicle.com/article/Faculty-Salaries-Vary-by/127073/.

Feldman, Maryann P. "The New Economics of Innovation, Spillovers, and Agglomeration: Review of Empirical Studies." *Economics of Innovation and New Technologies* 8 (1999): 5–25.

———. "Entrepreneurship and American Research Universities: Evolution in Technology Transfer." In *The Emergence of Entrepreneurship Policy: Governance, Start-ups, and Growth in the U.S. Knowledge Economy,* ed. David M. Hart. Cambridge: Cambridge University Press, 2003.

Finder, Alan. "Elite Colleges Reporting Record Lows in Admission." *New York Times,* 1 April 2008.

Florida, Richard. *The Rise of the Creative Class: And How it is Transforming Work, Leisure, Community, and Everyday Life.* New York: Basic Books, 2002.

Fogel, Daniel Mark. "In Search of a Sputnik Moment." *Washington Post,* 16 October (early edition) and 18 October 2005.

"For-Profit Colleges Capitalize on Pell Grant Revenue." *Chronicle for Higher Education,* 4 January 2010. http://chronicle.com/article/Data-Points-For-Profit/63388/.

Fossum, Donna, et al. *Discovery and Innovation: Federal Research and Development Activities in the United States.* Santa Monica: RAND, 2000.

French, Howard W. "China Spending Billions to Better Universities." *New York Times,* 27 October 2005, A1.

Friedman, Thomas L. *The World is Flat.* Farrar, Strauss and Giroux, 2005.

———. "Barack Kissinger Obama." *New York Times,* 25 October 2011.

Geiger, Roger L. *To Advance Knowledge: The Growth of American Research Universities, 1900–1940.* Oxford: Oxford University Press, 1986.

———. "Milking the Sacred Cow: Research and the Quest for Useful Knowledge in the American University since 1920." *Science, Technology, and Human Values* 13, no. 3–4 (Summer and Autumn 1988): 332–48.

————. "Organized Research Units: Their Role in the Development of the Research University." *Journal of Higher Education* 61, no. 1 (January/February 1990): 1–19.

————. "Science, Universities, and National Defense, 1945–1970." *Osiris*, 2nd series, no.7 (1992): 26–48.

————. *Research and Relevant Knowledge: American Research Universities Since World War II.* Oxford: Oxford University Press, 1993.

————. *Knowledge and Money: Research Universities and the Paradox of the Marketplace.* Stanford: Stanford University Press, 2004.

————. "Expert and Elite: the Incongruous Mission of Public Research Universities." In *Future of the American Public Research University,* ed. Roger L. Geiger et al. Rotterdam: Sense Publishers, 2007.

Gleason, Bill. "World-Class Greatness at a Land-Grant University Near You?" (Blog post). *The Chronicle of Higher Education,* 26 September 2010. http://chronicle.com/article/World-Class-Greatness-at-a/124591/.

Goldin, Claudia, and Lawrence F. Katz. *The Race Between Education and Technology.* Cambridge: Belknap Press of Harvard University Press, 2008.

Gordon, Larry. "Students ask Regents to Reject Proposed UC Tuition Hike." *Los Angeles Times,* 14 July 2011. http://articles.latimes.com/2011/jul/14/local/la-me-uc-regents-20110714.

————. Online Comments. *Los Angeles Times,* 14 July 2011. http://discussions.latimes.com/20/lanews/la-me-uc-regents-20110714/10?page=2.

Graham, Hugh Davis, and Nancy Diamond. *The Rise of American Research Universities: Elites and Challengers in the Postwar Era.* Baltimore: Johns Hopkins University Press, 1997.

Green, Madeline, Maura Porcelli, and Laura Siaya. *Public Opinion Poll: One Year Later: Attitudes about International Education Since September 11.* Washington, DC: American Council on Education, April 2000 and March 2002.

Guston, David H., and Kenneth Keniston. "The Social Contract for Science." In *The Fragile Contract: University Science and the Federal Government,* ed. Guston and Keniston. Cambridge: MIT Press, 1994.

Haddad, Georges. "The Importance of Internationalization of Higher Education." Presented at the International Association of Universities Conference on the Internationalization of Higher Education: New Directions, New Challenges. Beijing, China, 2006.

Hannah, John A. Address to the Association of Governing Boards. Ann Arbor, MI. October 11, 1962.

Hart, David M. "Entrepreneurship Policy: What It Is and Where It Came From." In *The Emergence of Entrepreneurship Policy: Governance, Start-Ups, and Growth in the U.S. Knowledge Economy,* ed. David M. Hart. Cambridge: Cambridge University Press, 2003.

Harvard University Web site. Research Funding, Office of the Vice Provost for Research. http://vpr.harvard.edu/content/research-funding.

Haycock, Kati. *Opportunity Adrift.* Washington, DC: Education Trust, 2010.

———, and Danette Gerald. *Engines of Inequality.* Washington, DC: Education Trust, 2008.

Heller, Donald E. "State Support of Higher Education: Past, Present, and Future." In *Privatization and Public Universities,* ed. Douglas M. Priest and Edward P. St. John. Bloomington: Indiana University Press, 2006.

"Higher Education Investment Act: An Open Letter to President-Elect Obama and His Administration." A Statement by Public Higher Education Leaders Convened by the Carnegie Corporation of New York. *New York Times,* 16 December 2008.

Higher Education Research Institute. "The American College Teacher, National Norms for the 2004–2005 HERI Faculty Survey." UCLA, 2005. http://www.gseis.ucla.edu/heri/PDFs/ACT-Research%20Brief. PDF.

Hill, Kent. "The Contribution of Arizona State University to the Arizona Economy, Fiscal Year 2009: A Report from the Office of the University Economist." Tempe: W. P. Carey School of Business, Arizona State University, November 2009.

Hoffmann, Roald. "Autobiography," http://www.nobelprize.org/nobel_prizes/chemistry/laureates/1981/hoffmann-autobio.html, accessed February 17, 2012.

Holland, Antonio. *The Soldiers' Dream Continued: A Pictorial History of Lincoln University.* Jefferson City, MO: Lincoln University Printing Services, 1991.

Holliday, Chad, chair, National Academies Committee on Research Universities. *Breaking Through: Ten Strategic Actions to Leverage Our Research Universities for the Future of America.* Washington, DC: National Academy Press, 2011.

Holm-Nielsen, L. B. "Promoting Science and Technology for Development: The World Bank's Millennium Science Initiative." Address delivered on April 30, 2002 to the First International Senior Fellows meeting, Wellcome Trust, London, UK.

Horowitz, David. *Reforming Our Universities: The Campaign for an Academic Bill of Rights.* Washington, DC: Regnery, 2010.

Hossler, Donald, et al. "State Funding for Higher Education: The Sisyphean Task." *Journal of Higher Education* 68, no. 2 (March/April 1997): 160–90.

Hudzik, John. "Comprehensive Internationalization: From Concept to Action." Washington, DC: NAFSA: Association of International Educators, 2011.

———, and Michael Stohl. "Modeling Assessment of Outcomes and Impacts from Internationalization." *Measuring Success in the Internationalization of Higher Education.* EAIE Occasional Paper 22, ed. Hans de Wit. Amsterdam: European Association for International Education, 2009.

———. "The Road to Comprehensive and Strategic Internationalization of U.S. Higher Education: Shaping Forces and Prospects." SAGE Handbook, anticipated 2012.

Institute for Public Policy and Social Research. 1999. State of the State Survey (SOSS)-25 (Fall). Michigan State University. East Lansing, MI. http://www.ippsr.msu.edu/SOSS.

———. 2002. State of the State Survey (SOSS)-19 (Spring). Michigan State University. East Lansing, MI. http://www.ippsr.msu.edu/SOSS.

Jefferson, Thomas. *Notes on the State of Virginia.* 1787. http://etext.virginia.edu/toc/modeng/public/JefVirg.html.

Johnson, Eldon L. "Misconceptions about the Early Land-Grant Colleges." *Journal of Higher Education* 52, no. 4 (July 1981): 333–57.

Jones, Charles I. "Sources of U.S. Economic Growth in a World of Ideas." *American Economic Review* 92, no. 1 (2002): 220–39.

Julius, Daniel J. "When Systems Evolve." *Inside Higher Ed,* 3 June 2011. http://www.insidehighered.com/views/2011/06/03/essay_on_the_evolution_of_flagship_universities.

Kane, Thomas, and Peter Orszag. "Funding Restrictions at Public Universities: Effects and Policy Implications." In *Brookings Institution Working Papers.* Brookings Institution, September 2003.

———. "Financing Public Higher Education: Short-Term and Long-Term Challenges." Ford Policy Forum. Brookings Institution, 2004.

———, and Emil Apostolov. "Higher Education Appropriations and Public Universities: Role of Medicaid and the Business Cycle." *Brookings-Wharton Papers on Urban Affairs.* Brookings Institution, 2005.

Kash, Don E. *Perpetual Innovation: The New World of Competition.* New York: Basic Books, 1989.

Kasper, Henry T. "The Changing Role of Community Colleges." *Occupational Outlook Quarterly* 46, no. 4 (Winter 2002-03): 14–21.

Kassicieh, Suleiman K., and H. Raymond Radosevich. *From Lab to Market: Commercialization of Public Sector Technology.* New York: Plenum Press, 1994.

Kellogg Commission on the Future of State and Land-Grant Universities. *Returning to Our Roots: The Student Experience.* Washington, DC: National Association of State Universities and Land-Grant Colleges, 1997. http://www.aplu.org/NetCommunity/Document.Doc?id=181.

———. *Returning to Our Roots: Student Access.* Washington, DC: National Association of State Universities and Land-Grant Colleges, 1998. http://www.aplu.org/NetCommunity/Document.Doc?id=182.

———. *Returning to Our Roots: The Engaged Institution.* Washington, DC: National Association of State Universities and Land-Grant Colleges, 1999. http://www.aplu.org/NetCommunity/Document.Doc?id=183.

———. *Renewing the Covenant: Learning, Discovery, and Engagement in a New Age and Different World,* Sixth Report. Washington, DC: National Association of State Universities and Land-Grant Colleges, Office of Public Affairs, March 2000.

———. *Returning to Our Roots: Executive Summaries of the Reports of the Kellogg Commission on the Future of State and Land-Grant Universities.* Washington, DC: National Association of State Universities and Land-Grant Colleges, 2001. http://www.aplu.org/NetCommunity/Document.Doc?id=187.

Kenney, Martin, and Urs von Burg. "Technology, Entrepreneurship, and Path Dependence: Industrial Clustering in Silicon Valley and Route 128." *Industrial and Corporate Change* 8, no. 1 (1999): 67–103.

Keohane, Nannerl O. "The American Campus: From Colonial Seminary to Global Multiversity." Wolfson College Lecture Series, "The Idea of a University," Oxford University, 3 February 1998.

Kerr, Clark. *The Uses of the University,* 5th ed. Reprint. Cambridge: Harvard University Press, 2001.

———. *The Gold and the Blue: Political Turmoil.* Berkeley: University of California Press, 2003.

Kerry, John, U.S. Senator for Massachusetts. "Press Conference—Introduction of the BUILD Act." 15 March 2011. http://kerry.senate.gov/press/speeches/speech/?id=5b9c0dc5-9c4d-4aae-b651-64a4f8c10c83.

Kirp, David. "Paul Ryan Hates Kids." *The Huffington Post*, 11 April 2011. http://www.huffingtonpost.com/david-kirp/paul-ryan-hates-kids_b_847134.html.

Kitcher, Philip. *Science, Truth, and Democracy*. Oxford: Oxford University Press, 2001.

Klenow, Peter J., and Andrès Rodríguez-Clare. "The Neoclassical Revival in Growth Economics: Has It Gone Too Far?" *NBER Macroeconomics Annual* 12 (1997): 73–103.

Kline, Ronald. "Construing 'Technology' as 'Applied Science': Public Rhetoric of Scientists and Engineers in the United States, 1880–1945." *Isis* 86 (1995): 194–221.

Knight, Jane, and Hans De Wit, eds. "Internationalisation of Higher Education." *Quality and Internationalisation in Higher Education*. Paris, France: OECD, 1999.

Koepplin, Leslie, and David Wilson, eds. *The Future of State Universities*. New Brunswick: Rutgers University Press, 1985.

Kotkin, Joel, and Ross DeVol. *Knowledge-Value Cities in the Digital Age*. Santa Monica: Milken Institute, 2001.

Kuznets, Simon. *Economic Growth and Structure*. New York: W. W. Norton, 1965.

———. *Economic Growth of Nations*. Cambridge: Belknap Press, 1971.

Leadership and Learning: An Interpretive History of Historically Black Land-Grant Colleges and Universities. A Bicentennial Study. National Association of State Universities and Land-Grant Colleges, 1990.

Lederer, William J., and Eugene Burdick. *The Ugly American*. New York: Norton, 1958.

Lederman, Doug. "Flexibility—But for (and From) Whom?" *Inside Higher Ed*, 28 February 2011. http://www.insidehighered.com/news/2011/02/28/wisconsin_debates_whether_madison_should_stay_within_university_system.

Lee, Jr., John Michael, and Anita Rawls. *The College Completion Agenda, 2010 Progress Report*. College Board Policy and Advocacy Center, 2010. http://completionagenda.collegeboard.org/sites/default/files/reports_pdf/Progress_Report_2010.pdf.

Lewis, Darrell R., and James Hearn. *The Public Research University: Serving the Public Good in New Times*. Lanham, MD: University Press of America, 2003.

Lin, Zeng, Richard Pearce, and Weirong Wang. "Imported Talents: Demographic Characteristics, Achievement, and Job Satisfaction of Foreign Born Full Time Faculty in Four-Year American Colleges."

Journal of Higher Education 57, no. 6 (June 2009): 703–21.

Lincoln, Abraham. *The Collected Works of Abraham Lincoln.* Ed. Roy P. Basler. New Brunswick, NJ: Rutgers University Press, 1953.

Long, Duward. "Financing in the Year 2000." In *The Future of State Universities,* ed. Leslie Koepplin and David Wilson. New Brunswick: Rutgers University Press, 1985.

Lucas, Robert E. "On the Mechanics of Economic Development." *Journal of Monetary Economics* 22 (1988): 3–42.

Lundvall, Bengt-Åke. "Innovation as an Interactive Process: From User-Producer Interaction to National Systems of Innovation." In *Technical Change and Economic Theory,* ed. Giovanni Dosi, Richard Nelson, Christopher Freeman, Luc Soete, and Gerald Silverberg. London: Pinter, 1988.

MacTaggart, Terrence, ed. *Academic Turnarounds: Restoring Vitality to Challenged American Colleges and Universities.* Westport, CT: Praeger, 2007.

Madsen, David. *The National University: Enduring Dream of the United States.* Detroit: Michigan State University Press, 1966.

Mansfield, Edwin. "Academic Research and Industrial Innovation." *Research Policy* 20 (1991): 1–12.

Mansfield, E., and J. Y. Lee. "The Modern University: Contributor to Industrial Innovation and Recipient of Industrial R&D Support." *Research Policy* 25 (1996): 1047–58.

Marklein, Mary Beth. "For-Profit Colleges See Major Gains in Past Decade." *USA Today,* 25 May 2011. http://www.usatoday.com/news/education/2011-05-26-for-profit-college-undergraduate-enrollment_n.htm.

Maryland Higher Education Commission. "Commission Responsibilities." http://mhec.maryland.gov/highered/about/commissi.asp.

Mayberry, B. D. *A Century of Agriculture in the 1890 Land-Grant Institutions and Tuskegee University—1890–1990.* New York: Vantage Press, 1991.

Mayr, Otto. "The Science-Technology Relationship as an Historiographic Problem." *Technology and Culture* 17, no. 4 (1976): 663–72.

McMahon, Walter. *Higher Learning, Greater Good.* Baltimore: Johns Hopkins University Press, 2009.

McMeans, Orlando. "The 1890 Land-Grant System: An Indispensable Investment." Presented 28 Sept. 2010 at the EES/SAES/ARD Annual Meeting and Workshop, Nashville, TN.

McPherson, Peter. "APLU's Recommendations to the NRC Committee on Research Universities." APLU, 2010. http://www.aplu.org/docu-ment.doc?id=2779.

McPherson, Peter, David E. Shulenburger, Howard Gobstein, and Christine Keller. *Competitiveness of Public Research Universities and Consequences for the Country: Recommendations for Change.* National Association of State Universities and Land-Grant Colleges discussion paper working draft, 2009.

Meara, Ellen, Seth Richards, and David Cutler. "The Gap Gets Bigger: Changes in Mortality and Life Expectancy, by Education, 1981–2000." *Health Affairs* 27, no. 2, (March/April 2008): 350–60. doi:10.1377/hlthaff.27.2.350.

Mestenhauser, Josef A. "International Education on the Verge: In Search of a New Paradigm." *International Educator* 7, no. 2–3 (1998): 68–76.

Metzger, Walter P. "The Academic Profession in the United States." In *The Academic Profession: National, Disciplinary, and Institutional Settings*, ed. Burton R. Clark.   Berkeley: University of California Press, 1987.

Miller, Charles, chair, The Spellings Commission, National Commission on the Future of Higher Education in America. *A Test of Leadership: Charting the Future of U.S. Higher Education.* Washington, DC: Department of Education, 2006.

Milton, John. *Paradise Lost.* New York: Norton, 2004.

Mokyr, Joel. *The Gifts of Athena: Historical Origins of the Knowledge Economy.* Princeton: Princeton University Press, 2002.

Moretti, Enrico. "Estimating the Social Return to Higher Education: Evidence from Longitudinal and Repeated Cross-sectional Data." *Journal of Econometrics* 121 (2004): 175–212.

Morrill Act of 1862, 37th Congress, 2nd session. 2 July 1862, sec. 4.

Morrill, James Lewis. *The Ongoing State University.* Minneapolis: University of Minnesota Press, 1960.

Morrill, Justin W. "Address." Ceremonies observing the 25th anniversary of the Land Grant Act. Massachusetts Agricultural College, June 1887.

———. "An address on behalf of the University of Vermont and State Agricultural College." Free Press Assoc.: Burlington, VT, 1888.

Mortenson, Thomas G., et al. "Why College? Private Correlates of Educational Attainment." *Postsecondary Education Opportunity: The Mortenson Research Seminar on Public Policy Analysis of Opportunity for Postsecondary Education* 81 (March, 1999).

Mowery, David C., Richard R. Nelson, Bhaven N. Sampat, and Arvids A. Ziedonis. "The Growth of Patenting and Licensing by U.S. Universities: An Assessment of the Effects of the Bayh-Dole Act of 1980." *Research Policy* 30 (2000): 99–119.

———. *Ivory Tower and Industrial Innovation: University-Industry Technology Transfer Before and After the Bayh-Dole Act.* Stanford: Stanford University Press, 2004.

Mowery, David C., and Nathan Rosenberg. *Technology and the Pursuit of Economic Growth.* Cambridge: Cambridge University Press, 1989.

———. *Paths of Innovation: Technological Change in Twentieth-Century America.* Cambridge: Cambridge University Press, 1998.

Mowery, David C., and Scott Shane. "Introduction to the Special Issue on University Entrepreneurship and Technology Transfer." *Management Science* 48, no. 1 (January 2002): v–ix.

NAFSA Task Force on Internationalization. *NAFSA's Contribution to Internationalization of Higher Education.* Washington, DC: NAFSA: Association of Internationalization, 2008. www.nafsa.org/uploaded-Files/nafsas_contribution.pdf?n=8167.

Narin, Francis, Kimberly Hamilton, and Dominic Olivastro. "The Increasing Linkage Between U.S. Technology and Public Science." *Research Policy* 26 (1997): 317–30.

National Academies. "Research Universities." Current Project Systems, Project Information. http://www8.nationalacademies.org/cp/projectview.aspx?key=49219.

National Academies Committee on Prospering in the Global Economy of the Twenty-First Century (U.S.). *Capitalizing on Investments in Science and Technology.* Washington, DC: National Academies Press, 1999.

———. *Rising Above the Gathering Storm: Energizing and Employing America for a Brighter Economic Future.* Washington, DC: National Academies Press, 2007.

———. *Rising Above the Gathering Storm Revisited: Rapidly Approaching Category 5.* Washington, DC: National Academies Press, 2010.

National Association of State Universities and Land-grant Colleges. "The Land-Grant Tradition." Washington, DC: NASULGC, 2008.

National Center for Education Statistics. *Digest of Education Statistics 2010, NCES 2011-015.* Washington, DC: U.S. Department of Education, National Center for Education Statistics, 2011. http://nces.ed.gov/pubs2011/2011015.pdf.

———. Table 201, "Total Fall Enrollment in Degree-granting Institutions, by Control and Type of Institution, Age, and Attendance Status of Student: 2009." National Center for Education Statistics, U.S. Department of Education. http://nces.ed.gov/programs/digest/d10/tables/dt10_201.asp.

———. Table 366, "Total revenue of private not-for-profit degree-granting institutions, by source of funds and type of institution: 1999–2000 through 2008–09." National Center for Education Statistics, U.S. Department of Education. http://nces.ed.gov/programs/digest/d10/tables/dt10_366.asp.

———. Table 368, "Total revenue of private for-profit degree-granting institutions, by source of funds and type of institution: Selected years, 1999–2000 through 2008–09." National Center for Education Statistics, U.S. Department of Education. http://nces.ed.gov/programs/digest/d10/tables/dt10_368.asp.

National Institutes of Health. *History of Congressional Appropriations, Fiscal Years 1938–1949; 2000–2010.* http://www.nih.gov/about/budget.htm.

National Research Council (U.S.) Commission on Human Resources. *Career Achievements of the National Defense Education Act (Title IV) Fellows of 1959–1973.* Washington, DC: National Academy of Sciences, 1977.

National Research Council (U.S.) Committee on the Education and Utilization of the Engineer. *Engineering Education and Practice in the United States: Foundations of Our Techno-Economic Future.* Washington, DC: National Academies Press, 1985.

National Research Council (U.S.) Committee on Management of University Intellectual Property. *Managing University Intellectual Property in the Public Interest.* Washington, DC: National Academies Press, 2011.

National Science Board (NSB). *Science and Engineering Indicators 2010.* Arlington, VA: National Science Foundation Board, 2010.

Nelson A. Rockefeller Institute of Government at the University at Albany and the University at Buffalo Regional Institute. "How SUNY Matters: Economic Impacts of the State University of New York." June 2011. http://regional-institute.buffalo.edu/projects/projects.cfm?ID=161.

Nelson, Cary. "Keep Your Hands Off the 'Fierce Humanities.'" *The Chronicle of Higher Education*, 28 August 2011. http://chronicle.com/article/Keep-Your-Hands-Off-the/128804/.

Nelson, Richard R. "The Simple Economics of Basic Scientific Research." *Journal of Political Economy* 67, no. 3 (June 1959): 297–306.

———, and Sidney G. Winter. *An Evolutionary Theory of Economic Change.* Cambridge: Harvard University Press, 1982.

Nevins, Allen. *The Origins of the Land-Grant Colleges and State Universities.* Washington: Civil War Centennial Commission, 1962.

———. *The State Universities and Democracy.* Urbana: University of Illinois Press, 1962.

Newby, Howard. "Sustaining World Class Universities: Who Pays and How?" Glion VIII Colloquium, ed. Luc Weber and James J. Duderstadt. Paris: Economica, 2011.

Newton, Jim. *Justice for All: Earl Warren and the Nation He Made.* New York: Riverhead, 2006.

Niosi, Jorge, Paolo Saviotti, Bertrand Bellon, and Michael M. Crow. "National Systems of Innovation: In Search of a Workable Concept." *Technology in Society* 15 (1993): 207–27.

Nussbaum, Martha. *Not for Profit: Why Democracy Needs the Humanities.* Princeton: Princeton University Press, 2010.

Oleson, Alexandra, and John Voss, eds. *The Organization of Knowledge in Modern America, 1860–1920.* Baltimore: Johns Hopkins University Press, 1979.

Organisation for Economic Co-operation and Development. "Technology, Productivity, and Job Creation: Best Policy Practices." Paris: OECD, 1998.

———. *Education at a Glance 2010: OECD Indicators.* Paris: OECD. 2010.

———. *Education at a Glance 2011: OECD Indicators.* Paris: OECD. 2011.

Paradeise, Catherine, Emanuela Reale, Ivar Bleiklie, and Ewan Ferlie. *University Governance: Western European Comparative Perspectives.* Dordrecht: Springer, 2009.

Peace Corps. "Stats, Facts, and Figures." Last updated Jan 27, 2011. http://www.peacecorps.gov/index.cfm?shell=resources.media.mediares.statsfacts.

"Percentages of Pell Recipients Stay Steady at Wealthy Colleges." *Chronicle for Higher Education*, 21 March 2011. http://chronicle.com/article/Interactive-Graphic-/126850/.

Peters, Tom. *Re-Imagine! Business Excellence in a Disruptive Age.* New York: DK Publishing, 2003.

Pew Research Center. *Is College Worth It?* 2011. http://www.pewsocialtrends.

org/2011/05/15/is-college-worth-it/2/#chapter-1-overview.

Pisano, Gary P., and W. C. Shih. "Restoring American Competitiveness." *Harvard Business Review* 87, no. 7–8 (July-Aug. 2009): 114–25.

Polanyi, Michael. *The Tacit Dimension.* Garden City, NY: Doubleday, 1966.

Porter, Michael E. "Clusters and the New Economics of Competition." *Harvard Business Review* 76, no. 6 (Nov.-Dec. 1998): 77–90.

Powell, Walter, et al., "The Spatial Clustering of Science and Capital: Accounting for Biotech Firm and Venture Capital Relationships." *Regional Studies* 36, no. 3 (2002): 291–316.

Prior, John, Sylvia Hurtado, Jessica Sharkness, and William Corn. *The American Freshman: National Norms for Fall 2007.* Cooperative Institutional Research Program, UCLA, 2008.

Pritchett, Henry S. "Shall the University Become a Business Corporation." *The Atlantic Monthly* 96, no. 3 (September 1905): 289–99.

PROPHE. "Country Data Summary (117 countries)." Last updated November 2010, http://www.albany.edu/dept/eaps/prophe/data/international.html.

Rhodes, Frank H. T. *The Creation of the Future: The Role of the American University.* Ithaca: Cornell University Press, 2001.

Ridge, Martin. "Frederick Jackson Turner at Indiana University." *Indiana Magazine of History,* 89, no. 3 (September 1993): 210–19.

Riley, Naomi Schaefer. *The Faculty Lounges: And Other Reasons Why You Won't Get the College Education You Paid For.* Lanham, MD: Ivan R Dee, 2011.

Rischard, J. F. *High Noon: Twenty Global Problems, Twenty Years to Solve Them.* New York: Basic Books, 2002.

Rittel, Horst, and Melvin Webber. "Dilemmas in a General Theory of Planning." *Policy Sciences* 4, no. 2 (1973): 155–69.

Rosenberg, Nathan. "America's Entrepreneurial Universities." In *The Emergence of Entrepreneurship Policy: Governance, Start-ups, and Growth in the U.S. Knowledge Economy,* ed. David M. Hart. Cambridge: Cambridge University Press, 2003.

———, and L. E. Birdzell. *How the West Grew Rich: The Economic Transformation of the Industrial World.* New York: Basic Books, 1986.

———, and Richard R. Nelson. "American Universities and Technical Advance in Industry." *Research Policy* 23, no. 3 (1994): 323–48.

Ross, Earle D. *Democracy's College: The Land-Grant Movement in its Formative Stage.* Ames: Iowa State College Press, 1942.

Ruby, Alan. *The Uncertain Future for International Higher Education in the Asia-Pacific Region.* Washington, DC: NAFSA Association of International Educators, 2010. www.nafsa.org/uploadedFiles/NAFSA_Home/Resource_Library_Assets/Networks/SIO/UncertainFuture.pdf.

Saxenian, Anna Lee. *Regional Advantage: Culture and Competition in Silicon Valley and Route 128.* Cambridge: Harvard University Press, 1994.

Schaefer, Samantha. "Middle Income Student Attendance Declines at UC." *Orange County Register,* 30 October 2011.

Schumpeter, Joseph A. *The Theory of Economic Development.* Cambridge: Harvard University Press, 1934.

Schwartz, Mosche. "Training the Military to Manage Contractors During Expeditionary Operations: Overview and Options for Congress." *CRS Report R40057,* 17 December 2008. http://stuff.mit.edu/afs/sipb/contrib/wikileaks-crs/wikileaks-crs-reports/R40057.pdf.

———. "Department of Defense Contractors in Iraq and Afghanistan: Background and Analysis." *Congressional Research Service Report R40835,* 13 May 2011. http://www.fas.org/sgp/crs/natsec/R40764.pdf.

"Scott: Florida doesn't need more anthropology majors." TampaBay.com, 10 October 2011. http://www.tampabay.com/blogs/the-buzz-florida-politics/content-scott-florida-doesnt-need-more-anthropology-majors.

Selingo, Jeffrey. "Americans Split on Government Control of Tuition." *Chronicle of Higher Education,* 4 April 2008. http://chronicle.com/article/Americans-Split-on-Government/32476/.

SHEEO. *State Higher Education Finance.* Washington, DC: State Higher Education Executive Officers, 2010.

Siciloff, Steven. "NASA Awards Second Round of Development Awards." National Aeronautics and Space Agency, 20 April 2011. http://www.nasa.gov/offices/c3po/home/ccdev2award.html.

Siegfried, John J., Allen R. Sanderson, and Peter McHenry. "The Economic Impact of Colleges and Universities." Working Paper no. 06-W12, Department of Economics, Vanderbilt University. Nashville: Vanderbilt University, May 2006.

Shils, Edward. "Order of Learning in the United States: The Ascendency of the University." In *The Organization of Knowledge in Modern America, 1860–1920,* ed. Alexandra Oleson and John Voss. Baltimore: Johns Hopkins University Press, 1979.

Shulenburger, David E., Christine Keller, and George Mehaffy. "The Voluntary System of Accountability: Responding to a New Era." *Liberal Education* 94, no. 4 (Fall, 2008): 48–53.

Siaya, Lauren, and Fred M. Hayward. *Mapping Internationalization on U.S. Campuses.* Washington, DC: American Council on Education, 2003.

Simon, Lou Anna K. "Constructive and Complex Tensions in the Art of Engagement." *Journal of Public Service and Outreach* 4, no. 2 (Fall 1999): 2–6.

———. "Embracing the World Grant Ideal: Affirming the Morrill Act for a Twenty-first Century Global Society." East Lansing: Michigan State University, 2009.

Slaughter, Sheila, and Gary Rhoades. *Academic Capitalism and the New Economy: Markets, State, and Higher Education.* Baltimore: Johns Hopkins University Press, 2004.

Slosson, Edwin E. *Great American Universities.* New York: MacMillan, 1910.

Smith, Woodruff D. *Public Universities and the Public Sphere.* New York: Palgrave Macmillan, 2010.

Solow, Robert M. "Technical Change and the Aggregate Production Function." *Review of Economics and Statistics* 39 (1957): 312–20.

"Some Universities Increased Internal Spending on Research—but Still Fell Behind." *Chronicle for Higher Education*, 8 May 2011. http://chronicle.com/article/Some-Universities-Increased/127437/.

Spencer, Herbert. *Social Statics: or, The Conditions Essential to Happiness Specified, and the First of Them Developed.* London: John Chapman, 1851.

State University of New York. *Functions of a Modern University: Proceedings of the First Symposium.* Albany: State University, 1950.

Steck, Henry. "Corporatization of the University: Seeking Conceptual Clarity." *Annals of the American Academy of Political and Social Science* 585 (2003): 66–83.

Stegner, Wallace. *The Sound of Mountain Water: the Changing American West.* New York: Penguin, 1997.

Straight Talk About College Costs and Prices. Report of the National Commission on the Cost of Higher Education, an independent advisory body created by act of Congress, 1 January 1998. http://www.eric.ed.gov/PDFS/ED416762.pdf.

SUNY Board of Trustees. *Resolution 2011-063.* 15 June 2011.

Supiano, Beckie. "Rise in Sticker Price at Public Colleges Outpaces That at Private Colleges for 5th Year in a Row." *The Chronicle of Higher Education*, 26 October 2011. http://chronicle.com/article/Rise-in-Sticker-Price-at/129532/.

Teixeira, Pedro. "Mass Higher Education and Private Institutions." *Higher Education to 2030, Volume 2: Globalization*. Paris: OECD, 2009.

Thelin, John R. *A History of American Higher Education*. Baltimore: Johns Hopkins University Press, 2004.

Thomas, S. L., "Longer Term Effects of College Selectivity and Control." *Research in Higher Education* 44, no. 3 (June 2003): 263–99.

Thompson, William O. "The Mission of the Land-Grant Colleges." *Office of Experiment Stations Bulletin 142*. Proceedings of the Seventeenth Annual Convention of the Association of American Agricultural Colleges and Experiment Stations. Washington, DC: U.S. Department of Agriculture, 1904.

Thorp, Holden, and Buck Goldstein. *Engines of Innovation: The Entrepreneurial University in the Twenty-First Century*. Chapel Hill: University of North Carolina Press, 2010.

Tobin, Eugene M. "The Modern Evolution of America's Flagship Universities," Appendix A. In William G. Bowen, Matthew M. Chingos, and Michael S. McPherson, *Crossing the Finish Line: Completing College at America's Public Universities*. Princeton: Princeton University Press, 2009.

Tocqueville, Alexis de. *Democracy in America*. Boston: John Allyn, 1876.

Toope, Stephen J. "Stephen Toope on Global Challenges and the Organizational-Ethical Dilemmas of Universities" [Blog post]. *Inside Higher Ed*, 5 December 2010. http://www.insidehighered.com/blogs/global-highered/stephen_toope_ubc_on_global_challenges_and_the_organizational_ethical_dilemmas_of_universities.

Tucker, Christopher, and Bhaven Sampat. "Laboratory-Based Innovation in the American National Innovation System." In Michael M. Crow and Barry Bozeman, *Limited By Design: R&D Laboratories in the U.S. National Innovation System*. New York: Columbia University Press, 1998.

Turner, Frederick Jackson. *The Frontier in American History*. New York: Henry Holt, 1921.

University of California Newsroom. "Record-setting enrollment of low-income students." 1 October 2010. http://www.universityofcalifornia.edu/news/article/24211.

University of California Office of the President. "The Facts: UC Budget Basics." July 2011. http://www.universityofcalifornia.edu/news/fact-sheets/thefacts_budget_07_14_11.pdf.

U.S. Census Bureau. "The Big Payoff: Educational Attainment and Synthetic Estimates of Work-Life Earnings." Current Population Survey P23-210, July 2002.

———. "As Baby Boomers Age, Fewer Families Have Children Under 18 at Home." 29 February 2009. http://www.census.gov/newsroom/releases/archives/families_households/cb09-29.html.

Vandenbussche, Jérôme, Philippe Aghion, and Costas Meghir. "Growth Distance to Frontier and Composition of Human Capital." *Journal of Economic Growth* 11, no. 2 (2006): 97–127.

Veysey, Laurence R. *The Emergence of the American University.* Chicago: University of Chicago Press, 1970, c1965.

Von Hippel, Eric. "Sticky Information and the Locus of Problem Solving: Implications for Innovation." *Management Science* 40, no. 4 (1994): 429–39.

Weber, Luc, and James Duderstadt, eds. *The Globalization of Higher Education.* VI Glion Colloquium. Paris: Economica, 2008.

———. *University Research for Innovation.* Glion VII Colloquium. Paris: Economica, 2010.

Wellman, Jane, and Charles B. Reed. "Mend, Don't End, State Systems." *Inside Higher Ed,* 28 March 2011. http://www.insidehighered.com/views/2011/03/28/wellman_reed_don_t_let_flagship_universities_leave_state_college_systems_wisconsin_oregon.

West Virginia University College of Agriculture, Forestry, and Home Economics. *The Development of the Land-Grant Colleges and Universities and Their Influence on the Economic and Social Life of the People.* Morgantown: West Virginia University Press, 1963.

Westwick, Peter J. *The National Labs: Science in an American System, 1947–1974.* Cambridge: Harvard University Press, 2003.

Wheeler, Benjamin Ide. "University Democracy." *University Chronicle* XV, Berkeley, 1901.

Widder, Keith. *Michigan Agricultural College: The Evolution of a Land-Grant Philosophy, 1855–1925.* East Lansing: Michigan State University, 2005.

Wiley, David. "Forty Years of the Title VI and Fulbright." *Changing Perspectives on International Education.* Bloomington: Indiana University, 2001.

Wilson, Edward W., Peter A. Hartman, and Karen M. Vander. "Strengthening 1890 Land-Grant Institutions." In *Report to the U.S. Department of Agriculture,* by presidents of 1890 Land-Grant Colleges and Universities, 11 March 1980.

Yusuf, Shahid. "University-Industry Links: Policy Dimensions." In *How Universities Can Promote Economic Growth,* ed. Shahid Yusuf and Kaoru Nabeshima. Washington, DC: International Bank for Reconstruction and Development, 2007.

———, and Kaoru Nabeshima, eds. *How Universities Can Promote Economic Growth.* Washington, DC: International Bank for Reconstruction and Development, 2007.

Zakaria, Fareed. *The Post-American World.* New York: W. W. Norton, 2008.

Zemsky, Robert. *Making Reform Work: The Case for Transforming American Higher Education.* New Brunswick: Rutgers University Press, 2009.

———, William Massey, and Gregory Wegner. *Remaking the American University: Market-Smart and Mission Centered.* Piscataway, NJ: Rutgers University Press, 2005.

Zhang, Liang. "Do Measures of College Quality Matter? The Effect of College Quality on Graduate Earnings." *Review of Higher Education* 28, no. 4 (summer, 2006): 571–96.

Zoghi, Cindy. "Why Have Public University Professors Done so Badly?" *Economics of Education Review* 22, no. 1 (2003): 45–57.

Contributors

CAITLIN CALLAGHAN is an executive communications specialist at the University of California office of the president. Prior to joining UC, she worked for two and a half years at D. E. Shaw Research in New York City. A San Francisco native, Callaghan holds a BA degree from Stanford University, an MSt degree from the University of Oxford, and a PhD in Medieval Studies from Cornell University.

COY F. CROSS II authored the Morrill biography, *Justin Smith Morrill: Father of the Land-Grant Colleges* (Michigan State University Press) after extensive research into Morrill's life, experiences, and accomplishments. Dr. Cross, employed as an U.S. Air Force historian from 1988 until 2007, received his PhD in United States Diplomatic History from the University of California, Santa Barbara. He also holds an MA in United States and American Civil War History from California State University, Stanislaus, and a BA from Florida State University. Dr. Cross has authored several other books and monographs, including his most recent, *Lincoln's Man in Liverpool: Consul Dudley and the Legal Battle to Stop Confederate Warships,* published by Northern Illinois University Press in 2007.

MICHAEL M. CROW became the sixteenth president of Arizona State University on July 1, 2002. He is guiding the transformation of ASU into one of the nation's leading public metropolitan research universities, an institution that combines the highest levels of academic excellence, inclusiveness to a broad demographic, and maximum societal impact—a model he terms the "New American University." Under his leadership ASU has established major interdisciplinary research initiatives such as the Biodesign Institute, Global Institute of Sustainability (GIOS), and more than a dozen new transdisciplinary schools, and witnessed an unprecedented academic infrastructure expansion, near-tripling of research expenditures, and attainment of record levels of diversity in the student body. He was previously executive vice provost of Columbia University, where he served as chief strategist of Columbia's research enterprise and technology transfer operations. A fellow of the National Academy of Public Administration, and member of the Council on Foreign Relations and U.S. Department of Commerce National Advisory Council on Innovation and Entrepreneurship, he is the author of books and articles analyzing science and technology policy and the design of knowledge enterprises. Crow received his PhD in Public Administration (Science and Technology Policy) from the Maxwell School of Citizenship and Public Affairs, Syracuse University, in 1985.

WILLIAM B. DABARS is Research Fellow for University Design in the Office of the President, Arizona State University. He has served in various research capacities for the University of Southern California, University of California, Santa Barbara, and Getty Research Institute, where he participated in editorial projects focused on nineteenth- and twentieth-century aesthetic and architectural theory. He has also served as an editorial consultant for the Getty Conservation Institute and University of Colorado, Boulder. He received a PhD in History from the University of California, Los Angeles. His dissertation and current research focus on the American research university.

JAMES J. DUDERSTADT is president *emeritus* and University Professor of Science and Engineering at the University of Michigan. A graduate of Yale and Caltech, Dr. Duderstadt's teaching and research areas include nuclear science, applied physics, cyber infrastructure, and science and education policy. He has served as chair of numerous National Academy and federal commissions, including the National Science Board and the Policy and Global Affairs Division of the National Research Council. At Michigan he currently directs the Science, Technology, and Public Policy program and the Millennium Project, a research center concerned with the impact of advanced technologies on society.

DANIEL MARK FOGEL served as the twenty-fifth president of the University of Vermont for nine years, beginning on July 1, 2002. During his tenure the university expanded significantly, with a 40 percent enrollment increase, while bringing in the academically strongest and most diverse student body in institutional history. At the same time, research productivity grew by 80 percent, the university's endowment nearly doubled, and the campus was physically transformed with new land acquisitions and a major building program. Before coming to UVM, he was executive vice chancellor and provost at Louisiana State University. A productive literary scholar and poet, Fogel holds a tenured professorship in English at UVM (and is professor emeritus at LSU). He was the founding editor of *The Henry James Review* and a co-founder of the Henry James Society. He has produced seven books (four authored, three edited, including one of the Henry James volumes in the Library of America) and numerous scholarly articles. He has served as president of the New England Association of Colleges and Schools and as chair of the board of the Association of Public and Land Grant Universities.

E. GORDON GEE returned to lead The Ohio State University in 2007, after serving as chancellor of Vanderbilt University. Prior to his tenure at Vanderbilt, he was president of Brown University, Ohio State, the University of Colorado, and West Virginia University. Born in Vernal, Utah, Gee graduated from the University of Utah with an honors degree in history and earned his JD and EdD degrees from Columbia University. He clerked for the U.S. 10th Circuit Court of Appeals before serving as a judicial fellow for the U.S. Supreme Court. Gee returned to Utah as an associate professor in the J. Reuben Clark Law School at Brigham Young University, where he achieved the rank of full professor. In 1979 he was named dean of the West Virginia University Law School, and was appointed to that university's presidency two years later. Gee is the co-author of nine books and numerous papers and articles on law and education.

JOHN HUDZIK is professor at Michigan State University and NAFSA Senior Scholar for Internationalization. He is past president and chair of the board of directors of NAFSA, Association of International Educators, and past president of the Association of International Education Administrators (AIEA). From 1995 to 2010, he was dean of international studies and programs at Michigan State University and then vice president for global engagement and strategic projects. He was acting university provost and vice president of academic affairs at MSU in 2005. He has served on numerous international policy and advisory boards for international development, regional studies, higher education internationalization, and education abroad; he is a frequently invited commentator and speaker at national and international conferences on the direction of global higher education and internationalization, and publishes frequently on these topics. He is an internationally recognized scholar and consultant on judicial reform and judicial administration and professor of criminal justice. He is the author of numerous books, monographs and articles on both international education and judicial administration and a member of the Academy of Criminal Justice Sciences and the National Association of State Judicial Educators, NAFSA, AIEA, EAIE, and APAIE. He is recipient of several national awards for his scholarly work in judicial systems and in international education.

CAROLYN R. MAHONEY has served since her appointment in February 2005 as the eighteenth president of Lincoln University in Missouri. She has also served as mathematics faculty at Denison University; founding faculty at California State University San Marcos; visiting scholar at the Mathematical Sciences Research Institute; dean, provost, and vice chancellor for academic affairs at Elizabeth City State University; and as visiting scholar with the Carnegie Foundation for the Advancement of Teaching in Menlo Park, California. She received the PhD degree in 1984 in mathematics from The Ohio State University.

ELIZABETH MALSON-HUDDLE teaches at the University of Vermont. She completed her doctorate in English at the University of Wisconsin-Madison in 2009. Currently, she is working on a book based on her dissertation that examines religious controversy in early modern utopian literature. Her research also addresses early modern women writers and religious radicalism in England; her article on Anne Askew, a Protestant martyr executed during the reign of Henry VIII, was published in 2010 in *Studies in English Literature, 1550–1900*. Additionally, she received an MFA in poetry from the University of Virginia in 1998, and recently her poems have appeared in the Summer 2011 issue of *Green Mountains Review*.

PETER McPHERSON has been president of the Association of Public and Land Grant Universities since 2004. Before joining APLU, he was president for more than eleven years (1993–2004) of Michigan State

University. He has also served as deputy secretary of the United States Treasury, as administrator of the U. S. Agency for International Development, and as director of economic policy for the Coalition Provisional Authority of Iraq. He is the former chair of the board of directors of Dow Jones and Company and the founding co-chair of the Partnership to Cut Hunger and Poverty in Africa. A special assistant in the White House to President Gerald Ford, he also has been a partner—and head of the Washington office—of the Ohio law firm Vorys, Sater, Seymour, and Pease. He has received numerous awards (from the departments of State and Treasury, UNICEF, and the Jewish National Fund, among others). He received a BA from Michigan State University, an MBA from Western Michigan University, and a JD from American University.

JESSICA FISHER NEIDL is senior writer and editor in the office of Chancellor Nancy L. Zimpher at The State University of New York. Before coming to SUNY, she held in-house writing, editing, and indexing positions in both the public and private sectors, and has also undertaken many independent projects. Neidl has written on a variety of subjects, including state politics, historic preservation, and local history, as well as aspects of education reform and economic revitalization. She holds a BA in English Literature and an MA in Classics, both from the University at Albany.

DAVID E. SHULENBURGER, APLU Senior Fellow, was APLU's first vice president for academic affairs. He served as provost and executive vice chancellor of the University of Kansas from 1993 to 2006. He was chair of the board of directors of the Center for Research Libraries, a member of the National Commission on Writing, and a BioOne board member. He currently serves as a consulting editor for *Change Magazine*. Shulenburger writes and speaks nationally and internationally on the economics of higher education and scholarly communications and accountability in higher education. He holds a PhD from the University of Illinois.

LOU ANNA K. SIMON is the twentieth president of Michigan State University. As president, Simon has engaged Michigan State University in a strategic and transformative journey to adapt the principles of the land-grant tradition to twenty-first-century challenges. This concept, which she calls the "World Grant Ideal," integrates the attributes and strengths of all segments of society for the sustainable prosperity and well-being of peoples and nations throughout the world. Simon's key initiatives, particularly in economic development and international engagement, reflect her commitment to applying knowledge to benefit society and further the global common good. She is a member of the Council on Competitiveness, a nonpartisan, nongovernmental organization working to ensure U.S. prosperity, and serves on the Blue Ribbon Panel for Global Engagement of the American Council on Education (ACE). She serves on the National Higher Education Security Advisory Board, a group of presidents and chancellors of several prominent U.S. universities that consults regularly with national agencies responsible for security, intelligence, and law enforcement. Additionally, President Simon serves on the executive committee of the NCAA, the board of directors for NCAA—Division I, and the NCAA Board of Directors of the Division I Academic Performance Program Historical Penalties Appeals Subcommittee. She is also a member of the Big Ten Council of Presidents and Chancellors, Structure/TV Committee, and a delegate to the NCAA Convention. She received her PhD from Michigan State in 1974.

MARK G. YUDOF is the nineteenth president of the University of California. He leads a university system with ten campuses, five medical centers, three affiliated national laboratories, a statewide agriculture and natural resources program, and more than 220,000 students. Yudof served as chancellor of the University of Texas System from August 2002 to May 2008, and as president of the four-campus University of Minnesota from 1997 to 2002. Before that, he served as dean of the law school at the University of Texas at Austin from 1984 to 1994, and as the university's executive vice president and provost from 1994 to 1997. Yudof is a distinguished authority on constitutional law, freedom of expression, and education law. A Philadelphia native, he earned both LLB and BA degrees from the University of Pennsylvania.

NANCY L. ZIMPHER became the twelfth chancellor of the State University of New York in June 2008. A nationally recognized leader in education, Chancellor Zimpher spearheaded and launched a new strategic plan for SUNY in her first year as chancellor. The central goal of the plan, called *The Power of SUNY*, is to harness the university's potential to drive economic revitalization and create a better future for every community across New York. Chancellor Zimpher is active in numerous state and national education organizations and is a leader in the areas of teacher preparation, urban education, and university-community engagement. As co-founder of *Strive*, a community-based cradle-to-career collaborative, Zimpher has been instrumental in creating a national network of innovative systemic partnerships that holistically address challenges across the education pipeline. She also currently leads the national Coalition of Urban Serving Universities and recently co-chaired NCATE's blue ribbon panel on transforming teacher preparation. Dr. Zimpher previously served as president of the University of Cincinnati, chancellor of the University of Wisconsin-Milwaukee, and executive dean of the Professional Colleges and dean of the College of Education at The Ohio State University.

Index

Note: An italicized *f*, *n* or *t* following a page number indicates a figure, endnote or table, respectively.